RICH AND STRANGE

RICH AND STRANGE

GENDER, HISTORY, MODERNISM

Marianne DeKoven

PRINCETON UNIVERSITY PRESS

PRINCETON, NEW JERSEY

Copyright © 1991 by Princeton University Press
Published by Princeton University Press, 41 William Street,
Princeton, New Jersey 08540
In the United Kingdom: Princeton University Press, Oxford
All Rights Reserved

Library of Congress Cataloging-in-Publication Data

DeKoven, Marianne, 1948–
Rich and Strange : gender, history, modernism / Marianne DeKoven
p.   cm.
Includes bibliographical references (p.) and index.
ISBN 0-691-06869-0 (CL) —ISBN 0-691-01496-5 (PB)
1. English fiction—20th century—History and criticism.
2. Modernism (Literature)—Great Britain.   3. American fiction—
History and criticism.   4. Modernism (Literature)—United States.
5. Authorship—Sex differences.   6. Sex role in literature.
I. Title.
PR888.M63D45   1991   823'.91091—dc20   91-3571   CIP

This book has been composed in Adobe Sabon

Princeton University Press books are printed
on acid-free paper and meet the guidelines for
permanence and durability of the Committee on
Production Guidelines for Book Longevity
of the Council on Library Resources

Printed in the United States of America

10 9 8 7 6 5 4 3 2 1

10 9 8 7 6 5 4 3 2 1
(Pbk.)

For Daniel, Maggie, and Julien
and for my parents,
Annabel and Maurice DeKoven

Whirl up, sea—
  —H.D., "Oread"

That dolphin-torn, that gong-tormented sea.
  —William Butler Yeats, "Byzantium"

CONTENTS

ACKNOWLEDGMENTS

I AM very grateful to the John Simon Guggenheim Memorial Foundation for the 1988–89 Fellowship without which I could not have written this book. I am also grateful to the Faculty Academic Study Program and the Research Council at Rutgers University for financial support and released time from teaching, and to the Center for Critical Analysis of Contemporary Culture at Rutgers for the 1986–87 Fellowship during which my initial work on modernism began to take on its current shape.

This book emerged from my participation in the group intellectual life of the community of feminist theorists and critics of modernism. Without that nurturant and challenging matrix, the issues, commitments, and ideas that shape this book would have no useful life. I would particularly like to thank Margaret Homans and Elaine Marks for their incredibly generous support, as well as for their groundbreaking work. I am also grateful, again both for support and for enabling work, to Rachel Blau DuPlessis, Susan Stanford Friedman, Christine Froula, Holly Laird, Jane Marcus, and Lisa Ruddick.

My general and permanent indebtedness to Albert Guerard and Thomas Moser, particularly to Albert Guerard, took on not only even greater scope and depth, but also specific shape in this book, in the way I see Conrad as central to the emergence of modernism, and simply in the way I see Conrad. I am also especially grateful to my Rutgers English Department colleagues Derek Attridge, Cora Kaplan, George Levine, and Barry Qualls, and former colleagues Gillian Brown and Miriam Hansen, for various sorts of insight, help, and support. I would like to thank Michael J. Hoffman, Bruce Kellner, Patrick Murphy, Garrett Stewart, and Neil Schmitz for their encouragement and editorial help during various stages of work on the manuscript. The Gender Group at Rutgers provided useful responses to my presentation of an initial version of chapter 1. The members of the graduate seminar on Early Modernist Narrative I taught at Rutgers in Spring 1990 were of material help to my final revisions of the manuscript, and I would like to thank them all: Debra Bertram, Kristin Bluemel, Monica Dorenkamp, Joan Eurell, Chris Goulian, Stephen Murdock, Amy Nelson, Eve Oishi, Priscilla Perkins, Sally Sevcik, Rachel Stein, Andre Stipanovic, and Mark Willhardt.

I find it impossible to categorize or assign adjectives to the myriad forms of essential life support provided by my husband, Julien Hennefeld; my children, Daniel and Maggie Hennefeld; and by Barbara Cohn Schlachet. Julien also provided patient and level-headed help with each day's tough decisions about the book. I am very grateful to my mother, Annabel DeKoven, for the strength of her devotion to me; to my parents-in-law, Edmund and Lillian Hennefeld, for their affection and kindness; and to Linda Bamber, Marjorie Berger, and Jonathan Strong, for friendship on which I can rely absolutely.

Finally, I would like to thank Beth Gianfagna and Alison Johnson for their fine editorial work, and my editor at Princeton University Press, Robert Brown, for his professionalism and humanity.

. . . . .

Portions of chapters 2 and 5 appeared in different form in "Gendered Doubleness and the 'Origins' of Modernist Form," *Tulsa Studies in Women's Literature* 8, no. 1 (Spring 1989). © 1989, The University of Tulsa. Reprinted by permission of publisher. A portion of chapter 3 appeared in different form in "Half In and Half Out of Doors: Gertrude Stein and Literary Tradition," *A Gertrude Stein Companion: Content with the Example*, ed. Bruce Kellner (New York: Greenwood Press, 1988). Portions of Chapter 6 appeared in different form in "Breaking the Rigid Form of the Noun: Stein, Pound, Whitman and Modernist Poetry," *Critical Essays on American Modernism*, ed. Michael J. Hoffman and Patrick Murphy (Boston: G. K. Hall, 1991).

Grateful acknowledgment is made to the following for permission to reprint:

H.D., "Sea Rose," in *Collected Poems, 1912–1944*. Copyright © 1982 by the Estate of Hilda Doolittle. Reprinted by permission of New Directions Publishing Corporation. Reprinted by permission of Carcanet Press Limited.

T. S. Eliot, excerpts from "The Love Song of J. Alfred Prufrock" and "The Waste Land" in *Collected Poems 1909–1962* by T. S. Eliot, copyright 1936 by Harcourt Brace Jovanovich, Inc., copyright © 1964, 1963 by T. S. Eliot, reprinted by permission of the publisher. Reprinted by permission of Faber and Faber Ltd.

Langston Hughes, from "The Negro Speaks of Rivers." Copyright 1926 by Alfred A. Knopf Inc. and renewed 1954 by Langston Hughes. Reprinted from *Selected Poems of Langston Hughes*, by permission of the publisher.

D. H. Lawrence, "After Dark" and "To Let Go or to Hold On—?" From *The Complete Poems of D. H. Lawrence*, edited by Vivian de Sola Pinto and F. Warren Roberts. Copyright (c) 1964, 1971 by Angelo Ravagli and C. M. Weekley, Executors of the Estate of Frieda Lawrence Ravagli. Reprinted by permission of Viking Penguin, a division of Penguin Books USA Inc. Reprinted by permission of Laurence Pollinger Ltd.

Ezra Pound, "In a Station of the Metro," in *Personae*. Copyright 1926 by Ezra Pound. Reprinted by permission of New Directions Publishing Corporation. Reprinted by permission of Faber and Faber Ltd. from *Collected Shorter Poems by Ezra Pound*.

Adrienne Rich, the lines from "Natural Resources" and "Diving into the Wreck" are reprinted from *THE FACT OF A DOORFRAME, Poems Selected and New, 1950–1984*, by Adrienne Rich, by permission of the author and W. W. Norton & Company, Inc. Copyright © 1984 by Adrienne Rich. Copyright © 1975, 1978 by W. W. Norton & Company, Inc. Copyright © 1981 by Adrienne Rich.

Gertrude Stein, from "Sugar," in *Tender Buttons*, in *Selected Writings of Gertrude Stein*, ed. Carl Van Vechten (New York: Random House, 1946). Copyright 1945, 1946, © 1962, by Random House, Inc. Reprinted by permission of the Estate of Gertrude Stein. Reprinted by permission of Random House, Inc.

RICH AND STRANGE

INTRODUCTION

Full fathom five thy father lies;
  Of his bones are coral made;
Those are pearls that were his eyes;
  Nothing of him that doth fade
But doth suffer a sea-change
Into something rich and strange.[1]

IN *THE TEMPEST*, the death of the father is an "Oedipal" (psychic-generational) fantasy, enabling rather than undermining the system of patriarchal power. Prospero, who pulls all the strings, displaces by means of his erudite (book-learned and image-controlling) magic Sycorax's lesser, earthbound sorcery. He becomes sole parent to Miranda when she is at the crucial age of three—the age of separation from the mother (I.ii.41). That mother is mentioned only once, when Prospero stipulates her virtue and therefore the legitimacy of his own paternity (I.ii.56–58). The plot is moved by the contestation of power among living men, none of whom have actually suffered the sea-change of Ariel's song. But the space this action occupies, in which the force of the tempest Prospero-Shakespeare plays with is contained, is the space of the maternal.

"Sea-change" has come to mean deep, pervasive change, encompassing all levels of life as it is lived. The advent of twentieth-century modernity was such a change. A sea-change, in the realm of the empowered maternal, in which "nothing" of the disenthroned but not annihilated father "doth fade," but instead is transformed "into something rich and strange," describes the emergence of modernism. Modernist writing *is* "rich and strange": its greatness lies in its density and its estranging dislocations.[2] The sea-change of the early twentieth-century, as represented in modernism, is, like the phrase "rich and strange" itself, irresolvably ambiguous. It encompasses at once death, suffering ("suffer a sea-change"), horror (the skeleton bones stripped bare to become coral, the gelatinous eyes themselves congealing into pearl), and at the same time a redemptive transformation not merely into coral and pearls, but "into something rich and strange," with its connotations on the one hand of fascination, luxury, indulgence ("jouissance"), and on the other of excess, transgression, and the bizarre. Arielian sea-change is different from the death and resurrection cycle of myth and religion, because it rewrites simple dualistic ("self-other") valorization, where death and suffering are the entirely negative price paid for an entirely positive redemption and rebirth. In

Ariel's song, death and transfiguration are both, simultaneously, with ir-reducible self-contradiction, terrible and wonderful.

In this study, I am interested in the connection, within the general sea-change of twentieth-century modernity, between literary modernism and political radicalism. Modernist formal practice has seemed to define itself as a repudiation of, and an alternative to, the cultural implications of late nineteenth- and early twentieth-century feminism and socialism. I will argue here that, on the contrary, modernist form evolved precisely as an adequate means of representing their terrifying appeal.[3] In chapter 1, I construct a formal paradigm I find characteristic of modernism: an unre-solved contradiction or unsynthesized dialectic ("rich and strange"; Julia Kristeva calls it an "impossible dialectic")[4] that enacts in the realm of form an alternative to culture's hegemonic hierarchical dualisms, roots of those structures of inequity that socialism and feminism proposed to eradicate. I adapt Jacques Derrida's formulation of "*sous-rature*" to label this paradigm.

The rest of the book analyzes pairs of female- and male-signed mod-ernist literary texts, first tracing the emergence of modernist *sous-rature* in turn-of-the-century and prewar fiction by James, Gilman, Stein, Con-rad, Chopin, and Woolf (chapters 2–5), then locating *sous-rature* in a range of canonical and noncanonical texts of the high modernist period (chapter 6), and finally positing the disintegration of the paradigm in early postmodernism, using texts by Adrienne Rich and John Barth (chapter 7). Since gender is my governing preoccupation and water im-agery, the locus of sea-change, is frequently gendered feminine (if gen-dered at all), I use water imagery as a touchstone of analysis through-out—although it has less importance in some texts than in others.

My purpose in structuring the book around pairs of female- and male-signed texts (with the exception of chapter 6, where I group the texts by authorial gender) is to make clear the way in which the paradigm of *sous-rature* was a function of the modernist writers' irresolvable ambivalence toward the possibility of radical social change promised/threatened by what Perry Anderson calls the "revolutionary horizon" of the twentieth century.[5] I argue that this ambivalence was differently inflected for male and female modernists. Male modernists generally feared the loss of hege-mony the change they desired might entail, while female modernists feared punishment for desiring that utter change.

The sequence of texts I analyze is loosely chronological, in accord with my sense of the uneven emergence of modernism in turn-of-the-century fiction from the nineteenth-century realism in which it was at first embed-ded (chapters 2–5), and of the shift to the "high modernism" of the teens and postwar period (chapter 6). I would emphasize the word "loosely" in "loosely chronological." I grouped these texts according to the predominance within them of modernist formal structures, not according to strict chronology, particularly of date of publication. For example, *The Voyage Out* was not published until 1915, though Woolf began work on it about the same time Stein was writing *Three Lives*. *The Turn of the Screw* was contemporaneous with the Conrad works I discuss here, all of which were written in the miraculous (for Conrad) last few years of the nineteenth century. Nonetheless, the Conrad works move (progressively, literally from year to year) much farther away from nineteenth-century realism than does *The Turn of the Screw*.

This loosely chronological sequence is not meant to indicate any upward progress in literary merit. It is, however, meant to indicate a sense of gradual, uneven movement from one literary-historical moment to another, where some works are "more modernist" than others. These judgments are intended as descriptive rather than evaluative, at least at the level of literary merit. Perhaps "high modernism" has unfortunate normative connotations as well, but it merely indicates, for me, fully modernist writing, no longer divided between realism and modernism.[6]

Although I claim a decisive linkage between the emergence of modernist formal practice and the revolutionary horizon of the early twentieth century, that linkage is historically general rather than chronologically specific. Modernist formal practice emerged unevenly within a general period, roughly 1890–1910; its development was not tied to any specific historical progression of events in radical history. In Perry Anderson's telling phrase, it was the "imaginative proximity" (104) of social revolution *throughout* this period, rather than any local, particular sequence of events in radical practice, that provided one of the key elements of the general historical situation within which modernism emerged.

It is difficult to discuss "modernism" or "modernity" without adverting to vexed questions of terminology and periodization. As Michael Levenson says, "Vague terms still signify. Such is the case with 'modernism': it is at once vague and unavoidable."[7] Most discussions of modernism acknowledge both the undefinability of the term and also the desirability of giving it a working definition, or at least periodization. A minority of Anglo-American critics (see for example Marshall Berman in *All That Is Solid Melts Into Air*)[8] follows the largely Continental version of modernism (or "modernity") that locates its starting point in the Enlightenment or in Romanticism. Other Continentally-aligned critics, notably Alice Jardine in *Gynesis*, equate "modernity" roughly with the twentieth century.[9] After remarking that "perhaps the oblique nature of Modernism explains why critics have found it so hard a movement to find a clear place or date for," Bradbury and McFarlane, in their influential book *Modernism*, go on to establish roughly 1890 and 1930 as its temporal boundaries.[10] Their dates come closest to a consensual Anglo-American periodization. I agree, however, with Ricardo J. Quinones' extension of the period to 1940.[11] He refers to "a serious loss if we stop that development short at around 1930"—a loss of *Four Quartets, Finnegans Wake, The Waves, Joseph and His Brothers*, and major works by Stevens (18); I would add *The Years, Between the Acts*, and major works by Barnes, H.D., Hurston, Stein, Colette, Faulkner, and Williams.

If it is possible to talk about "modernism" as the major movement in Western literature (and art in general) of the first half of the twentieth century, I would argue that it is also possible to talk about "modernist form," a shorthand term used to designate that cluster of stylistic practices that, more than any of modernism's other describable features, we use intuitively to identify literary works as modernist. In *Marxism and Modernism*,[12] Eugene Lunn lists four of the most important of those practices: (1) aesthetic self-consciousness; (2) simultaneity, juxtaposition, or "montage" (I would add the word "fragmentation"); (3) paradox, ambiguity, and uncertainty; and (4) "dehumanization" (following Ortega) and the demise of the integrated or unified subject (34–37). I would add to Lunn's list qualities that Bradbury and McFarlane, using a different kind of rhetoric, attribute to modernist form: "abstraction and highly conscious artifice, taking us behind familiar reality, breaking away from familiar functions of language and conventions of form . . . the shock, the violation of expected continuities, the element of de-creation and crisis"(24–25).

The term "form" itself, because of its critical history, might also require some comment in a book that seems to turn its back on New Critical modernism. I would account for my use of the term "form" both by pointing to Marxist and poststructuralist "formalism" and also by saying that, entirely apart from ideology or theoretical orientation, the work of the New Critics in making us *see*, as Conrad might say, the riches yielded by close reading of literary form, and in providing us with a set of analytical tools for doing it, remains invaluable.[13]

Issues of definition and periodization are closely connected to issues of canonization, and therefore to questions of modernism's relation to history and gender. All these questions have generated lately both controversy and a good deal of important criticism. This criticism, not to mention the century of work of which it is a continuation, is too diverse to summarize.[14] The debates over the political implications of modernist form have concerned the issue of the possibility of political efficacy for what many of us see as the most important modes of twentieth-century art: is modernist form oppositional, or does it reflect and support, either inadvertently or intentionally, the cultural and political status quo? The modernists themselves were highly self-conscious concerning the cultural and social implications of their "new" aesthetic practices, and the polemics they initiated have been extended by many of this century's most influential Western aesthetic theorists, from a widely diverse range of historical-cultural-ideological positions.

Some of these debates are famous, at least within Marxist intellectual circles: Brecht versus Lukács, Benjamin versus Adorno, Habermas versus Lyotard. Lukács, the most influential Marxist antimodernist (the terms "anti-" and "promodernist" are a shorthand I use here to designate, respectively, those who argue that the political implications of modernist form are negative and those who argue that they are positive), proclaimed nineteenth-century realism a model for all politically progressive art, condemning modernism, realism's antithesis, as a symptom of late capitalist reification, alienation, decadence, elitism, and fetishism. Brecht, Benjamin, Adorno, and Habermas have argued variously—including against one another—in favor of the progressive potential of certain kinds of modernist form (the debate between Benjamin and Adorno concerned *which* kinds) to defamiliarize (to use the Russian Formalist term) the "reality," or socially constructed cultural order, that bourgeois capitalism would have us believe inevitable or natural.

Among the Frankfurt School theoreticians, Marcuse is the least ambivalent, most programmatic defender of the progressive political implications of modernist formal innovation. In *The Aesthetic Dimension*, he argues that formal innovation is revolutionary because it is premised on a mode of subjectivity and a reality principle inimical to and beyond those of bourgeois capitalist society.[15] "Art cannot change the world," he says, "but it can contribute to changing the consciousness and drives of the men and women who could change the world" (32–33). More recently, Edward Said, while refraining from so vast a claim, links nineteenth-century realist narrative with the structures of authority that support imperialism, bourgeois class hegemony, and the male-dominated family, suggesting that modernist disruptions of realist narrative can also represent, and perhaps function as, disruptions of those structures of authority.[16]

Feminist theorists and critics have recently extended the boundaries of the debate and shifted its terms. Some American feminist critics, concerned particularly with the historical positioning and literary contributions of women writers, focus on resuscitating undervalued work by women modernists.[17] Asserting the stature of these works is an end in itself; it also contributes to establishing a tradition (or countertradition) of female modernism, defined either as separate from, or as intermingled with, canonical, male-dominated modernism. American feminist literary-historical analysis also focuses on the importance of women modernists' unacknowledged contributions to the development of modernism or, elsewhere, on the male modernists' deliberate suppression of women writers. In *The War of the Words*, Sandra Gilbert and Susan Gubar argue that male modernists, threatened by the advent of women in force into politics and literary high culture, invented modernist formal "classicism," with its cool, tough detachment, primarily as a move to rescue literary writing for masculinity from late-nineteenth-century "effeminacy."

Other feminist arguments, however, agree with the Marxist promodernist position that at least some types of modernist formal innovation, independent of the gender of the signature or the overt politics of the texts that employ them, have progressive or revolutionary implications. Certain modernist formal practices are seen to "inscribe" in culture modes that can be considered feminine or antipatriarchal. (I say "other feminist arguments" rather than "other feminists" because some feminists—including myself—make both kinds of arguments.) In addition to French theoreticians, a number of American writers and critics argue (again, as with the Marxists, from varying points of view, with varying emphases, and, perhaps most important, with varying and varyingly emphatic reservations) that modernist form's disruptions of hierarchical syntax, of consistent, unitary point of view, of realist representation, linear time and plot, and of the bounded, coherent self separated from, and in mastery of, an objectified outer world; its subjectivist epistemology; its foregrounding of the pre-Oedipal or aural features of language; its formal decenteredness, indeterminacy, multiplicity, and fragmentation are very much in accord with a feminine aesthetic or Cixousian écriture féminine.[18] As Rachel Blau DuPlessis says, "literature by women, in its ethical and moral position, resembles the equally nonhegemonic modernism in its subversive critique of culture."[19] And Julia Kristeva, the most influential promodernist theoretician of the feminine, claims that "in a culture where the speaking subjects are conceived of as masters of their speech, they have what is called a 'phallic' position. The fragmentation of language in a text calls into question the very posture of this mastery."[20]

The specific issues engaged within the general framework of these debates are remarkably consistent across a historical and ideological spectrum as broad as twentieth-century Western cultural history itself, and they remain the focus of contemporary polemics for and against modernist form. Not surprisingly, these issues have been and continue to be framed differently according to the varying ideologies, concerns, historical situations, and aesthetic or theoretical vocabularies informing any given articulation. Nonetheless, and, I hope, without doing violence to those differences or falling prey to ahistorical essentialism, I think it is possible to offer brief summaries of the key recurring issues in these debates. (This grouping together of positive and negative formulations of each issue is intended to reflect my sense that the debates have concerned the political import of modernist forms, not their nature.)

Antimodernists generally consider the fragmentation and disjunctiveness so broadly characteristic of modernist form a capitulation to nihilistic political despair concerning the possibility of representing a unified interpretive synthesis of the life of modern society. Promodernists consider the same phenomenon montage or polysemy: form that is nonlinear, decentered, or open and therefore antihierarchical and antiphallogocentric. Such form is seen as subversive because it challenges or undoes the linear, monologistic, hierarchical perceptual and aesthetic modes of the dominant culture. What antimodernists consider aestheticization, again a nihilistic retreat from art's mimetic political responsibility, promodernists consider artistic integrity, a self-reflexivity that is quite the opposite of sterile because it represents the only possible salvation in a society saturated or otherwise entirely dominated by hegemonic culture. (Here the Anglo-American modernists, the Frankfurt School, and the feminist avant-garde interestingly converge.)

A related problem for antimodernists is reification or fetishism: the displacement of the human onto inanimate or synecdochical objects. For nonfeminist Marxists, this case is made best by the correlation between the surrealist *objet trouvé* and the position of the object in consumer culture; for feminists, by the parallel with the cult of the phallus. The promodernist account of this phenomenon considers it an attack on Enlightenment (and therefore bourgeois and patriarchal) humanism and individualism, seeing in aesthetic programs ranging from Pound's Imagism or Vorticism, Eliot's objective correlative, Ortega's dehumanization, and the antihumanism of the *nouveau roman* an alternative to the order of the Father, that construction with the individual bourgeois white male at its head or center that is the premise of gender, class, and race hierarchies.

Alienation, a concomitant of reification for antimodernists and a crucial term for Marxists, damns modernism as capitulation to, or passive reflection of, one of the central conditions of labor under capitalism. For promodernists, alienation, again associated with the attack on humanist individualism, becomes the Russian Formalist "defamiliarization" or the Brechtian "alienation effect" or "distantiation"—a means of instituting critical distance from the illusionist-realist forms that make us think the social and cultural status quo is natural and inevitable.

Antimodernists find solipsism, excessive subjectivity, and artistic egomania in a wide range of modernist forms (expressionism, *roman fleuve*, surrealism, antirealist narrative and nontraditional poetic forms in general), seeing them as a reflection of a distorted, culturally pathological emphasis on the individual psyche and, again, a retreat from the life of society. For promodernists, these represent not exaggerated individualism but perceptual relativism, a mode of psychological and epistemological verisimilitude that challenges the dualism of subject and object, the latter entirely knowable and dominated by the former. That subject-object dualism is, again, seen as the basis of all hierarchically structured political oppression.

The Anglo-American modernists are commonly charged with obscurantism, with overuse of an erudition that is traditionally a male and upper-class educational prerogative, with an allusive difficulty smacking of elitism. For promodernists these modes represent a subversive complexity, a refusal of the facile, "easy" transparency of male-gaze-dominated, illusionist realism (again, this transparency reinforces hegemonic cultural ideology). In the promodernist view, difficulty is a vanguard cultural practice designed to change consciousness, forcing it in the direction of the complex critical thought that is necessary to repudiate the oppressive status quo, and to forge an appropriate literary language that would no longer be corrupted by service to the "master narratives."[21]

As is probably (though not intentionally) apparent in my tone, my own political-aesthetic sympathies are promodernist. It is clear to me, however, that promodernism as well as antimodernism necessarily reduce the complex political-cultural-historical provenance of modernist formal innovation. The preceding summary was, in fact, an attempt to deconstruct the dualism of the debate, revealing the dialectical relatedness of positions that define themselves as mutually exclusive. The debate over the politics of modernist form, like modernist form itself, inhabits the space of unresolved contradiction or unsynthesized dialectic that, as I will argue, makes modernist form exemplary of an alternative aesthetic politics.

The debate over the politics of modernist form has not flowed freely through the twentieth century. Like much else, it went underground in America in the late forties, fifties, and early sixties. History can help restore to modernism both a heterogeneity forfeited to New Critical ideology and a complexity that must characterize the assessment of the politics of modernist form that I hope to achieve here. It is particularly helpful to attend to the history of gender in modernism. Despite the patrilineality of what has become the high modernist canon, the literary wombs of women writers were just as important to the birth of modernism as the seminal ink of the modernist founding fathers. James, Yeats, Pound, Eliot, and Joyce are credited not with giving birth to modernism—that metaphor itself would change, and is intended to change, the picture— but with *inventing* modernism: the figure of "invention" locates modernism within the discourse of "male" technology. In his introduction to that influential work on American modernism, *A Homemade World*, Hugh Kenner aligns the Wright Brothers and their "Dedalian deed on the North Carolina shore" with Joyce and his invocation to the "Old Father, Old Artificer," locating them, along with technological modernity, at the originary moment of modernism.[22] But a formal analysis looking for the right things finds powerful evidence that, in texts such as Charlotte Perkins Gilman's "The Yellow Wallpaper," 1891, Kate Chopin's *The Awakening*, 1899, and Gertrude Stein's *Three Lives*, 1903–06, previously buried texts that have become crucial to the emerging feminist canon, women writers "invented" modernist form, "discovered" it "independently," to switch to the also frequently invoked scientific metaphor, *at just the same time* that male writers did.

Three Lives was composed at the same time as early versions of *Portrait of the Artist* (*Stephen Hero*). With its fluid, obtuse narration, detached, ironic tone, impressionist as well as spatial temporal structures, and disruptions of conventional diction and syntax, *Three Lives* has just as valid a claim to modernist "origination" as Joyce's *Portrait*. A decade earlier, "The Yellow Wallpaper" prefigures Kafka and the surrealists, with its deranged first person narration and its use of dream structure as an ordering principle. *The Awakening* employs several modernist formal strategies, such as ambiguous, shifting narrative stance, density and foregrounding of imagery, and passages of repetitive, incantatory, "poetic" language.

New Critical modernism not only omitted from its canon works like these by white women, and works by the black writers of the Harlem Renaissance,[23] but also valorized, at the expense of the progressive implications of its forms, modernism's reactionary features: hierarchical, totalizing myth, externally imposed order, ahistoricity, deadlocked irony, the idea of "well-wrought," perfectly balanced form as an end in itself, the only interesting end of art. Those characteristics do not constitute some transhistorical, essentialist modernism. Rather, they construct a version of modernism that, in history, as a result of unpredestined outcomes of cultural-political struggles, modernism has become.

In fact, modernism's affiliation with the political left predates, even in America, its absorption into the grainy fields of Southern agrarian reaction. (I say "even in America" because we are used to acknowledging a tradition of leftist modernism in Europe.) Modernism lived in New York before it moved to the Bible Belt. As we see in Leslie Fishbein's *Rebels in Bohemia*, for example, modernist formal innovation had been cultivated in the teens by Greenwich Village radicals associated with the journal *The Masses*.[24] In the thirties, some of the succeeding generation of New York radicals, such as Edmund Wilson and the *Partisan Review* writers, attempted to forge links between Marxist politics and modernist form. Although always wary of modernism's reactionary, ahistorical, and apolitical components, those critics were interested in both the modernist damnation of the bourgeoisie and its materialist culture and in the progressive potential of modernist formal innovation. As Daniel Aaron points out in *Writers on the Left*, the founding *Partisan Review* critics, unlike the older generation of American literary Communists, felt no unbridgeable gulf between Marxism and modernism:

> Writing in 1934, William Phillips . . . carefully distinguished his own "proletarian generation" from his immediate literary forebears. . . . The literary Marxists had been the guides and teachers of the young radicals throughout the dry years. But "the strain and exigencies of pioneering," Phillips thought, "kept them from assimilating the literary spirit of the twenties," which for good or ill was part of the literary heritage of the young radicals. Although his own proletarian group, he said, was tied up in some way with the Communist Party or the labor movement, its literary fathers were writers like Joyce and Eliot (from whose influence not even the most revolutionary writers were immune).[25]

Even though leftist interest in modernism never quite died in America, maintaining its life most notably in the person of Irving Howe, it was not the left intelligentsia but the New Critics who won the literary war of the thirties (see Aaron for a detailed account of this seldom discussed episode in our literary history). The triumph of New-Critical modernism has made it appear blunt, banal, even gauche to discuss modernist writing as a critique of twentieth-century culture—to approach it, in fact, as anything other than the altar of linguistic and intellectual complexity in search of transcendent formal unity.[26] It fell to the victorious New Critics, with the cooperation of those aspects of modernism indisputably in harmony with their project, to define modernism as the politically retrograde phenomenon—sexist, racist, elitist, fascist, even "royalist"—that has become so easy to condemn.

Again, my purpose is neither to condemn nor to praise modernism, but rather to understand the structures of its formal-political concatenations. Throughout almost all of the textual analyses in this book, I will use water imagery—not at all exclusively, but pivotally—to discuss those structures. Since water imagery is so pervasive in nineteenth-century literature, a brief demonstration of premodernist deployments of water imagery might be helpful here as a point of comparison.[27]

The climax of Henry James's *The Portrait of a Lady* (1881) both foreshadows modernism and reveals the distance from it of this late Victorian novel. Sea-change momentarily becomes a possible alternative for Isabel

Archer to her either/or trap, her nonchoice between self-annihilation (return to Osmond) and self-betrayal (union with Goodwood). In that moment, James uses water imagery to represent Isabel's desire for Good-wood as something other than self-betrayal, because that desire is a be-trayal only of the "self" constructed by the schooling of her subjectivity to the laws of marriage in patriarchy. For the space of half a page, Isabel's desire becomes a sign of feminine sexual empowerment, and the world available to her and to the text literally opens out:

> "The world is very small," she said, at random; she had an immense desire to appear to resist. She said it at random, to hear herself say something; but it was not what she meant. The world, in truth, had never seemed so large; it seemed to open out, all round her, to take the form of a mighty sea, where she floated in fathomless waters. She had wanted help, and here was help; it had come in a rushing torrent. I know not whether she believed everything that he said; but she believed that to let him take her in his arms would be the next best thing to dying. This belief, for a moment, was a kind of rapture, in which she felt herself sinking and sinking. In the movement she seemed to beat with her feet, in order to catch herself, to feel something to rest on.
>
> "Ah, be mine as I am yours!" she heard her companion cry. He had suddenly given up argument, and his voice seemed to come through a confusion of sound.
>
> This, however, of course, was but a subjective fact, as the metaphysicians say; the confusion, the noise of waters, and all the rest of it were in her own head. In an instant she became aware of this. "Do me the greatest kindness of all," she said. "I beseech you to go away!"[28]

In modernist writing, the distinction between "in her own head" and "reality" breaks down, as it begins to do in James's own *The Turn of the Screw* and, differently, in his Major Phase novels. In *The Portrait of a Lady*, the distinction still holds, and the terrible power of that mighty sea is recontained at the end of the novel as a mere "subjective fact." James must reject the narrative flooding released by Isabel's acknowledgment of her desire for Goodwood. She returns to her tragic choice, as James re-turns the novel to the traditional containing form of the tragic trajec-tory—Grace Paley's Faith calls it "the absolute line between two points which I've always despised. Not for literary reasons, but because it takes all hope away. Everyone, real or invented, deserves the open destiny of life."[29] James's narrator calls Isabel's final decision to return to Osmond "a very straight path." But within that flooding, before it is recontained and repudiated, James deploys the modernist configuration that I will call *sous-rature*.

The language James uses to describe the "fathomless waters" is thor-oughly ambiguous, reversing itself from one moment to the next. A phrase that is offered syntactically as supporting or extending the sense of the previous phrase in fact contradicts it. As the waters begin to rush in, the world becomes large rather than small; it "seemed to open out, all round her, to take the form of a mighty sea." Yet that positive opening out into a "mighty sea" causes her to float, after a comma, in terrifyingly "fathomless waters." In the next sentence, the sea is described as being the "help" that she "had wanted," yet, after a semicolon, that "help . . . had come in a rushing torrent," again a frightening image. Being taken in Goodwood's arms, in the next sentence, "would be the next best thing to dying"—a phrase whose perfect, ironic ambiguity needs no explication— and that belief is "a kind of rapture," but a rapture, after a comma, "in which she felt herself sinking and sinking." That sinking is her cue, and James's cue, that the flood has gone too far. In the very "movement" of sinking, she "seemed to beat with her feet," an image that foreshadows Stein's description in *Lord Jim* of how to move when immersed in the destructive element so as to keep oneself afloat. But James is not interested in keeping Isabel afloat; she must rather "catch herself" and be returned instantly to dry land. Note the dryness, the painfully abrupt distancing, that enters the narrator's tone in "This, however, of course, was but a subjective fact, as the metaphysicians say." The flood then becomes Isabel's tears: "'Ah, don't say that. don't kill me!' he cried. She clasped her hands; her eyes were streaming with tears. 'As you love me, as you pity me, leave me alone!'" (544).

In earlier Victorian fiction, water imagery does not have this irreducible undecidability. In George Eliot's *The Mill on the Floss* (1860), in Book 6, chapter 13, "Borne Along by the Tide," the river's current represents Maggie's illicit desire for Stephen, just as the flood represents Isabel's for Goodwood. But Eliot divides gratification very clearly from the danger of moral turpitude, and morality triumphs. There is none of the oscillating, moment-to-moment ambiguity we saw in the James passage. Being borne along by the tide is purely wonderful at first, as they float "between the silent sunny fields and pastures, which seemed filled with a natural joy that had no reproach for theirs" (487). It remains wonderful as long as "memory [is] excluded" (487). But when memory returns to Maggie with a sudden jolt, being borne along by the tide switches suddenly from wonderful to awful: "She clasped her hands and broke into a sob" (488).

Maggie's illicit desire for her brother Tom, which floods at the end of the novel, can also be compared to Isabel's for Goodwood: both are forms of female desire that are taboo within patriarchy. Again, unlike the language in the passage narrating Isabel's flood, the negative, ominous language in the narration of Maggie and Tom's climactic drowning is clearly separated from the positive, triumphant language, with the latter definitively succeeding, and vanquishing, the former:

> Some wooden machinery had just given way on one of the wharves, and huge fragments were being floated along. The sun was rising now, and the wide area of watery desolation was spread out in dreadful clearness around them—in dreadful clearness floated onwards the hurrying, threatening masses. . . . Tom, looking before him, saw death rushing on them. Huge fragments, clinging together in fatal fellowship, made one wide mass across the stream.
>
> "It is coming, Maggie!" Tom said in a deep hoarse voice, loosing the oars and clasping her.
>
> The next instant the boat was no longer seen upon the water, and the huge mass was hurrying on in hideous triumph.
>
> But soon the keel of the boat reappeared, a black speck on the golden water.
>
> The boat reappeared, but brother and sister had gone down in an embrace never to be parted, living through again in one supreme moment the days when they had clasped their little hands in love and roamed the daisied fields together.[30]

The word "golden" marks the shift from negative to positive representation.

Positive representation certainly did not always prevail in Victorian water imagery. What I am emphasizing here is clear separation of clusters of positive and negative connotation and decidability between them. In Dickens's *Our Mutual Friend* (1864–65), for example, the serenity and beauty of the river mask, like idealizing art, the horrible truth realism must reveal:

> Perhaps the old mirror was never yet made by human hands, which, if all the images it has in its time reflected could pass across its surface again, would fail to reveal some scene of horror or distress. But the great serene mirror of the river seemed as if it might have reproduced all it had ever reflected between those placid banks, and brought nothing to the light save what was peaceful, pastoral, and blooming.[31]

The illicit drowning embrace of Riderhood and Headstone provides just such a scene of horror, and also a neat foil to the drowning embrace of Maggie and Tom:

> Bradley was drawing to the Lock-edge. Riderhood was drawing away from it. It was a strong grapple, and a fierce struggle, arm and leg. Bradley got him round, with his back to the Lock, and still worked him backward. . . .
>
> Riderhood went over into the smooth pit backward, and Bradley Headstone upon him. When the two were found, lying under the ooze and scum behind

one of the rotting gates, Riderhood's hold had relaxed, probably in falling, and his eyes were staring upward. But, he was girdled still with Bradley's iron ring, and the rivets of the iron ring held tight. (874)[32]

Dickens's and Eliot's deployments of water imagery can encompass both horror and serenity, and the two may even cohabit the same scene, but fair remains fair and foul foul. The reader always knows which is which, and which is meant to govern the interpretation of the sequence.[33] Momentarily for Isabel Archer, and pervasively in modernism, that knowledge is transformed.

PART I

TOWARD THE MODERNIST NARRATIVE

Chapter 1

MODERNISM UNDER ERASURE

ERRY ANDERSON considers modernism the last Western movement in the arts to achieve profound cultural significance: social scope as well as aesthetic stature.[1] That scope and stature result, in Anderson's "conjunctural" Marxist framework, from modernism's historical position at the "intersection of three temporalities" (which might be labeled, after Raymond Williams, residual, dominant, and emergent):[2]

> In my view, "modernism" can best be understood as a cultural field *triangulated* by three decisive coordinates. The first of these . . . was the codification of a highly formalized *academicism* in the visual and other arts, which itself was institutionalized within official regimes of states and society still massively pervaded, often dominated, by aristocratic or landowning classes: classes in one sense economically "superseded," no doubt, but in others still setting the political and cultural tone in country after country of pre–First World War Europe. . . . The second coordinate is . . . the still incipient, hence essentially *novel*, emergence within these societies of the key technologies or inventions of the second industrial revolution: telephone, radio, automobile, aircraft and so on. Mass consumption industries based on the new technologies had not yet been implanted anywhere in Europe. . . . The third coordinate . . . was the imaginative proximity of social revolution. . . . In no European state was bourgeois democracy completed as a form, or the labour movement integrated or coopted as a force. The possible revolutionary outcomes of a downfall of the old order were thus still profoundly ambiguous. . . . European modernism in the first years of this century thus flowered in the space between a still usable classical past, a still indeterminate technical present, and a still unpredictable political future. . . . It was the Second World War—not the First—which destroyed all three of the historical coordinates I have discussed, and therewith cut off the vitality of modernism. (104–6)

Modernism was able to appropriate aesthetic classicism and at the same time use it against itself and against capitalist degradation of culture; to appropriate the energy and dynamism of the machine age while abstracting them *for aesthetic practice* from its relations of production under capitalism;[3] to appropriate the "apocalyptic light" of nascent social revolution for "a violently radical . . . rejection of the social order as a whole" (105). For Anderson, modernism was the last great moment of Western literature. Although I do not agree with his blanket condemnation of postmodernism, I do agree with his unashamed argument for modernism's greatness, and find compelling his account of the historical configuration that enabled it.

I am particularly interested in the "apocalyptic light" (105) of the third element of this tripartite conjuncture. The ambivalence that, as I will argue, generated the most salient features of modernist form was an ambivalence toward the radical remaking of culture and represented these writers' response precisely to Anderson's "profoundly ambiguous possible revolutionary outcomes of the downfall of the old order." The downfall of the old order, linked to the radical remaking of culture, was to be the downfall of class, gender, and racial (ethnic, religious) privilege; revolution was to be in the direction of egalitarian leveling on all those fronts. This utter change was embodied in the social-political sphere in the various left-wing revolutionary movements—anarchism, communism, socialism—and in feminism. For the sake of convenience, I will designate these two forces socialism and feminism.[4] The period from 1880 to World War I, during which modernism evolved, encompassed the heyday of these movements on the Anglo-American political scene, allowing of course for important national differences and for specific historical sequences of success and defeat, revolutionary activity and state suppression, and for the diversity of organizations and leaders within these general movements. What I am postulating is a profound connection between this radical history and the development of modernist form. The irresolvable ambivalence (fear and desire in equal portion) of modernist writers concerning their own proposals for the wholesale revision of culture, proposals paralleled in the political sphere by the programs for wholesale social revision promulgated by socialism and feminism, generated the irreducible self-contradiction, what I will call the *sous-rature*, of modernist form. I will argue that male modernists generally feared the loss of their own hegemony implicit in such wholesale revision of culture, while female modernists generally feared punishment for their dangerous desire for that revision.

I will attempt a characterization of modernist form adequate to such an assessment of its political significance, beginning with an alternative to Jameson's reading of Conrad's style, and therefore of modernist form in general. At the opening of his brilliant chapter on Conrad in *The Political Unconscious*, Jameson quotes, as I will, an early passage of *Lord Jim*: "His station was in the fore-top, and often from there he looked down, with the contempt of a man destined to shine in the midst of dangers, at the peaceful multitude of roofs cut in two by the brown tide of the stream, while scattered on the outskirts of the surrounding plain the factory chimneys rose perpendicular against a grimy sky, each slender like a pencil, and belching out smoke like a volcano."[5]

Jameson claims that he sees Conrad as a transitional figure of what he calls "nascent modernism," where history and the world, though displaced and marginalized, are not yet entirely repressed, as they will be in what he calls "the more fully achieved and institutionalized modernisms of the canon" (210). Jameson's actual reading of this passage, however, puts Conrad squarely in that canon. He finds in it evidence of "the impulse of Conrad's sentences to transform such realities [the realities of society's life under late capitalism] into impressions" (210). Jameson continues: "These distant factory spires may be considered the equivalent for Jim and, in this novelistic project, for Conrad, of the great Proustian glimpses of the steeples of Martinville" (210–11). The connection to Proust seems to me to obliterate, at least for this moment of the argument, Jameson's distinction between Conrad's "nascent modernism" and the "fully achieved and institutionalized modernisms of the canon." Even though he attempts to maintain the distinction by means of a parenthetical remark in which he points to "the one obvious qualification that the latter [Proust's steeples] are already sheer impression" and therefore require no "aesthetic transformation," Jameson represents Conrad's style here, I think correctly, as fully modernist.

What Jameson omits from his analysis of Conrad's passage, and therefore from his characterization of modernist form, is what I would call its *sous-rature*, its unresolved contradictoriness or unsynthesized dialecticality. As Derrida uses it, *sous-rature* indicates a verbal sign that is discredited but has no adequate replacement, whose meanings are inimical to deconstruction—are in fact precisely what deconstruction deconstructs—but that is nonetheless necessary to indicate an intellectual position, germane to Derrida's argument, that cannot otherwise be named.[6] I appropriate this term here for its emblematic quality: it represents in a visually compelling way (a word that is visible but at the same time crossed out) unresolved contradiction, unsynthesized dialectic, resulting from a historical transition in intellectual paradigms. In fact, modernist writing enacts in literature the same historical moment that deconstruction enacts in philosophy: a moment not of "paradigm shift" but of the simultaneous coexistence of two mutually exclusive paradigms. Though Derridean deconstruction comes half a century later, it produces and reproduces the same "suspense between two ages of writing"[7] as modernism, evolved as it is from the late nineteenth- and early twentieth-century thought of Nietzsche and Heidegger. Deconstruction simultaneously uses and undoes bourgeois Enlightenment modes of thought and argument, just as modernist writing simultaneously uses and undoes bourgeois Enlightenment modes of narrative and poesis. As characterization of modernist form, *sous-rature* indicates a system that coexists within one figure with its own undoing.[8]

A system that coexists within one figure with its own undoing: what sort of animal is that? In his preface to *William Shakespeare*, Terry Eagleton explains, with enviable succinctness and simplicity, what critical practice is involved in applying the tools of New Criticism to literary form in order to find complex historical-intellectual structures: "The book is in no direct sense an historical study of its topic, but is, I suppose, an exercise in *political semiotics*, which tries to locate the relevant history in the very letter of the text."[9] The political-semiological study of representations of gender and history in modernist form I undertake here depends on the claim that modernist writing, at the level of form, is characterized most saliently by *sous-rature* (self-cancellation, unresolved contradiction, unsynthesized dialectic), a claim I will explain and illustrate by returning to Jameson and *Lord Jim*.

Conrad is not Jim, any more than he is Marlow (note how Jameson, in equating Conrad with Jim "in this novelistic project," does away with precisely the distinction most important to modernist form), and yet it is from Jim's or Marlow's point of view that Conrad writes. It is modernist form that allows Conrad to refuse not history, not the "realities" of life under imperialist, misogynist late capitalism, but to refuse epistemological determinacy. It is *from Jim's point of view* that, to use Jameson's term again, "realities" become impressions. Jim, not Conrad, has his station "in the fore-top," from which he can "look down, with the contempt of a man destined to shine in the midst of dangers"; the irony of the tone here is characteristic and crucial. The novel is about to show us just how little Jim "shines," just how "grimy" he becomes "in the midst of dangers": Jim's failure to assist his fellow students on the training ship in an actual rescue immediately follows the sequence Jameson quotes, and it is precisely the "griminess" of the skipper of the *Patna* that Jim obsessively dissociates himself from but that the novel insists taints him.

It is from this extremely problematical perch "in the fore-top" that Jim redeems the "grimy" material world by converting it into the "shining" impression. Jim never learns what the novel, via Stein, so emphatically shows us: that beetles must be collected (another destabilizing figure in its ironic representation of reification) along with butterflies. If repressed, they return in the lethal form of Gentleman Brown. Conrad clearly separates himself not only from Jim's "fore-top" point of view, but from the "impressions" he gets there: the escapist, megalomaniacal fantasy idealizations his perch allows Jim to substitute for life in the world.

Moreover, in those impressions themselves we can see Conrad's representation of the fragility and explosive instability of Jim's *un-self-critically* impressionist point of view. The factory chimneys are "slender like a pencil," pointing to the fragility of the pencil that converts, through simile, a smokestack into a pencil, a full-bodied phallic "reality" into "slender" effeminate writing. The smokestacks are also "belching out smoke like a volcano." First we note the wonderful disparity, the impossibility, of fragile pencils belching out smoke like volcanoes: the power of *modernist* writing to represent, through self-erasure, the irreducibility of a "reality" whose explosive force would be effaced, not revealed, by a *realist* language constructed as transparent. By itself that particular contradiction undercuts Jim's rewriting of industrial reality as harmlessly lovely "artistic" impression. But beyond that, the connotations of barely contained, potentially monstrously destructive violence in the image of the volcano near eruption speak of the representation in Conrad and, I would argue, in all modernist writing, of precisely the impossibility, the ludicrousness, and the danger of attempting to convert the facticity of history into harmless (or transcendent) art.

Modernist form, again, continually puts itself, including its own self-consciousness, under erasure. Eliot has Prufrock represent himself with an effete fatalism, but at the same time undercuts that representation with an angry contempt for it: the "ragged claws" tear the smooth, ironic urbanity of "I have known them all already, known them all"; the crucified insect "pinned and wriggling on the wall," who angrily and with harsh, staccato consonants wonders how it will "spit out all the butt-ends of [its] days and ways," radically disrupts "the taking of a toast and tea." The representation and its own negation coexist in the text in an oscillating simultaneity, an unresolved contradiction—not a "tension" resolved or contained by "organically unified" form, as the New Critics have it, but something entirely different: a coexistent doubleness that is resolved nowhere, that is reinforced in, rather than eased of, its contradictoriness by the radically disjunctive, juxtapositional *modernist* form of the poem.

Eugene Lunn, who, as a Marxist, is not interested in resolution of "tension" through organically unified form, lists as some defining characteristics of modernist form "paradox, ambiguity, uncertainty."[10] *Sous-rature* is different in degree rather than kind from Lunn's, and many other, formulations. I am not claiming to have discovered something new about modernist form. Rather, to use Lunn's formulation as characteristic of consensual thought about modernism, I am separating "paradox" from the weaker "ambiguity" and "uncertainty" and emphasizing its self-canceling or self-contradictory implications as the most salient aspect of modernist form, not necessarily in every context, but in the context that concerns me here: the relationship of the emergence of modernist formal practice to turn-of-the-century feminism and socialism.

I would also like to emphasize the distinction between the American deconstructionist version of all (literary) writing, which finds unresolved contradiction everywhere, and my thesis here concerning the *sous-rature* of modernist writing. American deconstructionism finds, and in fact perhaps prefers to find, unresolved contradiction in texts that offer or construct themselves as noncontradictory or consistent. I am arguing not merely that we can find instances, even many instances, of unresolved contradiction in modernist writing, but that modernist writing *constitutes itself as* self-contradictory, though not incoherent: incoherence is the province of avant-garde experimentalism and some postmodernism.

Jameson cites Proust, with justification, as the ultimate impressionist or high modernist. But representation of late capitalist bourgeois social history is clearly one of Proust's central narrative intentions. This representation puts under erasure Marcel's self-transfiguring elevation, by means of the madeleine and the uneven flagstones—the eucharist and altar of the religion of literary impressionism—from moribund history to immortal Time(lessness). Again, let me make my position clear: I am not arguing that Marcel's transcendent impressionism is discredited. Rather, the text is constructed as a juxtaposition of that impressionism with its own negation or contradiction. While passages might be cited, particularly the very end of *The Past Recaptured*, demonstrating Proust's (Marcel's) wholehearted endorsement of the impressionist religion, it is just as important to remember that Proust is not Marcel as it is to remember that Conrad is not Jim (or, for stricter parallelism, not Marlow). Also, it is clear elsewhere, throughout the text, that Proust *uses* Marcel's penchant for rapturous idealization—the tone in which the famous impressionist sequences, including Martinville and the final movement of the text, are written—to provide ironic contrast to the text's tough-minded comic-grotesque representations of the rottenness and impending demise of the French aristocracy and upper middle class. The text represents that demise as desirable as well as inevitable, at the same time that it participates in Marcel's acolytic worship of the Guermantes and the Faubourg Saint-Germain.

Most definitions and descriptions of modernism, and many of the modernists' own statements on aesthetic practice, resort to tropes that bespeak an aesthetic of *sous-rature*, tropes such as the famous irony, tension, ambiguity, and paradox of the New Criticism. I would argue that those tropes dehistoricize the modernist aesthetic situation, essentializing it as the condition of all (great) literature. Cleanth Brooks's characterization of all poetic language as the language of paradox defined this New-Critical aesthetic, and Empson's "seventh type of ambiguity" is perhaps its ultimate formulation: "An example of the seventh type of ambiguity . . . occurs when the two meanings of the word, the two values of the ambiguity, are the two opposite meanings defined by the context, so that the total effect is to show a fundamental division in the writer's mind."[11] F. Scott Fitzgerald claimed that "the test of a first-rate intelligence is the ability to hold two opposed ideas in the mind at the same time, and still retain the ability to function."[12] Maurice Merleau-Ponty described "Cézanne's doubt" as, in part, his "aiming for reality while denying himself the means to attain it."[13] One thinks immediately as well of Wilde's famous paradoxes, particularly his statement that "a Truth in art is that whose contradictory is also true."[14] One thinks also of Stevens's formulations of the interrelations of imagination and reality in *The Necessary Angel* or his "Let be be finale of seem," Moore's "imaginary gardens with real toads in them," Williams's "no ideas but in things," and, perhaps the clearest, most schematic representation of *sous-rature*, Yeats's interlocking gyres.[15]

So far I have cited, as textual evidence of the aesthetic of *sous-rature*— the unsynthesized dialectic or unresolved contradiction that characterizes modernist form—modernists canonized by the New Critics. It is not necessary to stay so securely within that canon to find such evidence; moreover, one of my purposes here is to participate in the current rethinking of "canon," arguing at the least for an opening of the "modernism" produced by New Critical ideology to the full heterogeneity of the modernism that historical analysis can recover. For example, in chapter 5 I will argue that Kate Chopin's *The Awakening* is an originary modernist work. Its protagonist, Edna Pontellier, stands in precisely the same relation to Chopin and her narrator that Jim does to Conrad and Marlow: a relation of irresolvable and continuous oscillation between identification and distance, approval and disapproval, endorsement and repudiation. By the end of the novel, Edna is simultaneously a figure of feminist affirmation and of feminist despair, since swimming "far out where no woman has swum before" is, literally, suicide.

It would be impossible, and a serious distortion of the modernist text, to claim that it resolves its dualisms in favor of one term over the other. Instead, the text enacts precisely the modernist moment of simultaneity, of dualism that seeks neither a unitary resolution (one term over the other) nor a transcendent third term, a dialectical synthesis, but rather a simultaneity that, from within dualism, imagines an alternative to it: not an obliteration or replacement of dualism—I would argue that all modes of doing away with dualism are ultimately versions of dialectical synthesis[16]—but an alternative to it that maintains difference while denying hierarchy. Derrida articulates this idea most pointedly in *Positions*; with such efficacy, in fact, that I will quote him at length:

> Therefore we must proceed using a double gesture, according to a unity that is both systematic and in and of itself divided, a double writing. . . . On the one hand, we must traverse a phase of *overturning*. To do justice to this necessity is to recognize that in a classical philosophical opposition we are not dealing with the peaceful coexistence of a *vis-à-vis*, but rather with a violent hierarchy.

One of the two terms governs the other (axiologically, logically, etc.), or has the upper hand. To deconstruct the opposition, first of all, is to overturn the hierarchy at a given moment. To overlook this phase of overturning is to forget the conflictual and subordinating structure of opposition. Therefore one might proceed too quickly to a *neutralization* that *in practice* would leave the previous field untouched, leaving one no hold on the previous opposition, thereby preventing any means of *intervening* in the field effectively. We know what always have been the *practical* (particularly *political*) effects of *immediately* jumping *beyond* oppositions, and of protests in the simple form of *neither* this *nor* that. When I say that this phase is necessary, the word *phase* is perhaps not the most rigorous one. It is not a question of a chronological phase, a given moment, or a page that one day simply will be turned, in order to go on to other things. The necessity of this phase is structural; it is the necessity of an interminable analysis: the hierarchy of dual oppositions always reestablishes itself. . . .

Hegelian idealism consists precisely of a *relève* of the binary oppositions of classical idealism, a resolution of contradiction into a third term that comes in order to *aufheben*, to deny while raising up, while idealizing . . . while *interning* difference in a self-presence.[17]

Julia Kristeva, describing in *About Chinese Women* an ideal cultural order of gender, has called it an "impossible dialectic" ("time," "identity," and "history" in the following are culturally masculine, the obverse of each is culturally feminine): "a constant alternation between time and its 'truth,' identity and its loss, history and the timeless, signless, extraphenomenal things that produce it. An impossible dialectic: a permanent alternation: never the one without the other."[18] Modernist form represents this impossible dialectic, not in the mythologized matrilineal Chinese past or utopian avant-garde/feminist future projected by Kristeva, but in historical twentieth-century time.

Appropriating Kristeva's language can be a risky enterprise for an American critic. This discourse assumes that time, identity, and history lie on the dominant, masculine side of a massive Western-cultural gendered dualism, constituted by and constitutive of their feminine other of "truth," loss, timelessness, signlessness, the extraphenomenal. Moreover, here is a discourse in which one writes freely of time, identity, and history, "truth," loss, and timelessness, without disclaimer, qualification, explanation, or footnote. Perhaps the greatest risk of this discourse lies in its potential for "essentializing" gender, thereby suppressing the historical, cultural particularity of actual women and men. I would especially like to make explicit at this point my (and many others') sense of the difference between woman, or the cultural feminine, as the repressed other of hegemonically masculine Western culture, and actual, historical women, who have, as individuals and in movements, resisted suppression and struggled against oppression throughout history, in varying degree, and differently, from period to period and place to place. Since "masculine" and "feminine" are cultural abstractions—forces functioning pervasively in culture and representation, within historically specific configurations—they operate in a different register from the almost limitlessly multiple, complex, mixed, and indeterminate gender positions occupied by actual people. Finally, "the feminine" is often conflated in this discourse, and in my study here, with "the maternal," generally when the maternal aspect of the cultural feminine is the primary consideration in a particular segment of the argument. That conflation is a function of the cultural construction of these gender abstractions.

The most thoroughgoing archeology of the Western cultural *longue durée* produced within this risky discourse is Luce Irigaray's *Speculum of the Other Woman.*[19] It is a remarkable book, a work of enormous ambition and high seriousness in a very traditional sense, nothing less than an intellectual history of Western culture from Plato to Freud (or, in her structure of return as political counter to "progress," from Freud to Plato). With one exception, Irigaray's view in *Speculum* of gender relations as constitutive of Western culture is ahistorical: she believes that from Plato to Lacan, nothing much has changed. The one exception is precisely the modernist historical moment, when, in the work of Freud, Irigaray finds the insights that have the potential to explode the hegemony of masculine self-representation in Western culture. However, instead of allowing those insights to do any subversive work, Freud represses them by means of a cruel, because nearly self-conscious, reinscription of masculine hegemony.

The narrative that emerges over and over again in *Speculum* can be summarized fairly simply, and in its précis form it is a familiar story to Continentally-educated, deconstructive-psychoanalytic feminist theorists.[20] Phallogocentric Western culture has been created by masculine self-representation, which is driven by the necessity to produce an image of the self-same, and therefore to suppress the feminine, particularly the maternal. The maternal feminine, as we have been hearing for over a decade now (*Speculum* was published in France in 1974), is the repressed other of Western culture. More specifically, for Irigaray, the maternal feminine is the "origin" so threatening to masculine subject-formation in its generative power that it must be recast as a chaotic nothing out of which the something of masculine self-representation reproduces its endlessly reiterated upright form. This anxiously repressed maternal feminine "nothing" continually returns in emptied-out versions of otherness, which serve both to reinforce masculine representations of the self-same and also to mark the place of the absented feminine. This is, not surprisingly, a Lacanian story in its privileging of the phallus as the prime locus of representation, but it is a story relativized or politicized in the consensual feminist appropriation of Lacan, to deprive the phallus of representational inevitability, linking it not to "the" development of "the" unconscious, language, and all symbolization, as Lacan does, but to the unrelenting (if variegated across time, place, differential subjectivity) history of male dominance in the West.

The importance of *Speculum* lies not just in its pride of place as one of the first extended articulations of these ideas. Rather, Irigaray's method implants her analysis of Western culture so forcefully in some of its key texts that the book seems to offer not so much an analysis of the Western "Great Tradition" as a wholesale reappropriation of it to her vision. Irigaray finds her pattern everywhere she looks, but one does not feel that the texts she inhabits are being reduced or distorted to fit themselves around it; quite the contrary, one feels that they have been reborn as Irigaray's book.

The first part of the book, "Blind Spot of an Old Dream of Symmetry," inhabits in great detail Freud's essay "Femininity." The third part, "Plato's *Hystera*," inhabits in even more remarkable detail Plato's parable of the cave. The central section, "Speculum," takes on fragments of Plato, Aristotle, Plotinus, Descartes, Kant, and Hegel in a series of essays. In one particularly powerful case, the essay "Une Mère de Glace," Irigaray does nothing but quote from Plotinus, with no commentary of her own. Plotinus does Irigaray's work with admirable efficiency, as if, in a Borgesian twist, he were writing her essay in retroactive self-mockery. That essay brings into sharpest focus the version of Irigaray's story most relevant to my concerns here. But to prevent the reading of the position of gender in Western representation that emerges from that essay from seeming arbitrary, it helps to establish the terms of the analysis, as Irigaray does, by means of the discourse most deeply cathected for her: that of Freud.

Three of Freud's premises in "Femininity" strike Irigaray with particular force. The first two are the assumption of early bisexuality in children of both genders and the claim that the etiology of female sexual subjectivity is a mystery: "And now you are already prepared to hear that psychology too is unable to solve the riddle of femininity."[21] Irigaray finds a telling contradiction in Freud's insistence on assigning all sexual mystery, despite his assumption of early bisexuality, to the feminine: "Why . . . wish to reserve the mystery to women? As if, for the argument to be possible, 'male sexuality' at the very least had to impose itself as clearly defined, definable, even practicable" (20), while female sexuality is relegated to undefinability, invisibility ("castration").

The third element of Freud's meditation on feminine sexuality of peculiar significance for Irigaray is his vision of the crucial stage of femininity's evolution not as a process of self-constitution in relation to an other, as in the evolution of masculine sexual subjectivity, but as a process of self-annihilation in relation to—a becoming-invisible as necessary mediator between—two others who jointly occupy the only available subject position: the father and the male baby.[22] Again, in Freud's familiar story, the girl's inherently "masochistic" (self-annihilating) sexuality is defined by her desire for the father's phallus. In compensation for her inability to acquire it for herself, she wants to be impregnated by it and to give birth to a male child, which becomes a substitute for it, the closest to having it that she can get. Irigaray sees this story as placing women always between two men (father-and-son is really an infinite regress of masculine specular self-regarding), the mediation that enables their confrontation with one another, which is really the masculine subject's endless confrontation with himself. Woman is the obliterated term in a "specula(riza)tion" (Irigaray's usage "specula(riza)tion" connects this construction of masculine identity to the history of Western thought) that allows the masculine subject reconstruct himself endlessly: the father giving birth to the son, that image at which he must look in order to see himself, through the "passive," "mysterious" medium of the mother/daughter.[23]

The masculine terror of "nothing to see," crucially viewed by Freud and Lacan as the fear of castration, makes it necessary for the masculine subject to confirm self-presence (the presence of his own phallus) by means of endless specularization, thus engendering a representational economy of presence and of the self-same that is identified and attacked by deconstruction as the bastion of phallogocentric Western culture. For Irigaray, this masculine terror is not a fear of losing the phallus, but a fear that having something else, something that cannot be seen, is the true condition of power (the "phallic mother," in this analysis, would become not a projection of castration fear but a desire to remake power in the masculine image of self):

> But it seems, all the same, that one might be able to interpret the fact of being deprived of a womb as the most intolerable deprivation of man, since his contribution to gestation—his function with regard to the origin of reproduction— is hence asserted as less than evident, as open to doubt. An indecision to be attenuated both by man's "active" role in intercourse and by the fact that he will mark the product of copulation with *his own name*. Thereby woman, whose intervention in the work of engendering the child can hardly be questioned, becomes the anonymous worker. . . . And the desire that men here displays [sic] to determine for himself what is constituted by "origin," and thereby eternally and ever to reproduce him (as) self, is a far from negligible indication of the same thing. (23)

Man must substitute himself, symbolized as the name-of-the-Father, for woman, as the "origin" of life. The "mystery" of man's role in reproduction is reassigned to the "passive" woman; her terrible power to engender life is repressed and reassigned to the man as a necessity, made violent by the repression on which it is based, for self-representation (literally engendering the self).[24] The vigilant repression and exclusion of the feminine "origin" results in the starkness of the familiar normative gendered self/other dualisms of Western culture: their obsession, familiar from deconstruction, with maintaining the purity and integrity of the self-same and repudiating a contaminating other.

Dualism itself, the entire construct of asserted self and repressed-returning other, is a function of this masculine economy of representation. From a perspective of some barely imaginable feminine economy, a different regime would obtain. Irigaray at times uses the language of multiplicity and diffusion to characterize such a feminine economy; I would argue that multiplicity and diffusion are themselves contaminated by the self-other structure and stand in the place described by Derrida in *Positions* of the dialectical-synthetic third term, illusory and therefore falsely reassuring, inviting complacency in seeming to offer something entirely different from dualism. Again, it is Kristeva's "impossible dialectic," simultaneously acknowledging dualism and repudiating both its hierarchical imbalance and its rigid self-other exclusivity, that, in my opinion, offers (in a term crucial to Irigaray, as we will see) a *passage* out of our masculine economy of representation, given the fact that we are now inevitably located within it and can only see a passage out within its terms.

In its compulsion to repress the maternal origin, masculine (self-)representation defines (refines) itself in opposition to maternal materiality as pure intellect, ideality, and reason. Irigaray's recapitulation of her version of Freud, in "Any Theory of the 'Subject' Has Always Been Appropriated By the 'Masculine'," the first essay in the "Speculum" section, begins to emphasize this aspect of her story, an aspect that, for obvious reasons, will become crucial in "Plato's *Hystera*": "He [Freud, as representative theorist of masculine subjectivity] must challenge her ["mother/nature"] for power, for productivity. He must resurface the earth with this floor of the ideal" (140). Or, in "How to Conceive (of) a Girl," the fourth essay in "Speculum," based on four fragments from Aristotle's *The Generation of Animals* and *The Physics*:

> The state of existence of the "beginning" from which being will emerge and stand apart [in Aristotle] is not predictable; being traces its lineage back first to a male parent who already rejoices in a specific form, and then, if we go back over the causes of generation, to that father's desire and love for God: "origin" of pure property. *For God, the intelligible will be identified with intellection, thus avoiding the aporia that may arise out of the boundlessness of a "first matter"* as a result of her eternal and perfect autonomy. (161, italics added)

This anxious and obsessive elevation of God, the father, form, and reason over their other, matter-mother-earth-blood-chaos-*physis*, is most crudely elaborated by Plotinus, the lesser thinker who institutionalizes the repressive ideological content of the greater, and therefore more complex and open-ended, Socratic-Platonic texts.[25] It is an elevation based, as Irigaray (in the tradition of Engels) repeatedly says, on the historical-material fact of male dominance over property and capital, production and reproduction.[26] But the myth Western culture has used to explain the system that results from this gender dominance suppresses its material history, substituting emanations of its own elevation of ideality. This myth, constructed by Plato, is deconstructed by Irigaray in "Plato's *Hystera.*"

In Plato's parable of the cave,[27] his story of movement from benighted prison of illusory shadows to, literally, enlightened vision of truth enabled by reason, Irigaray finds the prime representation of her account of representation. Plato's cave immediately reveals itself as the earth-womb, the denigrated maternal origin that the masculine subject must deny, leave, and replace by logos.

The men in the cave are chained in such a way that they can only look at what is in front of them. At the outset of the story, the move toward the masculine-dominant economy of representation has already begun. The back of the potential male subject is already turned on the maternal origin, even while he is still within her womb: "Heads forward, eyes front, genitals aligned, fixed in a straight direction and always straining forward, in a straight line. A phallic direction, a phallic line, a phallic time, backs turned on origin" (245). Behind them, at the back of the cave, the male "magician-imagemakers" (264), having already co-opted the function of representation, project distorted, reversed shadows. They also generate "an echo which [comes] from the other side" (Plato, 254). These distorted representations depend (they are distorted *because* they depend) on the participation of the made-invisible "other side" of the cave—the already denied, repressed maternal origin. The participation of the feminine in the scene of its own silencing is required if the masculine economy is to establish itself by suppressing it: "The feminine, the maternal are instantly *frozen* by the 'like,' the 'as if' of that masculine representation dominated by truth, light, resemblance, identity. By some dream of symmetry[28] that itself is never ever unveiled . . . The *womb*, unformed, 'amorphous' origin of all morphology, is transmuted by/for analogy into a circus and a projection screen, a theater of/for fantasies" (265).

The masculine subject emerges from the cave of illusion into the light of sun, truth, reason, form, the ideal, the logos, the Father. In Plato's myth, this emergence marks a total repudiation of the cave: "And when he remembered his old habitation, and the wisdom of the den and his fellow-prisoners, do you not suppose that he would felicitate himself on the change, and pity them? . . . Would he not say with Homer, 'Better to be the poor servant of a poor master,' and to endure anything, rather than think as they do and live after their manner?" (256). But, as Irigaray argues, this too-much-protested exclusivity of the masculine subject's fealty to the father-sun (father-son) bespeaks its necessary containment of/contamination by the suppressed maternal feminine:

> Even though it has been decided that these struggles will die out in the Sun, that light will conquer darkness and truth fantasy, that *the father* in other (?) words will hold the monopoly on procreation, will alone sow the "good" seed and be able to give it a "proper" name, nonetheless, underground, in the dim light of the cave, or else in the *captive consciousness of the child*, the fight will go on. The second birth, secondary origin, renaissance or reminiscence of truth will never, simply, defer the *hysterical tropism.*[29] The discourse of reason, solar and paternal metaphor, will never oust the fantasy structure of the cave completely. (274)

The maternal origin, the feminine, "stripped of [her] function as cause," is repository of this fantasy structure; her "burning, incendiary chambers" that "may produce change" become "mere dark holes in which lucid reason risks drowning" (302). At the same time, her boiling waters are chilled into ice, an "ice in which he mirrors himself, without coupling. Such frigidity is required for an exact self-knowledge, for the maintenance of self-identity. She is just chilled enough to prevent his being deformed in her waters, lost in her ever receding depths, but not so chilled that she might shine with tenfold radiance, multiplying the light's power. A mild, mat frost. A cold whiteness that will send back the light" (302).

The threat to the patriarchal hegemony of reason and the self-same constituted by those roiling, originary feminine waters, waters that must be subdued into an icy reflection of masculine self-representation if it is to maintain itself, is clearest in Plotinus's angry, contemptuous attack on "Matter" in his Sixth Tractate, "The Impassivity of the Unembodied," from his *Enneads*,[30] quotations from which constitute the entirety of Irigaray's "Une Mère de Glace." Water is the feminine element par excellence, for Irigaray[31] as for (Western) mythology and iconography in general.[32]

Matter is, for Plotinus, at once liquid and feminine-maternal. It is incapable of form, but is the necessary medium upon which form imprints itself. "Authentic Existents . . . pass through it [Matter] leaving no cleavage, as through water; or they might be compared to shapes projected so as to make some appearance upon what we know only as the Void" (169). Liquid and formless void, matter is also, in Plotinus's direct appropriation of Plato's language, "the receptacle and nurse of all generation" (173): very explicitly the maternal feminine—"The Ideal Principles entering into Matter as to a Mother affect it neither for better nor for worse" (179).[33]

Particularly remarkable in Plotinus's text, as edited (but not altered) by Irigaray, is the tone of scornful attack and violent repudiation in the treatment of matter. It is this suspiciously violent need to deny the generativity of matter as the maternal feminine that Irigaray emphasizes by her choice of quotes:

> Matter is not Soul; it is not Intellect, is not Life, is no Ideal-Principle, no Reason-Principle; it is not limit or bound, for it is mere indetermination; it is not a power, for what does it produce? It lives on the farther side of all these categories and so has no title to the name of Being. . . . not even strong enough to withdraw, so utterly has it failed to accept strength from the Intellectual Principle, so absolute its lack of all Being. Its every utterance, therefore, is a lie. . . . Feeble in itself, a false thing and projected upon a falsity, *like an image in a dream or against water or on a mirror*, it [the "visible thing" as opposed to the ideal form] can but leave Matter unaffected. . . . Perhaps we have here the solution of the difficulty as to how Matter, essentially evil, can be reaching towards The Good: there would be [in this "seeming"] no such participation as would destroy its essential nature. (168–71, italics added)

Plotinus, in his scornful reductionism, culls the essential misogyny of the informing myth of phallogocentric metaphysics, a myth that depends on converting the threat of the seemingly all-encompassing materiality of the maternal feminine into a powerless, propertyless (in both senses) void of nonbeing, characteristically, and crucially for this study, imagined and imaged as water.

My decision to use water imagery as the focus for textual analysis in this study was founded partly in Irigaray, partly in Conrad, and partly in the daily presence on my desk, at a crucial phase of work on this project, of the Metropolitan Museum of Art's 1987 engagement calendar, which is organized around water imagery.[34] This decision preceded my reading of Klaus Theweleit's *Male Fantasies*, Volume I: *Women, Floods, Bodies, History*, but his book reinforced, and gave further theoretical-historical justification for, that decision (as is evident in his title, he finds water imagery a locus of representation of the feminine).[35] Theweleit historicizes Irigaray's deconstructed metaphysics, discovering it first in narratives written by Nazi soldiers, then reconstructing in its light the entire history of bourgeois culture. Since Theweleit was working on this book at approximately the same time that Irigaray was writing *Speculum*, he was unaware of her work, as he was unaware of French feminist thought in general (though he made extensive use of Deleuze and Guattari's *Anti-Oedipus*[36]). He begins with documentation of the Nazi soldiers' attitudes toward women and self as revealed in letters, memoirs, journals, pamphlets, and more standard genres of literary and nonliterary writing.

The written texts of these Nazi men reveal versions of self and attitudes toward femininity that Theweleit finds not an exception to, or a pathological distortion of, some more benign norm, but rather an extreme point *within* a continuum of characteristic masculine gender subjectivity in patriarchal culture. The texts construct a self rigorously defended, armored, rigidified—a self in terror of dissolution in the "abyss" associated with sexuate woman and vaginal fecundity. For the most part, women are entirely omitted from the conscious universe of these men as revealed in their writings. Sons are born, just as in Irigaray's formulation, without the acknowledged participation of their mothers. Daughters are not mentioned. Wives are omitted from accounts of weddings; the emphasis is rather on the father-in-law. Positive versions of femininity are associated with the chaste purity of virgins in white. All that so terrifyingly threatens the fragile, and therefore violently defended, upright armored rigidity of these men is associated with the liberation of desire as embodied by the overtly, genitally erotic woman. It is important that this threatening desire, gendered female, is imaged as turbulent flood, either of water as a general element or, more specifically, as unleashed red flood of all that dangerous, repressed sexual-political matter; it is crucial for my argument here that this is *simultaneously* the *red* flood of socialist revolution and of menstruation and childbirth. The rising flood of the working class, and, historically proximate, of the "dark" races, is conflated symbolically with that of the repressed maternal feminine, as we will see throughout this study.

The Nazi evidence is presented and interpreted in chapter 1, "Men and Women." In chapter 2, "Floods, Bodies, History," Theweleit elaborates his (highly ambitious, like Irigaray's) history of bourgeois Western culture in relation to the phenomena discovered in chapter 1. Using two dialectically related terms of Deleuze and Guattari (*Anti-Oedipus*), drawn from their Marxist argument about the simultaneous liberation and alienation of human productivity under capitalism, Theweleit establishes his conceptual-historical framework:

> The contradiction runs as follows: the process of primary accumulation in industry opens up the borders of a hitherto unknown human productive potential, setting in motion streams of money, commodities, and workers, and propelling itself forward on the streams of sweat and blood of workers and non-European peoples. Running parallel to that is a process of *limitation*, directed against the evolution of human pleasures. Deleuze and Guattari call the first process *deterritorialization*—the opening up of new possibilities for desiring-production across the "body with organs"—and the second process *reterritorialization*, which is mobilization of dominant forces to prevent the new productive possibilities from becoming new human freedoms [Theweleit has a reference here to *Anti-Oedipus*, 34ff.]. We'll look next at the course taken by reterritorialization in bourgeois history as a whole; that is, at how anything that flowed came to inspire the kind of fear we have seen in our soldier [wonderfully misprinted as "solider"] males. (264)

Theweleit goes on to assert that "in all European literature (and literature influenced by it), desire, if it flows at all, flows in a certain sense *through women.* . . . in relation to the image of woman. . . that image lives in water" (272–73). The bourgeois "reterritorialization" of this flowing woman-desire coincides with the bourgeois enforcement of monogamy and the contemptuous relegation of overt female sexuality to the working class: "The newly constructed edifice of the bourgeois-absolutist state is founded upon the restructured sexuality of the 'high-born' woman, who is to become a model for all women. The flowing of the streams of desire is captured and held in a fountain; it bubbles up to please man in his own garden. It is desensualized, 'white' water, perfect for irrigating the new ordered state" (316).[37]

It is crucial for this study that class oppression, imperialism, and the subordination of woman are all part of the same bourgeois economy: "Thus the expansion of the European world outward beyond old boundaries found expression in imperialist drives against 'primitive peoples.' I submit that this corresponded to an inner imperialism that took as its territories lands formed from the subjugated nature of female bodies. . . . The patriarchal bourgeoisie, arming itself for a new departure toward world domination, depended equally on both forms of subjugation" (323). Theweleit postulates here a crucial symbolic concatenation operative during the bourgeois period (modern Western culture since the Enlightenment), where race and class are frequently suppressed co-referents of representations of woman and the feminine. I will assume or work explicitly with that co-reference throughout this study.

At the turn of the century and in the first half of the twentieth century, woman is simultaneously reduced to the vagina and enlarged to the sea of seas, becoming the utopian site of the absence of lack, deterritorialization of gender-class-race, repository of all desire. At the same time, she is both punished for man's defeat, his disappointment in her (bourgeois culture's) inability to provide such a utopian plenitude in reality, and also functions as site of reterritorialization. I would argue that this simultaneity, this unresolved contradiction or dialecticality, arises in this period from the presence on the historical scene of the "revolutionary horizons" of socialism and feminism, offering when taken together a new utopian/dystopian scenario in which the threat and the promise of the "red flood" have become inseparably connected.

Irigaray, again, pointed to *the potential for* an undoing of the hegemonic masculine representational economy in Freud. I would point again to Freud's position as a figure of the modernist moment. Irigaray finds in Freud not just an overlooked or undeveloped potential for subversion but a deliberate suppression of it, as if Freud, realizing precisely what his own insights would overthrow and seeing where his self-interest lay, reinscribed the old narrative with all the more insistence. Irigaray's account of this double structure in Freud is very similar to Theweleit's adaptation of "deterritorialization-reterritorialization" in relation to woman:

> For whereas the man Freud ... *might have been able* to interpret what the overdetermination of language (its effects of deferred action, its subterranean dreams and fantasies, its convulsive quakes, its paradoxes and contradictions) owed to the repression (which may yet return) of maternal power ... whereas he might have been able also to interpret the repression of the history of female sexuality, we shall in fact receive only confirmation of the discourse of the same, through comprehension and extension. With "woman" coming once more to be embedded in, enclosed in, impaled upon an architectonic more powerful than ever. (141)

And, Theweleit might add, she becomes the flowing world of desire, the maternal "oceanic feeling" of absence-of-lack, for the continual frustration of which she must be continually punished. And, I would add, she also becomes the history of the simultaneous possibility and threat of her own liberation from this deadlocked idealization. For modernist writing, the "overdetermination of language (its effects of deferred action, its subterranean dreams and fantasies, its convulsive quakes, its paradoxes and contradictions)" is foregrounded as definitive of literary form just at the moment when its constitution by the "repression (which may yet return) of maternal power" is most radically challenged. Again, this returning repression is collapsed with, as co-representation of, the promised/threatened liberation of lower classes and darker races. The position of the Platonic earth-cave, and of the maternal womb, as "lower" and "darker" achieve this co-representation at the symbolic level.

Without paying attention to history in anything but the vastest sense, Irigaray, as we have seen, locates Freud at/as the one moment of potential but suppressed rewriting of patriarchal Western culture—historically, the modernist moment—reproducing in her paradigm of simultaneous liberation and suppression the double structure of modernist *sous-rature*.[38] Within this structure, the very psychoanalytic insights *about language*, and procedures for applying those insights to a subversive mode of interpretation, that could generate the release of the maternal (with its co-referents of repressed others of class and race) into culture, become instead the means of its firmer resuppression. In another sequence, in "Plato's *Hystera*," Irigaray provides a wonderful version of the phenomenon of "path" or "passage." This version accounts for the quality of *sous-rature* that, much more explicitly than Kristeva's "impossible dialectic, never the one without the other," makes modernist *sous-rature* different from the traditional dualistic "both/and":

> Thus, in that cave, inside that cave, burns *a* fire "in the image of" *a* sun. But there is also *a path*. ... A repetition, representation, figuration reenacted

within the cave of that passage which we are told leads in and out of it. Of the path *in between*. Of the "go-between" path that links two "worlds," two modes, two methods, two measures of replicating, representing, viewing, in particular the sun, the fire, the light, the "objects," and the cave. Of this passage that is neither outside nor inside, that is between the way out and the way in, between access and egress. This is a key passage, even when it is neglected, or even especially when it is neglected, for when the passage is forgotten, by the very fact of its being reenacted *in* the cave, it will found, subtend, sustain the hardening of all dichotomies, categorical differences, clear-cut distinctions, absolute discontinuities, all the confrontations of irreconcilable representations. . . . But what has been forgotten in all these oppositions, and with good reason, is how to pass through the passage, how to negotiate it—the forgotten transition. The corridor, the narrow pass, the neck. *Forgotten vagina.* . . . (246–47) Obliteration of the passage between outside and inside, up and down, intelligible and sensible . . . the "father" and the "mother." (344)

The biologism of this vaginal "passage" is, I would argue, enabling rather than vitiating here (as opposed to some of the biologism in *This Sex Which Is Not One*)[39] because it is so vividly present in, and such a crucially suppressed and sublated component of, Plato's allegory:

> Behold! human beings living in an underground den, which *has a mouth open towards the light* and reaching all along the den . . . And suppose once more, that he is *reluctantly dragged up a steep and rugged ascent,* and held fast until he is forced into the presence of the sun himself . . . you will not misapprehend me if you interpret the journey upwards to be the ascent of the soul into the intellectual world . . . (*Republic* VII: 514, 516, 517; italics added)

Cultural accessibility of this vaginal "passage" would not substitute a "feminine" multiplicity for phallogocentric unity or duality. Quite the contrary, two terms—"father" and "mother" as symbolic type of the self-other—are retained. What changes is the relationship between them: no longer either/or, asserted and excluded, superior and inferior, higher and lower, nor a simple both/and, but a simultaneity enabled by the open "passage" between them. This passage recalls the culturally suppressed originary birth canal and opens into the modernist literary text.

Chapter 2

A DIFFERENT STORY: "THE YELLOW WALLPAPER"

AND *THE TURN OF THE SCREW*

I BEGIN with a pair of 1890s works neither of which is generally included in the modernist canon, even the protomodernist canon (if there is such a thing). Although mainstream critical consensus has certainly made James at least a modernist precursor, if not a full-fledged member of the order, it is generally the great Major Phase novels *The Wings of the Dove* (1902), *The Ambassadors* (1903), and *The Golden Bowl* (1904) that are discussed in connection with modernist epistemology and narrative practice, not *The Turn of the Screw* (1898), which has been of enormous interest, for obvious reasons, to psychoanalytically oriented criticism.[1] Yet *The Turn of the Screw* anticipates the modernist formal conventions of the unreliable narrator who generates irreducible interpretive uncertainty—notoriously, the apparitions the narrator of this story sees are of indeterminate status, as are her imputations of "evil" to the children—and the conventions of narrative framing or distancing: she tells her story in a "manuscript" delivered to the mysterious Douglas, who then reads it aloud to a group including the narrator who opens the text. This is a triple narrative frame, similar to those sequences in *Lord Jim* where we hear Jim's story in his voice but as mediated by Marlow's retelling to the group of listeners.[2]

The critical provenance of Charlotte Perkins Gilman's "The Yellow Wallpaper" (1892) is even farther removed from the precincts of modernist canonization. A lost text until it was revived by second-wave feminist criticism, via Feminist Press reprint in 1973, it has been treated almost exclusively as a cautionary or inspirational parable of the possibilities, limits, and dangers of women's liberation, feminist reading, and feminist criticism itself.[3] Yet, like *The Turn of the Screw*, it palpably qualifies as a work of modernist origination.[4] It inherits Poe's (and Melville's, in *Benito Cereno*) premodernist form of pathologically unreliable first-person narrative, marking the progressive derangement of an initially plausible narrative voice, and it anticipates Kafka's and the surrealists' use of dream structure, notably condensation and displacement, as an ordering principle of narrative. Further, it makes both chronology and agency undecidable—who rips the wallpaper behind the bed? when is it ripped? who is responsible for the "smooch" around the perimeter of the room? for gnawing the bedstead?—and offers other unassimilable detail, for example, the mysterious "Jane," who appears for the first time at the end of the text (wonderfully, undergraduates frequently decide that the protagonist herself is "Jane").[5]

I too, like other feminist readers of this text, will analyze the wallpaper figuration in relation to feminist paradigms of freedom, autonomy, desire, and female subject-construction through writing. But the purpose of that analysis will not be to locate "The Yellow Wallpaper" as either a cautionary or an exemplary fable for contemporary feminists. Rather, I will analyze the self-contradictory doubleness, the formal *sous-rature* of the wallpaper figuration as an instance of Gilman's attempt to write a different story. I will read both these works as incipiently modernist expressions of profound ambivalence concerning the radical changes in society and culture promised by the "revolutionary horizon" of socialism and feminism, changes overtly desired by Gilman and overtly feared by James.[6] This ambivalence, reflected in water, forged, here and in the texts I discuss in Part II, the *sous-rature* of early modernist narrative.

The gothic provides controlling conventions for both tales: "uncanny" apparitions and an old, "ancestral," "haunted" house in an isolated rural setting as location and metaphor of the female protagonist's confrontation with those apparitions.[7] In each of the texts, though more conclusively in "The Yellow Wallpaper," the apparitions are figures of the protagonist's repressed anger at her capitulation to male authority and of her frustrated desire for an eroticized power. The female protagonist's domination by a distant, authoritarian male figure is a determining narrative fact in both texts, a motivator of her psychological struggle. Both texts *are* the female protagonist's narration of her own attempt to write a different story and of that attempt's defeat. In both, this attempt corresponds to (produces, is produced by, figures) insanity.

Gilman's nameless narrator-protagonist is a young invalid wife infantilized by a bullying doctor-husband who, generally absent, nonetheless sets the regimen that absolutely controls her life. James's similarly nameless narrator-protagonist is the standard gothic young woman, the condition of whose employment as governess (another familiar fictional convention) at "Bly" is that she acquiesce totally and unquestioningly to her dashing, handsome employer's desire never to be troubled by her.[8] She does so because she falls in love with him at the job interview, a situation that fixes in the reader's mind the unequal power relations between them.[9] James thus establishes a paradox as the determining condition of his story: she loves her employer and therefore agrees never to see him.

Gilman's oppressive husband supplies two narrative-generating paradoxes, one of them the historical fact of S. Weir Mitchell's notorious "rest cure."[10] This "cure" for a depressed woman involves, in this story, forcing her to sleep in a room she dislikes and forbidding her any creative outlet or enlivening human contact. Concomitantly, the narrator's depression is postpartum, and the hateful room she is forced to inhabit is a nursery. Maternity, just as the Irigarayan story would predict, instead of confirming her generative power, her full-fledged adulthood, further infantilizes her—makes her even more childlike in relation to her husband's paternalistic authority. In the haunted, quasi-dispossessed ancestral funhouse of patriarchy, it is explicitly she, rather than her baby, who is forced into the hideous nursery: "There's one comfort, the baby is well and happy, and does not have to occupy this nursery with the horrid wall-paper" (22).

Gilman's primary figure of ambivalence toward female freedom and a world in which it might flourish is that "horrid wallpaper." But the narrator's oppression by patriarchal marriage is so forcefully represented that most feminist readers overlook the ambivalence informed by the narrator's own fear of freedom. In the action of the story, which is the same as the writing of the story, the narrator at once rebels and reimprisons herself.

The representation of oppression governs the opening of the story. The "horrid wallpaper" is only the most notable torment in a room that is established as evocative more of a torture chamber than of the chldren's nursery it is supposed to be.[11] In fact, the nursery *is* patriarchy's torture chamber for the disenfranchised mother. It has "rings and things in the walls" (12) and bars on the windows. Its only piece of furniture is a heavy bedstead that is nailed to the floor, and there is a gate at the head of the stairs. These details are planted among distracting effusions about the beauty of the house and garden, the airiness of the nursery, and the kindness of sinister husband John, but Gilman makes sure we get the point about him: "John laughs at me, of course, but one expects that in marriage. . . . I sometimes fancy that in my condition if I had less opposition and more society and stimulus—but John says the very worst thing I can do is to think about my condition, and I confess it always makes me feel bad" (9–10).

The "opposition" she has, in place of "society and stimulus," is that of her husband and brother, both doctors, to her writing. The writing of the narrative is itself the narrator's most successful act of rebellion. But she cannot *feel* successful: "I did write for a while in spite of them; but it *does* exhaust me a good deal—having to be so sly about it, or else meet with heavy opposition" (10). Although she "disagree[s] with their ideas" and "believe[s] that congenial work, excitement and change, would do [her] good" (10), these attitudes do not help her combat that "exhaustion" any more than they alleviate the "bad feeling" induced by thinking about her "condition." These are the exhaustion and bad feeling of self-destructive internal conflict—of needs and impulses pushed back by frightened repression.[12]

The narrator has internalized the punitive, constraining voices of paternalism so successfully that the story's battle is primarily her own against herself. Gilman dramatizes that ambivalence by means of the narrator's symbolic projections onto the wallpaper. When the wallpaper first appears, it is already a figure not only of the narrator's repressed anger, sexuality, and desire for freedom, but of that repression itself.

The wallpaper first appears as "one of those sprawling flamboyant patterns committing every artistic sin" (13). Its color is a "smouldering unclean yellow, strangely faded by the slow-turning sunlight. It is a dull yet lurid orange in some places, a sickly sulphur tint in others" (13). The yellow-orange of anger and sexuality, the patternlessness and flamboyance of freedom, are alienated and contaminated for the narrator by her fear of them: the color is "unclean," "repellent, almost revolting"—dangerously angry and sexual—but it is also "faded" by the (masculine) sun, "dull," "sickly," nearly extinguished by repression.[13]

The "sprawling flamboyant pattern" is "dull enough to confuse the eye in following, pronounced enough to constantly irritate and provoke study": in the very act of condemning the wallpaper's freedom here, the narrator cannot help but express her fascination. But expressing it immediately brings on a fit of self-repressive fear. Just after she says the pattern is "pronounced enough to constantly irritate and provoke study," she goes on to say, "and when you follow the lame uncertain curves for a little distance they suddenly commit suicide—plunge off at outrageous angles, destroy themselves in unheard of contradictions" (13). The "sprawling and flamboyant" pattern has suddenly become "lame" and "uncertain." Its dangerous assertions—its "outrageous angles"—can only "destroy themselves" in the "suicide" of "unheard of contradictions": a summary of this text's self-contradiction and a foreshadow of the story's deadlocked end.

The theme of self-destructive repression is elaborated in the wallpaper's next appearance. The narrator has been lamenting again the strictures her husband places on her freedom, just as she had been before her first mention of the wallpaper. He has told her she must curb her "imaginative power and habit of story-making" (15), in other words, her creativity, her impulse to write. Her response begins with capitulation, then moves rapidly to rebellion, frustration, defeat, and, finally, denial: "I wish I could get well faster. But I must not think about that" (16).

The moment she voices that final denial—"I must not think about that"—the narrator turns to the wallpaper: "This paper looks to me as if it *knew* what a vicious influence it had!" (16). The "vicious influence" of her own dangerously rebellious feelings—the feelings that prevent her from "getting well" in a way that will satisfy her husband—combats repression through projection onto the wallpaper. The personified wallpaper's guilty knowledge of its "vicious influence" is, of course, the narrator's own knowledge of both her anger and her fear. The two combine to impel her to elaborate the theme of suicide, initiated in the first passage about the wallpaper, now clarified as death by strangulation: "There is a recurrent spot where the pattern lolls like a broken neck and two bulbous eyes stare at you upside down." (By the end of the story, the narrator has actually made an unsuccessful attempt to hang herself: "I've got a rope up here that even Jennie did not find. . . . But I forgot I could not reach far without anything to stand on!" [34].)

The eyes staring upside down are a wonderful invention. They stare at her as projections of her own knowledge, but they are dead, both denying that knowledge and killed by it. Further, they are grotesquely "bulbous," swollen with the pressure of unallowable feeling. Knowledge and feeling together have been killed by strangulation, and they are upside down, inverted, products as they are of denial and displacement.

The narrator's relation to the wallpaper progresses as her "condition" deteriorates:

> I don't feel as if it was worth while to turn my hand over for anything, and I'm getting dreadfully fretful and querulous.
>
> I cry at nothing, and cry most of the time. . . . I am alone a good deal just now. . . .
>
> I'm getting really fond of the room in spite of the wall-paper. Perhaps *because* of the wall-paper.
>
> It dwells in my mind so! (19)

Only in the wallpaper, which, quite literally, "dwells in [her] mind," can she allow herself a displaced representation of her desire for freedom from repressive "laws": "I know a little of the principle of design, and I know this thing was not arranged on any laws of radiation, or alternation, or repetition, or symmetry, or anything else I ever heard of" (20). She must, of course, separate herself from this representation of freedom, in a desperate attempt both to check or contain her defiance and at the same time to allow it to play itself out: "I determine for the thousandth time that I *will* follow that pointless pattern to some sort of a conclusion" (19). The disapproval evident in her tone here becomes suffused with the disgust attendant on denied sexual feeling. Again, she sees the wallpaper as "bloated," presumably by the pressure of that repressed desire:

> Looked at in one way each breadth stands alone, the bloated curves and flourishes—a kind of "debased Romanesque" with *delirium tremens*—go waddling up and down in isolated columns of fatuity.

But, on the other hand, they connect diagonally, and the sprawling outlines run off in great slanting waves of optic horror, like a lot of wallowing seaweeds in full chase. (20)

Beneath the surface tone of conventional sarcasm, Gilman's diction develops the narrator's dilemma. "Delirium tremens" connotes madness resulting from excess, revealing again the narrator's fear of her feelings (if she "lets them loose," they will both elude control and become addictive, like liquor to the alcoholic). "Waddling," "sprawling," and "wallowing" suggest female sexual self-disgust, and these adjectives joined with "bloated" suggest pregnancy; "debased" and "isolated" describe the narrator's condition itself.

As the narrator's torment intensifies, the wallpaper can no longer provide her with release. She is losing the battle against her desire, against herself. The wallpaper's "lack of sequence," its "defiance of law," is now "a constant irritant to a normal mind" (25). She is becoming desperate because she knows she can rely less and less on the defenses she has constructed against what she has projected onto that lawless wallpaper:

> The color is hideous enough, and unreliable enough, and infuriating enough, but the pattern is torturing.
>
> You think you have mastered it, but just as you get well underway in following, it turns a back-somersault and there you are. It slaps you in the face, knocks you down, and tramples upon you. It is like a bad dream. (25)

The mastery provided by denial is defeated—slapped, knocked down, and trampled—by the projected "bad dream" her desire has become, which, in its "back-somersault," escapes repression.

The imagery Gilman uses to represent that repressed desire continues to point to sexual expression as a component of liberation from repressive "laws." The pattern, in an image that combines both phallic and vaginal suggestions with terrifyingly uncontrolled fecundity, has become a "toadstool in joints, an interminable string of toadstools, budding and sprouting in endless convolutions" (25). Finally, the wallpaper acquires a foul, "yellow" smell, which "creeps all over the house. I find it hovering in the dining-room, skulking in the parlor, hiding in the hall, lying in wait for me on the stairs" (28–29). The yellow smell of the narrator's sexual disgust, the foul yellow smell of the repressed sexuate maternal body, is described in the same terms, in its creeping, hovering, skulking and hiding, as the "woman behind bars," the "back pattern" of the wallpaper, which Gilman has been developing throughout the story in tandem with the "front pattern" of similarly denied desire.[14] Susan Lanser's reading of "yellow" in this story as a repressed racial other makes clear the conflation of the nonwhite with the female within the ambivalence of modernist *sous-rature*.[15] I would add to that conflation the suggestion of class sub-ordination in the "back pattern" (back stairs) woman's perpetual stooping and skulking, which suggest not only the position but, literally, the movements of the female servant's labor. That labor is actually the most important element of the political unconscious of this story, because without it the upper middle class woman's infantilization, as well as the rest cure, the story's premises, would be impossible.

The caged woman first appears as a "kind of sub-pattern in a different shade, a particularly irritating one . . . a strange, provoking, formless sort of figure, that seems to skulk about behind that silly and conspicuous front design" (18). This "sub-pattern" is visible only in "certain lights." At its next appearance, as the narrator's self-division progresses, the "sub-pattern" has become, dimly or faintly, but unmistakably, "a woman stooping down and creeping about" (22), who only appears in moonlight and who seems to "shake the pattern, just as if she wanted to get out" (23). The moonlight and its effect on the narrator are described in the same terms as the caged woman herself: "I hate to see it sometimes, it creeps so slowly. . . . I kept still and watched the moonlight on that undulating wall-paper till I felt creepy" (23).

Almost immediately—the narrator's deterioration has accelerated—the sub-pattern becomes just as constitutive of the wallpaper for her as the outside pattern. She connects the outside pattern to the male sun and the sub-pattern, again, to the female moon:

> There is one marked peculiarity about this paper, a thing nobody seems to notice but myself, and that is that it changes as the light changes.
>
> When the sun shoots in through the east window—I always watch for that first long, straight ray—it changes so quickly that I never can quite believe it.
>
> That is why I watch it always.
>
> By moonlight—the moon shines in all night when there is a moon—I wouldn't know it was the same paper.
>
> At night in any kind of light, in twilight, candle light, lamplight, and worst of all by moonlight, it becomes bars! The outside pattern I mean, and the woman behind as plain as can be.
>
> I didn't realize for a long time what the thing was that showed behind, that dim sub-pattern, but now I am quite sure it is a woman.
>
> By daylight she is subdued, quiet. I fancy it is the pattern that keeps her so still. It is so puzzling. It keeps me quiet by the hour. (25–26)

By the end of the story, the narrator has "resolved" her dilemma by entirely disowning the rebellion she had projected onto the wallpaper, redefining it as "front pattern," and *becoming* the caged woman of the sub-pattern: "It is the same woman, I know, for she is always creeping, and most women do not creep by daylight. . . . I always lock the door when I creep by daylight" (30–31). The ending depicts the narrator's "success" in "freeing" herself, the caged woman, from the prison of the wallpaper, so that she can creep around and around the nursery, tied, presumably, to the nailed-down nursery/marriage bed by her suicide rope.

To be male, the sun/moon imagery tells us, is to "shoot . . . a long straight ray"; to be female is to creep. Women skulk in their prisons, as anyone in prison might, but when they are freed, they simply go on skulking, no different outside the bars than in. Gilman has constituted, in the remarkable figure of the wallpaper, a false duality of prison and prisoner. Even the narrator hints at the spuriousness of that duality when she says she "lay there for hours . . . trying to decide whether that front pattern and the back pattern really did move together or separately" (25). In our empathy with the narrator, we want her to succeed in "freeing" the woman of the sub-pattern, who shakes the bars of her prison as if she wants to get out. That image of shaking the bars and coming out from behind them is so compelling that it can make us forget what the bars actually are. There is some indication that Gilman forgets too, since she allows the narrator to connect the front pattern with the male sun. Gilman seems to be participating in the narrator's increasing hopelessness about taking possession of anything that she has projected onto the wallpaper, seeing health and freedom as available only to men. No wonder she finds the front pattern's imprisonment of the back pattern's woman, her hopeless dilemma, "so puzzling" (26); a statement, in its modesty, of unbearable pathos.

The false duality inscribed in the wallpaper is the figure of the story's ambivalence about female freedom and sexuate-maternal empowerment, and, concomitantly, linkage of that threatening empowerment to liberation of the other of race and class. The front pattern and the back pattern *are* one—they do "move together" as the narrator suspects. They are the twin offspring of the narrator's internalization of her own oppression. The assertion and empowerment stifled by paternal law erupt onto the wallpaper. When that projection of denied anger, sexuality, and self-assertion becomes too threatening to the self-jailer who enforces the stifling, the eruption itself becomes, ironically, the "prison" whose bars must be pulled down. The woman it imprisons, the victor who escapes from behind the bars, is in fact also the victim—the trusty her capitulation to paternal authority has made her.

The impulse toward freedom and empowerment—the identification with the promise of the "revolutionary horizon"—invents the wallpaper; the fear of that horizon divides it into front and back patterns and sets them at war against one another. Because the narrator writes on/in the wallpaper a different story, using a different—modernist—mode of representation deploying the dream-structures of the unconscious, locus of the erupting sexuate maternal and its co-referents of race and class, she must tear the wallpaper off the wall of the nursery/prison within the ancestral patriarchal house, destroying her own textual creation, in order to "liberate" her own defeat. The modernist mode of representation does not survive in the world of this text. Gilman is more afraid of the liberation promised by the new order she herself is working to bring about than she is eager for it.

That liberation is connected with water and with female apparitions who seek it. The gothic house that encloses the story is located on a "bay," which is potentially accessible to the narrator by "a little private wharf belonging to the estate" (15). Wharf and bay are suggestive, I would argue, of uterine figuration. The place that imprisons her also gives her unthreatening, controllable ("little, private") access to freedom and to the empowerment of female sexuality. The lane and bay, and the surrounding overgrown garden, are another figure of freedom, which the narrator describes in clearly positive imagery suggesting an association of freedom with the feminine: "Those mysterious deepshaded arbors, the riotous old-fashioned flowers, and bushes and gnarly trees" (15). Lane and bay are immediately connected by the narrator to the exercise of her imaginative gifts and to her husband's disapproval of them: "I always fancy I see people walking in these numerous paths and arbors, but John has cautioned me not to give way to fancy in the least. He says that with my imaginative power and habit of story-making, a nervous weakness like mine is sure to lead to all manner of excited fancies"(15–16). John fears the "excited fancies" that might undermine not only his control over her erotic-creative "excitement" but his power to define for her what is real and what is not: his power over narrative.

The bay and the shaded lane running to it disappear through the middle section of the story, as the narrator's struggle turns entirely inward, locking itself in the nursery/prison of her mind. But in the final movement, when she has let go into madness, they reappear as figures of terrifying, unachievable freedom. First, the "yellow smell" is connected to "a week of fog and rain" (28)—water is no longer safe, pleasant, accessible, and figurally female. The lovely bay with its little wharf has become a dismal, powerful, ubiquitous atmospheric force of fog and a heavy rain traditionally associated with masculinity that alienate her sexuate maternal body and make it contaminate every atom of her world.

The bay's presence in the story is recalled only synecdochically, by means of the shaded lane that "runs" to it. This lane becomes by the end of the story the site of a female freedom unattainable by, and also terrifying to, the narrator. She decides the woman behind bars "gets out in the daytime" because she "sees" her creeping "on that long road under the trees" (30). Though this apparition still creeps, she also "runs," or even flies: "I have watched her sometimes away off in the open country, creeping as fast as a cloud shadow in a high wind" (31).

By the end of the story, the creeping apparition has multiplied in conjunction with the release of the narrator's anger. That anger is associated, though of course suicidally, with going through the window (toward what she sees outside it): "I am getting angry enough to do something desperate. To jump out of the window would be admirable exercise, but the bars are too strong even to try" (34).

That statement instantaneously evokes a guilty, almost finicky retraction that is Kafkaesque in its paranoid self-consciousness: "Besides I wouldn't do it. Of course not. I know well enough that a step like that is improper and might be misconstrued" (34–35). This repression turns her attention again to what is outside the window:

> I don't like to *look* out of the windows even—there are so many of those creeping women, and they creep so fast.
>
> I wonder if they all come out of that wall-paper as I did?
>
> But I am securely fastened now by my well-hidden rope—you don't get *me* out in the road there! (35)

She cannot bear the speed of her escaping doubles. She is so afraid of what they offer her that she must literally tie herself down. Her substitute for freedom is a (presumably very temporary) triumph over her husband. Taking on her hysteria, he faints—he does not collapse with anything even remotely fatal—when he sees her in her full-blown madness. She ends the story creeping repeatedly over his fallen body in her trapped, bound circuit around the perimeter of her cage.

James's parallel distrust of the "revolutionary horizon" was clear by 1886, the year he published *The Princess Casamassima* and *The Bostonians*. In *The Turn of the Screw*, issues of female power, sexuality, and autonomy and issues of class inequality are muted but crucial. They are also linked. In the 1908 New York Edition Preface to *The Turn of the Screw*, an extended metaphor that could have been taken straight from Theweleit uses water to represent the impossible dialectic of unleashing and at the same time restraining the imagination. This metaphor serves as an apt introduction to my argument here:

> Nothing is so easy as improvisation, the running on and on of invention; it is sadly compromised, however, from the moment its stream breaks bounds and gets into flood. Then the waters may spread indeed, gathering houses and herds and crops and cities into their arms and wrenching off, for our amusement, the

whole face of the land—only violating by the same stroke our sense of the course of the channel, which is our sense of the uses of a stream and the virtue of a story. Improvisation, as in the Arabian Nights, may keep on terms with encountered objects by sweeping them in and floating them on its breast; but the great effect it so loses—that of keeping on terms with itself. (119)

Note the flood's femininity, both in its implied association with Scheherezade and in "floating them on its breast," and its concomitant suggestiveness of revolution. Again, the feminine revolutionary horizon promises/threatens to write a wholly new story, which is precisely how James describes *The Turn of the Screw* elsewhere in the Preface: "The thing had for me the immense merit of allowing the imagination absolute freedom of hand, of inviting it to act on a perfectly clear field, with no 'outside' control involved, no pattern of the usual or the true or the terrible 'pleasant' (save always of course the high pleasantry of one's own form) to consort with" (118).

This narrative, says James, must be at once totally free and strictly restrained; subsequently, the critical history of *The Turn of the Screw* has made it a locus classicus of "ambiguity."[16] The 1930 essay by Edmund Wilson that instituted the interpretive controversy that still rages in relation to his essay almost sixty years later is entitled "The Ambiguity of Henry James."[17] The controversy of course concerns whether it is the protagonist or the children who are "guilty," whether the ghosts are "real" or projections, as Wilson argues, of the protagonist's repressed sexuality.

This controversy has spawned the remarkable terms "apparitionist" and "antiapparitionist," and on several counts, terminological self-consciousness is important in approaching criticism of this story. By convention, the character I have been calling the "narrator" or the "protagonist" is referred to as the "Governess." The framing narrator who introduces the tale is referred to as "*the* narrator" or the "I" (we consider Marlow, not the framing narrator, *the* narrator of *Heart of Darkness*). Evidently, such a view fixes the protagonist in, and defines her by, her subordinate class-gender status, while it confers on the male framer the privileged status of centered subjectivity, of reader-identified selfhood. James, however, makes *her* the focal narrative agency, the organizing Jamesian consciousness. One might argue that James emphasizes so explicitly the authorial prowess of the protagonist—"Douglas . . . had begun to read with a fine clearness that was like a rendering to the ear of the beauty of his author's hand" (14)—that he has made some of his readers uncomfortable enough to reascribe his authorization.[18]

Much of the "antiapparitionist" criticism is highly critical of the "Governess," frequently in a way that invokes misogynist stereotypes, emphasizing her "vanity," her pushiness, her delusional sexual frustration (like the "old maid" who is imagined to imagine rapists), her supposedly aggrandized notion of her position at Bly.[19] If the ghosts are not "real," then one must feel a combination of pity and contempt for the hysterical, repressed, deluded and deluding "Governess." One must also ultimately judge her guilty at least of tormenting innocent children, at most of murder. (But what can one expect of a poor, badly educated country parson's daughter.) James's strong statements on behalf of his protagonist's strength, intellect, and probity, and of the "reality" of his ghosts, are easily dismissed by these "antiapparitionists." (I am not suggesting, of course, that his statements be given either unquestioning credence or the unquestioned authority of "authorial intention"; rather, that such easy dismissal of them becomes readable as an act of repression.)

The debate over *The Turn of the Screw* reproduces the hierarchical either/or paradigm that has covered and distorted modernist ambivalence. *The Turn of the Screw* moves into a realm beyond ambiguity, a realm of pure irresolvable contradictoriness, where powerful evidence of the ghosts' reality *coexists* in the text with equally powerful evidence of their unreality.[20] As Leo Bersani says, in *A Future for Astyanax*, "the very question of what is 'true' is made irrelevant . . . the questions of the ghosts' reality and of the governess's repressions are unanswerable."[21]

Bersani also claims that those questions are unanswerable "because *The Turn of the Screw* raises no questions at all" (139). Bersani's emphasis is on the power of the Jamesian consciousness to generate narrative virtually unaided by standard fictional impedimenta. The protagonist is the Jamesian character par excellence, who, as assimilated to Jamesian authorship, "released from the obligation of having to operate within a clearly and distinctly given world of fictional events, assumes the function of novelizing" (140). Bersani gives her almost unlimited power, more even than she claims for herself, but in doing so he suppresses the "questions" of gender and class that this text clearly "raises."

Reading *The Turn of the Screw* in conjunction with "The Yellow Wallpaper" and in relation to Jamesian ambivalence concerning the concomitant claims to power and equality of women and of the "lower orders" yields no "definitive" reading of the text—needless to say, and particularly here, there is no such thing—nor is it intended to replace psychoanalytic, epistemological, or deconstructive readings.[22] But such a reading does constitute the text in suggestive ways not otherwise apparent (all that any reading can finally hope to do).

James postulates, in this story, a protagonist disadvantaged by gender and class, who nonetheless rises determinedly to the frightening challenge posed by the class advantage of both "master" and children and the absolute hereditary cultural proprietorship represented by Miles, the "little gentleman," heir to the haunted ancestral house. These children need not be seen as the helpless innocents they appear when class issues are elided from a reading of this text. In fact, one might argue that if they were not lowered, as it were, nearer their governess's status by their age, there would be no story for this protagonist—no possibility of such a poignantly valiant self-assertion on her part. The gulf would be too great.

The protagonist displaces her erotic engagement with the unreachable "master" onto his house and its inhabitants, his other dependents, as James concomitantly displaces the master's chilling power over the narrative and the protagonist to the same location.[23] The plot is generated by the protagonist's battle to bridge, by an eroticized self-assertion, the distance the master has imposed between her and his world of hereditary masculine upper-class privilege. Peter Quint and Miss Jessel always appear to the protagonist in relation to episodes or situations that make this self-assertion problematic. I would argue that they are figures of her fear of, and James's ambivalence about, such a gender- and class-specific claim to power.

As figures, their particularity constitutes a multiple or overdetermined representation. Like the "governess" and the beautiful, angelic-demonic orphan children, they are stock types of Victorian melodramatic fiction. Peter Quint, with full name but no title, is the licentious, drunken, presumptuous seducer, with red hair and a bold expression. Miss Jessel, with no first name but the "Miss" of her own governess position, is the tragic, doomed, darkly beautiful female victim-monster.[24] They are apparitions of the Victorian past of narrative and political possibility. Quite literally, they represent the past of this narrative: the dark secret of this haunted house, the limits against which the protagonist attempts to define a new order of narrative and social power, where the consciousness and *vision* of a poor, badly educated woman of undistinguished birth can shape a fiction that defies both "the master's" power and the spectres of Victorian sexual and narrative scenarios (in fact, the narrative is set at midcentury). The apparitions simply haunt the protagonist's acts of self-assertion. She is at war with them for control of the children, the future.

She first sees Peter Quint when she is in the act of claiming various prerogatives of power. Issues of power are frequently figured for her by images of water. At the end of the first chapter, in "possession" of Bly, she says she "had the fancy" that she, the children, Mrs. Grose, and the other servants are "almost as lost as a handful of passengers in a great drifting ship. Well, I was, strangely, at the helm!" (18). She represents her position here in a telling paradox: she is "at the helm" of a "drifting" ship. She has all power; she has no power.

In the sequence leading up to her first encounter with Quint, she says that the summer after Miles returns from school is "the first time, in a manner, that I had known space and air and freedom" (24), but then compares her charges to "little grandees, princes of the blood" (25), as if reminding herself of their actual position relative to her. In these long summer days, she allows herself "what I used to call *my own hour*, the hour when, for my pupils, tea-time and bed-time having come and gone, I had, before my final retirement, a small interval alone. Much as I liked my companions, this hour was the thing in the day I liked most. . . . I could take a turn into the grounds and enjoy, *almost with a sense of property* that amused and flattered me, the beauty and dignity of the place" (25, italics added).

She strolls through the estate, feeling that she possesses it, possesses herself, possesses at least a small piece of time. As she strolls, she thinks with complacency, even self-flattery (and her language here is used against her by some "antiapparitionists"), of her success in fulfilling the requirements of the absent master for whose sake she is undertaking her difficult assignments, the man "to whose pressure I had responded" (25). Precisely in her moment of claiming power, she thinks erotically of her absolute subordination to him. She concludes that she is "a *remarkable* young woman"—a very ambiguous word that is used repeatedly to describe the children, a word that encompasses James's simultaneous approval and disapproval of her claims.

"Plump, one afternoon, in the middle of my very hour," just as she is fantasizing that the master will suddenly appear to her, smiling and approving, his knowledge of her successful sacrifices for him shining in his handsome face, she sees instead Peter Quint, the embodiment not only of the male sexual aggression she is both suppressing and representing in her benign fantasy of the master's approval, but also of the melodramatic fictional scenario and the Victorian scenario of gender relations that she is attempting to rewrite and redress in her claims to authorship, power, autonomy, even a sort of equality with the master, figured for her by her fantasy of their mutual understanding.

Just when she thinks she will encounter the master at mutual eye-level, the double of his questionable and sinister power appears in a position of *illegitimate* superiority. The symbolic significance of Peter Quint's location, or the protagonist's placing of him, is almost parodically overloaded. He is standing high above her in a tower, specifically the "old" tower (there are two towers, "old" and "new"); he "fixes" her with a bold "scrutiny," he is "very erect."[25] He becomes almost a textbook illustration of phallic symbolism, and as a phallus he is clearly invested with power and proprietorship. The overdone quality of this symbolism, like the characterization and behavior of the master whom Quint hideously duplicates, is in line with the "old tower" itself—the bankrupt conventions of the fiction and society dominated by such an extreme of male power.

Most tellingly, with the statement "I saw him as I see the letters I form on this page" (28), James reminds us that the protagonist is the authorial sensibility, and also literally the author of the manuscript that *is* the story. At the same time, her stature as author is undermined, along with the other power and freedom she claims, by this emanation of the killing "old" story from which hers must be wrested. The apparition of Quint, both punishing and monitory, appears like an earlier version in a palimpsest, threatening to blot out the narrative she is trying to write.

The first encounter with Quint establishes a structure opposite to that of "The Yellow Wallpaper," where apparitions were generated by the narrator's self-repression. The second encounter with Quint establishes a counter-structure within *The Turn of the Screw* similar to the structure of "The Yellow Wallpaper." The situation of this encounter is precisely opposite to that of the first. Rather than feeling her freedom and power, the narrator is feeling oppressed, troubled by the mystery of Miles's dismissal from school—the painful challenge to which she is not at all sure she can rise—and by reminders of her origin, her past, rather than feeling elevated by fantasies of her empowering present or gratifying future: "I was in receipt in these days of disturbing letters from home, where things were not going well" (31).

As in "The Yellow Wallpaper," it is rain—masculine water overwhelming and permeating the atmosphere—that precipitates this development: "There was a Sunday—to get on—when it rained with such force and for so many hours that there could be no procession to church" (31). Church is a locus, of course, of convention, tradition, the old, established hierarchies of class and gender. Deluging rain prevents the orderly *procession* to church, but only temporarily, long enough to enact for the protagonist the agon of her rebellion against orderly procession. The rain stops; they are on their way to evening service; she has forgotten her gloves—left them in "that cold, clean *temple* of mahogany and brass, the 'grown-up' dining room" (31–32, italics added). This dining room, "temple" of legitimate authority, becomes the very important setting of the protagonist's final struggle. Here it is the setting of her humility: rather than presiding in dignity over the formal Sunday dining room tea, she had been enacting her lowly status by sewing her (worn-out?) gloves: "I remembered a pair of gloves that had required three stitches and that had received them—with a publicity perhaps not edifying—while I sat with the children at their tea" (31). Reminded of her "perhaps not edifying" position, as she is about to join the procession to church, she sees Quint through the dining room window: "One step into the room had sufficed;

my vision was instantaneous; it was all there" (32). Her position—"it was all there"—is revealed to her in a moment of "instantaneous vision." Quint, embodiment of that position, appears to her "with a *nearness* that represented a forward stride in our intercourse" (32, italics added): instead of striking us as the master's dark double, he now strikes us as hers. Like her, he is now positioned as the excluded, in the classic posture of the disenfranchised, outside the window looking in. His bold stare through the window is now a challenge to constituted authority identical to her challenge. He figures her fear of, and uncertainty about, her claim, that is, James's own ambivalence about it.

With hindsight, we can now see him as having been her double, as well as the master's, in the first encounter too. He appeared then in a position of threatening, illegitimate proprietorship just when she was feeling the fullness of her own, illegitimate(?) claim to equality and proprietorship. In the first encounter, the sight of Quint undermined her too-easy, self-flattering sense of successful mastery. In the second encounter, the consolidation of her knowledge of her marginality, the falseness of her claim to be an insider—to see Quint looking in from outside the window is to see it all clearly—brings to her a new knowledge: "On the spot there came to me the added shock of a certitude that it was not for me he had come there. He had come for someone else" (32).

She disavows her direct connection to Quint, even as she literally puts herself in his position: she immediately runs outside to stand just where he had stood, looking through the window. Mrs. Grose comes into the dining room, sees her there, and is terrified in her turn (the hierarchical "procession" of intimidation). Her decision that Quint has "come for someone else" is just as much an act of identification with him as it is a denial of that identification. Like Quint, she has "come for someone else": come to Bly for the master's sake and for service to the children. But "come for" is of course also a statement of a sinister desire to take possession. The object of that desire, the "someone else," now becomes Miles, the inheritor of patriarchal upper-class authority, power, autonomy, legitimacy. Miles's name reminds us of that echt-masculine stock character, *Miles Gloriosus*. He is, of course, usually "little Miles," putting him within her reach. Flora's name evokes a feminine vegetation goddess, an evocation reinforced by her association with water and plants. The first initials of the two names, M and F, make them together an allegory of gender.

The narrator's new knowledge, the displacement or focusing of her struggle for power onto possession of Miles, strengthens her shaken resolve: "The flash of this knowledge—for it was knowledge in the midst of dread—produced in me the most extraordinary effect, started, as I stood there, a sudden vibration of duty and courage" (32). This "vibration of duty and courage," courage acceptable because imagined as being in the service of duty rather than ambition, focuses itself, in subsequent conversation with Mrs. Grose (whose name wonderfully exonerates her from all trials of consciousness) as a determination to assert her power in order to "save" the children—a goal not questionable, troubling, frightening, as her desire to be generally in charge of Bly evidently was. Her fantasy of noble self-sacrifice, with the master, one imagines, always in mind as admiring audience and instigator, puts her right back in the masochistic Victorian feminine scenario: "I had an absolute certainty that I should see again what I had already seen, but something within me said that by offering myself bravely as the sole subject of such experience, by accepting, by inviting, by surmounting it all, I should serve as an expiatory victim and guard the tranquillity of my companions. The children, in especial, I should thus fence about and absolutely save" (39).

But the desire for power leaks through the many cracks in this safe masochistic fantasy. She will continue to "see": to be the sole governing consciousness ("sole subject of such experience"). She will offer herself "bravely"; she will invite, surmount, and guard: verbs of active power. She will "fence about and absolutely save" the children: a vision of absolute control, asserted more safely in the service of her ostensible repudiation of self-assertion.

She is now ready to meet the double of her (partial) acceptance of the Victorian feminine position. Her vision of noble self-sacrifice generates the apparition of the doomed, tragic, ruined former governess. Her first and last encounters with Miss Jessel take place across a body of water, the small lake or pond of the estate. Like the first two encounters with Quint, they reverse the relative positions of protagonist and apparition. In the first encounter, Miss Jessel appears to the protagonist with the body of water and Flora herself, her back turned to the site of the apparition, between them.

This encounter is preceded by a consolidation for the protagonist of her position of power gotten paradoxically by self-sacrifice. Masochism is always an obverse form of power, of course, but here the "secondary benefit" is foregrounded emphatically: "I was in these days literally able to find a joy in the extraordinary flight of heroism the occasion demanded of me. I now saw that I had been asked for a service admirable and difficult; and there would be a greatness in letting it be seen—oh, in the right quarter!—that I could succeed where many another girl might have failed" (42). She delivers herself over to the children, she "walk[s] in a world of their invention" (43), and they make her, in their fantasy games, "some remarkable person" of "superior . . . exalted stamp" (43).

The protagonist is playing some such game with Flora, "on the edge of the lake," which, in the game, is the "Sea of Azof": a wonderful figure of putative or hypothetical possession. They are sitting where the "old trees, the thick shrubbery, made a great and pleasant shade": overgrown, shady verdure, the world of "Flora," adjacent to a body of water; precisely the site of female freedom and eroticized empowerment imagined by Gilman in "The Yellow Wallpaper." She is again sewing, reminding us of her position in her last encounter with Quint.

The language in which she afterward describes to Mrs. Grose the appearance of Miss Jessel is straight from the melodramatic mode into which she has temporarily lapsed: "a figure of . . . unmistakable horror and evil: a woman in black, pale and dreadful—with such an air also, and such a face!" (46). But during the encounter itself, what she focuses on, and describes calmly, with restraint, is Flora's activity:

> She had picked up a small flat piece of wood, which happened to have in it a little hole that had evidently suggested to her the idea of sticking in another fragment that might figure as a mast and make the thing a boat. This second morsel, as I watched her, she was very markedly and intently attempting to tighten in its place. My apprehension of what she was doing sustained me so that after some seconds I felt I was ready for more. Then I again shifted my eyes—I faced what I had to face. (45)

Flora's action suggests "the turn of the screw"—that multifarious figure of aggressive sexuality, associated with children, that governs the text. Peter Quint and Miss Jessel are damnable seducer and damned seduced; in turn they become seducers of the children. The protagonist's struggle is with her own "illicit" desire for the master and for mastery, displaced onto his future heirs and haunted by his past retainers. Flora's neat objective correlative of the sexual consummation that would provide a "boat"—a means of actually embarking on the dangerous waters of these desires without being overwhelmed by them—gives the protagonist the courage to face, and face down by splitting the image off from herself, the embodiment of her own inscription in melodrama.

The encounter with Miss Jessel marks the end of the first movement of the story. The protagonist has detached from herself, as apparitions, the threatening aspects of her claims to power, autonomy, sexual self-expression. Peter Quint, the seducer, is "no gentleman";[26] he is an illegitimate usurper of the master's position, even to the point of appearing to the protagonist in the master's stolen clothes. Miss Jessel, a "lady"—respectable like the protagonist—has been dragged down to Peter Quint's class level by her sexuality.

In the middle section of the book, once the protagonist has decided that the children "know"—that they are Quint's and Miss Jessel's accomplices—she sees Quint *below* her on the stairs, faces him "in our common intensity" (59), and feels no fear. She has joined him in the quest for socially and sexually illegitimate power, even as the overt version of that quest takes a noble, self-sacrificing, orthodox form: "dread had unmistakably quitted me and . . . there was nothing in me there that didn't meet and measure him" (59).

Miss Jessel appears to her as only pathetic, sitting, again on the staircase *below* the protagonist—these issues of relative positioning are crucial—and then sitting wretchedly at the nursery table. She becomes an expression of the protagonist's own increasing wretchedness at her total abandonment by the master. Miss Jessel seems at first to be a servant "writing a letter to her sweetheart" as she sits at the nursery table—a displacement and reversal, as well as an echo (servant) of the protagonist's own hopeless erotic position. She cannot bring herself to write to the master; when she does at last, the letter is stolen by Miles, the heir.

The despair she feels at her decision that the children "know"—that they are demonic rather than angelic, though potentially savable—enables her to redouble her efforts at control. She will enclose them, win them over, possess them. Her impulse toward self-assertion has found a socially, fictionally, and theologically acceptable channel, but a channel that *James* presents as having become sinister and frightening just when the apparitions have become so much less so.

In fact, the apparitions cease for the moment to appear. The climactic episode of this section begins with the protagonist discovering Flora looking out of the window. She assumes Flora is communing with Miss Jessel, but the girl is in fact looking at Miles, who has gone outside and is looking at some point on the tower above the grand, stately, chillingly empty (master?) bedroom that the protagonist has decided is the best vantage point for her to observe an apparition on the lawn that she thinks will be Miss Jessel. The protagonist is literally not positioned at this moment to see what Miles is looking at on the tower, though she assumes it is Quint. This episode enacts the futility of the protagonist's position: she cannot inhabit the master bedroom legitimately; she is not entitled to encounter the children directly—they are looking elsewhere. Although hers is the authorial consciousness, the only consciousness capable of vision, that vision can only be partial and misdirected, compromised as it is both by the illegitimacy of her claims and by her capitulation to her fear of that illegitimacy.

The narrative turning point comes in the appropriately gothic churchyard, on another aborted procession to church. Miles asserts, against the protagonist's assertion of power over him, his ineluctable class and gender rights, rights that would inevitably be reasserted once the protagonist acceded to the domain in which they hold sway by redefining her struggle within such orthodox narrative-political boundaries. It is not James who elides or even suppresses issues of class and gender privilege in this text:

"Turned out for Sunday by his uncle's tailor . . . Miles's whole title to independence, the rights of his sex and situation, were so stamped upon him that if he had suddenly struck for freedom I should have had nothing to say" (77). On Sunday, on his way to church, legitimately appareled in his own version of his uncle's clothes, his title and his rights, if openly claimed, would obliterate hers. They would in fact silence her, terminating her continuing effort, however compromised, to write a different story.

In the final movement of the text, the now openly acknowledged power struggle between the protagonist and the children is organized around two culminating episodes, the first involving Flora and the closing episode, of course, Miles. In these two episodes, first Mrs. Grose and then Miles himself fail to see, respectively, Miss Jessel and Quint, leaving the protagonist entirely alone, except for Mrs. Grose's crucial continuing faith in her vision. (It is certain my conviction gains infinitely, the moment another soul will believe in it," says Novalis in Conrad's epigraph to *Lord Jim.*)

The penultimate episode releases the protagonist from both the earthbound, nonvisionary, traditionally female world of motherly "Mrs. Grose" and also from the melodramatic plot within which she has self-defeatingly cast herself as noble, piteous heroine. This episode is saturated with water: there has been a storm the previous night (in which the protagonist has confronted Miles, inconclusively, with his guiltly "knowledge"); the afternoon is "damp and grey" (94). On this rainy day, Miles beguiles the protagonist with music, drawing her into his privileged world of high culture and accomplishment. Flora meanwhile "escapes" to the lake; at last missing her, the protagonist annexes Mrs. Grose and goes to look for her. She opens the first of the two chapters that narrate this episode with a digression on "sheets of water":

> We went straight to the lake, as it was called at Bly, and I dare say rightly called, though I reflect that it may in fact have been a sheet of water less remarkable than it appeared to my untravelled eyes. My acquaintance with sheets of water was small, and the pool of Bly, at all events on the few occasions of my consenting, under the protection of my pupils, to affront its surface in the old flat-bottomed boat moored there for our use, had impressed me both with its extent and its agitation. (94–95)

Throughout the text, the protagonist's overall situation is described in water imagery, particularly as "depths" to be "sounded" or "plunged" into (recall the "great drifting ship" of which she is "strangely at the helm" of the first chapter). The emphasis here is on the protagonist's inexperienced vision—her "untravelled" eyes—and the shallowness of the water (a "sheet" is a flat surface, suggesting, moreover, both beds and shrouds), an emphasis that is reiterated a paragraph later: "the depth is, I believe, nowhere very great" (95). It is also important to note the intimidating, threatening quality of the pool, despite its shallowness: "its extent and agitation." The female element is hostile; it is shallow but unfamiliar and threatening; it is aggrandized by the terminology of Bly, made a "lake" rather than the mere "pool" it really is. The protagonist is simultaneously intimidated by and contemptuous of it. I would argue that, at this point in the text, the negative component of James's ambivalence toward the feminine—his fear and contempt of female sexuality, in particular—is mobilized on behalf of the protagonist's coming battle with the social and narrative conventions of the feminine that, during the middle section of the story, have worked against her vision and her new narrative of power.

The protagonist's subsequent description of the "pond" (a compromise between "lake" and "pool") confirms it as, at this moment of the text, a figure of female sexuality: "The pond, oblong in shape, had a width so scant compared to its length that, with its ends out of view, it might have been taken for a scant river" (96). In this fairly explicit vaginal image, the repetition of the word "scant" signals a defense, by belittlement, against the clearly threatening quality of what is called in the very next sentence "the empty expanse."

Fairly dragging Mrs. Grose behind her, the protagonist must skirt the rough perimeter of the pond, since Flora has taken the homely, reassuring "old flat-bottomed boat," leaving the two women with no means to cross the hostile body of water. (The protagonist immediately knows that Flora has gone to the spot across the pond where Miss Jessel first appeared: see n. 20.) The protagonist's valor in the face of the threatening watery oblong and its surrounding tangle of nearly impenetrable vegetation is asserted here in her fortitude at braving the "ground much broken" and the "path choked with overgrowth" (96), just as it is earlier, when she tells Mrs. Grose they are going to look for Flora at the lake: " 'You're going to the water, Miss?—you think she's *in*—?' 'She may be, though the depth is, I believe, nowhere very great' " (95). James is establishing the protagonist's ability to overcome what he represents as the watery grave of feminine superficiality, which he, again, associates here with the dangers of female sexuality and the inability to *see* that Mrs. Grose and Flora demonstrate in this episode—as we know from Irigaray, vision is masculine, blank watery embodiment feminine.

What they are unable to see (or, in the case of Flora, what she perhaps refuses to acknowledge the sight of) is the alternative femininity that Miss Jessel has come to represent. While Flora was a figure simultaneously of a bankrupt Victorian narrative and also of a potentially new future, she had been allied with Miss Jessel. During this episode she openly repudiates both the vision of Miss Jessel and also the real presence of the protagonist, aligning herself instead entirely with Mrs. Grose. James figures the bankruptcy of her mode of femininity by mocking her mythological name—as the protagonist and Mrs. Grose approach her, where she stands "on the grass" in a "copse," she "stoop[s]" to pick "quite as if it were all she was there for—a big, ugly spray of withered fern" (97). Her "floral" loveliness has "withered," become "ugly"; moreover, it is now "all she is there for"—she no longer offers the protagonist anything of worth.

The word "ugly" is important, signaling the end of the protagonist's enchantment with Flora's Victorian angelic-demonic-melodramatic beauty. Flora first becomes "old," a description of her that is repeated several times during the course of the episode. She has become, literally, the embodiment of the "old" order, like the "old" tower. As she turns toward Mrs. Grose and against the protagonist and the vision she offers, looking at the protagonist with "an expression of hard, still gravity, an expression . . . that appeared to read and accuse and judge me," "united" with Mrs. Grose "in pained opposition to me," Flora becomes to the protagonist not only "ugly" but "common": "I prayed God to forgive me for seeming to see that, as she stood there holding tight to our friend's dress, her incomparable childish beauty had suddenly failed, had quite vanished. I've said it already—she was literally, she was hideously hard; she had turned common and almost ugly" (101). Flora's speech repudiating the protagonist "might have been that of a vulgarly pert little girl in the street" (101). The beautiful fairy princess (one thinks of the fantasy games they play in the middle section of the book) has turned into a plain, vulgar commoner, fit only to be carried off by Mrs. Grose. The negative component of James's ambivalence about the "revolutionary horizon" of redress of class inequity—his contempt for the lower orders—is mobilized here concomitantly with the negative component of his ambivalence toward women's new claims to equality. They are both deployed in the service of the protagonist, a relatively lowly woman, who is to be exempted from the negative judgment against women and the lower orders because of her saving power of consciousness, the writer's power of authorship, that power so prized by the modernists as the hope of redemption from cultural bankruptcy, the vision she has attained in the course of this story.

That vision, embodied in this episode as Miss Jessel, presents itself to her again across water; the female element of water both separates and unites the two women. The language of identification between the protagonist and Miss Jessel is heavily emphasized here: she appears just where the protagonist had sat with Flora in the first encounter; in insisting that Flora sees Miss Jessel, the protagonist says, "you see her as well as you see me!" (99). The protagonist's first reaction to the sight of Miss Jessel "on the opposite bank" is a "thrill of joy": "she was there, and I was justified" (98).

Miss Jessel is no shining figure of triumphant femininity, however. The protagonist establishes in her vision of Miss Jessel simultaneously her own power and her own "evil." To repudiate the conventional feminine is not at all, in this incipiently modernist text, to be free of it; quite the contrary, as Gilman's protagonist has already poignantly taught us. Where Gilman's protagonist pays the price of madness for capitulation to patriarchal authority, James's protagonist pays the price of "damnation" for defiance of it.

Miss Jessel is a "pale and ravenous demon" (99), suggesting now vampirism rather than melodramatic victimhood. She rises "erect on the spot my friend and I had lately quitted," a figure of masculinized power, "and there was not, in all the long reach of her desire, an inch of her evil that fell short" (99). An "erect," potent, efficacious figure of "evil desire," she simultaneously embodies and makes hideous the protagonist's libidinal and social ambitions. The phrase "she's as big as a blazing fire" (100) suggests, obviously, uncontrolled, destructive desire, damnation, and also the antithesis of water: to repudiate the feminine is to become a hideous, destructive, damned version of the masculine.[27]

When the protagonist turns "to communicate again" with Miss Jessel, she is "as vividly there for my disaster" as she is "not there for my service" (101). Nonetheless, she had felt a "thrill of joy" at seeing her, and she sends her an "inarticulate message of gratitude" (99). The joy and gratitude are ostensibly for the "service" the protagonist thinks Miss Jessel will render by finally showing herself to Mrs. Grose and to Flora in her presence, thereby confirming the protagonist in her increasingly desperate control over the children. Similarly, the "disaster" is presumably Mrs. Grose's failure to see and Flora's failure, or refusal, to acknowledge the sight. But this language focuses, apart from, and in conjunction with, this issue, the paradox of the protagonist's situation: this appearance of Miss Jessel *is* simultaneously the protagonist's triumph and her disaster. The protagonist says, without explanation, precisely that. Mrs. Grose's failure to see Miss Jessel, followed immediately by her annexation of Flora, marking the end of the protagonist's compromise with the old plots, produces this remarkable passage:

> with this hard blow of the proof that her [Mrs. Grose's] eyes were hopelessly sealed I felt my own situation horribly crumble. I felt—I saw—my livid predecessor press, from her position, on my defeat, and I was conscious, more than all, of what I should have from this instant to deal with in the astounding little attitude of Flora. Into this attitude Mrs. Grose immediately and violently en-

tered, breaking, even while there pierced through my sense of ruin *a prodigious private triumph*, into breathless reassurance. (100, italics added)

Through her sense of the "ruin" of the painfully achieved status quo of the middle section of the book, a ruin marked by her separation from Mrs. Grose and Flora, newly allied within the conventional feminine, pierces the "prodigious private triumph" of her full allegiance with Miss Jessel, explicable only as the triumph of her emergence from that compromise into a fully realized, and fully damned, claim to power.

The crisis in this episode had been brought on by the protagonist's allowing herself at long last to utter Miss Jessel's name to Flora, thereby literally summoning her presence. When Flora asks her "And where's Miles?" she responds: "There was something in the small valour of it that quite finished me: these three words from her were, in a flash like the glitter of a drawn blade, the jostle of the cup that my hand, for weeks and weeks, had held high and full to the brim and that now, even before speaking, I felt overflow in a deluge" (98). Drawn blade and overflowing cup: heavily conventional symbols of the masculine and the feminine—the masculine invoked by the name of Miles, the feminine cup overflowing in a deluge at the summoning of Miss Jessel. After Mrs. Grose whisks away the transformed Flora, who does not appear again in the narrative, the protagonist swoons. When she comes to, she is on the ground, aware only of "an odorous dampness and roughness" (101). She gets up and sees "the grey pool and its blank, haunted edge" (102): clearly (to me) a figure of antifemale sexual disgust. The deluge has receded, leaving in its damp, blank residue a foreshadow of the protagonist's empty triumph, avatar of a damned empowered maternal feminine, over the heir.

Mrs. Grose and Flora fly to London and, presumably, the master's protection, reintegrated into the order he represents. The protagonist assumes full command: "It was precisely, in short, by just clutching the helm that I avoided total wreck; and I daresay that, to bear up at all, I became, that morning, very grand and very dry" (109). Far from finding herself "strangely at the helm" of a "great drifting ship," she is "clutching the helm" of a ship on the point of "total wreck." Saving the ship by means of such desperate but firm and determined self-assertion keeps her "very dry" and also makes her "very grand." She becomes the lady of the house, taking meals with Miles, who has assumed almost fully the position of the master: with evident erotic displacement, she compares their embarrassed silence in the presence of the maid to that of "some young couple who, on their wedding-journey, at the inn, feel shy in the presence of the waiter" (112).

These silent meals are eaten in that crucial formal dining room. (In case we have forgotten, the protagonist reminds us of its significance: "I had been waiting for him [Miles] in the ponderous pomp of the room outside of the window of which I had had from Mrs. Grose, that first scared Sunday, my flash of something it would scarce have done to call light" [110].) She renounces the "fiction that I had anything more to teach him" (110)—he has attained to the rights of his gentlemanly status. It is with a young man, a gentleman and putative proprietor, not an orphaned child, that she has her final contest.

The final episode is a fight to the death in the ring of the formal, traditional, domestic interior, with the illegitimate claim to power represented by Quint again relegated to marginality, positioned outside looking in through the window. The language of this episode is highly eroticized, and characterized by an intensification of water imagery. The protagonist begins by eliciting from Miles a reluctant "surrender," yielded up with "the finest little quiver of resentful passion" (115): an acknowledgment that there is something for him to confess. This surrender thrills her: "I can't begin to express the effect upon me of an implication of surrender even so faint. It was as if what I had yearned for had come at last only to astonish me" (115). She is delighted that he seems to be afraid of her, which is "perhaps the best thing to make him" (115). She describes herself as "nearly reaching port" (115), dry and in command.

Fortified by these successes, she works herself up to asking Miles whether he stole the letter she finally wrote to the master from the hall table the previous day, an act that officially confirms his "evil," but also serves to place him literally in the master's position, the usurping but nonetheless functional recipient of the protagonist's letter to the master. As soon as she asks this question, Peter Quint appears at the window, embodiment of the illegitimacy not of Miles's theft of the master's right, because he is its legitimate heir, but rather the illegitimacy of the protagonist's claims. Only she can see Quint now: it is clear to her, and James confirms for the reader (by having Miles ask whether Miss Jessel is at the window) that Miles cannot see him. She is alone with Quint in the presence of Miles, just as she was alone with Miss Jessel in the presence of Mrs. Grose and Flora.

Quint no longer offers a bold, challenging stare. His is now the "white face of damnation" (116), now that the protagonist has asserted mastery, taken on not just Flora but Miles himself, and is to be damned for it. The sight of Quint reconfirms her in her self-assertion: she is going to play the drama out to the end. She experiences her self-assertion sexually, "enfold[ing]" Miles "with a moan of joy" (117). Her "quickened courage" brings her a "success" that is measured by the severing of "communication" between Miles and Quint, itself again a measure to her of her empowerment as authorial consciousness, the only one who *sees*. With the damned, outcast usurper Quint as her dark double, she has taken command: "I felt that the cause was mine and that I should surely get *all*" (118; note the ambiguity of "cause" and of the emphasized "all," also the grammatical ambiguity of "should").

She turns on Miles to press home her victory, shaking him, "but it was for pure tenderness" (118), to get from him a full confession, a total "surrender." Miles is suddenly submerged: "He looked in vague pain all round the top of the room and drew his breath, two or three times over, as if with difficulty. He might have been standing at the bottom of the sea and raising his eyes to some faint green twilight" (119). The protagonist is no longer at the helm of her ship, dry, near port. His "surrender" (repeated again) and her "victory" bring her for the first time into the water, the "sea," first floating on the surface and then foundering in bottomlessness with Miles: "I seemed to float not into clearness, but into a darker obscure, and within a minute there had come to me out of my very pity the appalling alarm of his being perhaps innocent. It was for the instant confounding and bottomless, for if he *were* innocent, what then on earth was *I*?" (119). She is precisely *not* "on earth," and there is no longer even any ship whose helm she can clutch. "It," the consequence of her self-assertion, is "confounding and bottomless." The wreck has come, she is going down. The sea bordered by the "revolutionary" class and gender "horizon," across which she had hoped to steer her authorial ship to the port of a new social and narrative order, has become "confounding and bottomless," enforcing its threat rather than yielding up its promise. Her victory is complete—she "dispossesses" the gentleman-proprietor-heir— but she can do so only by killing him. If he is innocent, legitimate, then what on earth is she: doomed either to marginality and illegitimacy or to damnation. In "The Yellow Wallpaper," a female-signed text fearing what it desires, female capitulation is damnation; in *The Turn of the Screw*, a male-signed text desiring what it fears, female (and subaltern) victory is damnation.

PART II

CONRAD AND OTHERS

Chapter 3

DARKER AND LOWER DOWN: THE ERUPTION
OF MODERNISM IN "MELANCTHA" AND
THE NIGGER OF THE "NARCISSUS"

NEITHER Irigaray nor Theweleit considers race, a category of otherness crucial to the formation of modernist narrative. As Jameson has made clear, Conrad occupies a privileged position in the history of that formation; quite possibly because he does consider the issue of race. Plato's cave is dark; the masculine subject moves from the dark maternal cave into the brilliant white sunshine of the father's truth. Dark race and low class (the cave, like the womb, is under, lower; the sun is above, higher), together with the maternal itself, erupt in a troubled conjuncture at the birth of modernist narrative.

The Nigger of the "Narcissus", 1897, and "Melanctha," 1906, partly achieve modernist narrative: they undermine realism, though without yet establishing the modernist configuration of *sous-rature*.[1] In both texts, race, class, and childbirth figure together in the disruption of traditional narrative form. Nineteenth-century narrative forms persist, however, as structuring frames, sources of narrative impulse, in both texts: the heroic seagoing tale of masculine solidarity in gale-defying toil of the sailors on the *Narcissus* and the naturalist antibildungsroman of Melanctha's thwarted life. These frames are sufficiently functional, in fact, to control most responses to the texts. Criticism generally sees them as defining the two texts, allowing for some lapses, or complications, or inconsistencies. I would argue that the impact of modernist disruption is so great that it prevents the ostensible narratives from dominating the effect of the two texts.

In both texts, the source of disruption is the lure of what the ostensible narrative must discredit. Conrad is fascinated by the cowardly subjectivity of Wait, the "nigger," and the attendant infamy of his double, Donkin, self-appointed spokesman of the proletariat. Stein is fascinated by Melanctha's point of view, which justifies her selfishness as she wanders in the realm of dangerous knowledge.[2]

Wait and Donkin are, of course, the bad guys of, and therefore crucial to, the heroic tale of the sea—theirs is the existential abyss over which the solidarity of the crew constructs itself. But their power in the text overwhelms that subordinate role and overwhelms at the same time the narrative structure that relies on it. Similarly, Melanctha's self-justification, the reasonableness of her view of her own self-destructive behavior, is necessary to Stein's nonjudgmental naturalist saga of thwarted aspiration. It must seem to Melanctha, and to the reader's sympathy (if not to the reader's ultimate judgment), that she does nothing wrong; fate is simply against her, as in the Laforguian epigraph to *Three Lives*: "Donc je suis un malheureux et ce / n'est ni ma faute ni celle de la vie." ("Thus I am an unfortunate, and this is neither my fault nor life's.") But Stein, by entering as fully as she does into the construction of that self-justification, unleashes into the text material too subversive to be contained by the detached, cool, fatalistic narrative she is ostensibly writing.

By Stein's own assessment, "Melanctha" was "the first definite step away from the nineteenth century and into the twentieth century in literature."[3] All the characters in "Melanctha" are black; black characters appear nowhere else that I can think of in Stein's oeuvre.[4] "Melanctha"was an adaptation of an earlier, fully conventional autobiographical work, *Q.E.D.*, the story of Stein's painfully unresolved triangular relationship with May Bookstaver, the prototype of Melanctha, a white woman of Stein's own educated upper middle class.[5] Transposing her story to the black working and middle classes coincided for Stein with the initiation of those remarkable reinventions of literary form that characterize her career in the twentieth century. (I would argue that "Melanctha"is the point at which Stein's work coincides most closely with modernism—after the [almost] modernist "Melanctha," Stein moves beyond or outside modernism into avant-garde experimentalism.)[6]

By contrast, nonwhite characters inevitably appear throughout that portion of Conrad's work based on his experiences in Africa and in Eastern seas, work in which the interaction of white denizens of various imperialist "outposts of progress" with the native populations they are meant to "civilize" is a central recurrent theme, as it is of so much Conrad criticism.[7] But in *The Nigger of the "Narcissus"* the uncharacteristic dominance of a black character in the narrative, as in the title, coincides with Conrad's own first "definite step away from the nineteenth century and into the twentieth century in literature" (in fact, the Preface to *The Nigger of the "Narcissus"* stands as Conrad's own modernist manifesto, in power and significance comparable to Wordsworth's Preface to *Lyrical Ballads*).

Racial otherness, specifically the "blackness" we can connect to the dark and darkly suppressed maternal origin, functions chaotically in these texts. Race is a highly ambiguous force of disruptive fascination or fascinating disruption, contributing to the generic indeterminacy (ostensible story undermined, modernist alternative inchoate) of these narratives rather than to any racist or antiracist, conservative or subversive, thematic configuration.[8]

James Wait's famous entry into *The Nigger of the "Narcissus"* is marked by darkly comic confusion: the mate, Mr. Baker, hears as a rude challenge Wait's cry of his own name as he arrives late for the ship's first muster. Conrad deliberately puts the reader in the same position as Mr. Baker, so that we experience sequentially Wait's challenge to authority, his characteristic imposition of delay, and his unassailable explanation, which makes him "right as ever, and as ever ready to forgive" (15). The initial description of Wait is a marvel of complexity, encapsulating as it does this character's polysemous position in the text. One element of this opening characterization establishes Wait as a majestically superior being. He is a "tall figure" with a "sonorous voice . . . His head was away up in the shadows of lifeboats. . . . The nigger was calm, cool, towering, superb. . . . He overtopped the tallest by half a head. . . . The deep, rolling tones of his voice filled the deck without effort." At the same time, Wait's superiority is ironized: "he stood in a swagger that marked time. . . . He was naturally scornful, unaffectedly condescending, as if from his height of six foot three he had surveyed all the vastness of human folly and had made up his mind not to be too hard on it."

The notoriously pervasive light/dark imagery of this story (important for the patriarchal paradigm of Plato's cave) is ambiguous in this description of Wait: "The lamplight lit up the man's body. . . . His head was away up in the shadows . . . The whites of his eyes and his teeth gleamed distinctly, but the face was indistinguishable. . . . He held his head up in the glare of the lamp—a head vigorously modeled into deep shadows and shining lights." In the ostensible narrative, light is good and dark is bad, just as sea is good and land is bad. Any responsible reading of this text would then note the complications and ambiguities that interrupt this predominant pattern. But the ambiguity of light/dark imagery here—the sheer overdetermined excessiveness of it—goes well beyond interruption.

The description culminates in a deliberate gesture of racial stereotyping: "a head vigorously modeled into deep shadows and shining lights—a head powerful and misshapen with a tormented and flattened face—a face pathetic and brutal: the tragic, the mysterious, the repulsive mask of a nigger's soul" (15). That final phrase has a powerfully defining impact, in the word "repulsive" itself, strong for Conrad, and in the suggestion that "a nigger's soul" cannot be seen directly, it is too dark and obscure, but it can be represented at a distance by a barbaric, simultaneously revealing and concealing "mask." Negative as the overall impact of this characterization undeniably is, however, it is also marked by an ambiguity generated by the strong positive modifiers: "vigorously," "shining," "powerful," "tragic," and "mysterious."

"Mysterious" is clearly a key word, designating Wait's dangerous appeal. Again, in the ostensible narrative, Wait represents the moral darkness of the soul, the abyss of self-indulgence, cowardice, and stagnation against which the crew must define itself in masculine solidarity of seaworthy endeavor. Through much of the narrative, we perceive Wait in that light (or darkness). During the ludicrous "mutiny," for example, Wait is described as "that moribund carcass, the fit emblem of their [the mutinous crew's] aspirations" (94). But his death sequence is narrated (part of it, indeed, from his own point of view) with moving power and for the most part with sympathy. We enter fully into his compelling, damned subjectivity, much as we do Jim's in his account of the *Patna* episode. It is not merely a matter of the pity Captain Allistoun feels for Wait, "standing there, three parts dead and so scared—black amongst that gaping lot—no grit to face what's coming to us all . . . Sorry for him—like you would be for a sick brute" (98). Allistoun's subsequent, less distanced comment is more revealing: "One lone black beggar amongst the lot of us, and he seemed to look through me into the very hell" (98). As "nigger," Wait is privileged to look through all of us into "the very hell," to make accessible the dark substratum (cave) from which the subversive material of modernism is erupting, projecting its darkness onto the Father's light itself, making it "a luminous, arid space where a black sun shone" (87, Jimmy's deathbed nightmare).

Similarly, the crew's attitude toward Jimmy is not simply one of weak pity and self-destructive susceptibility, as it must be in the ostensible narrative. In fact, the narrative characterizations of the crew's attitude are deliberately, recurrently, and often perfectly ambivalent. The narrator accords Wait great stature even when damning most forcefully his corrupting influence:

> He fascinated us. He would never let doubt die. He overshadowed the ship. Invulnerable in his promise of speedy corruption he trampled on our self-respect, he demonstrated to us daily our want of moral courage; he tainted our lives. Had we been a miserable gang of wretched immortals, unhallowed alike by hope and fear, he could not have lorded it over us with a more pitiless assertion of his sublime privilege. (37)

Other expressions of the crew's attitude are more neatly, perfectly ambivalent: "We hesitated between pity and mistrust" (29). "We knew he was dry and comfortable within his little cabin, and in our absurd way were pleased one moment, exasperated the next, by that certitude" (41). "We could not scorn him safely—neither could we pity him without risk to our dignity. So we hated him, and passed him carefully from hand to hand" (57).

Dr. Jefferson Campbell, the transformation in "Melanctha" of the Gertrude Stein character in the autobiographical *Q.E.D.*, might say just the same thing (though in different language) of his ambivalent feeling toward Melanctha. The position of race in the configuration of ambivalence in "Melanctha" is in many ways very different from that in *The Nigger of the "Narcissus"*—the characters in "Melanctha" are all black. However, the visibility of the characters' race disappears and reappears throughout the text. In long sequences, particularly in the central movement of the novella that treats the love affair of Jeff and Melanctha, racial specificity (except in the speech rhythms) is suspended—we enter into what Conrad might call the truth of the characters, independent of racial stereotype or antistereotype, as we do into the truth of Jimmy's dying.

Nonetheless, it is clear that the race of Stein's characters enables her, as Wait's blackness enables Conrad, simultaneously to undo her own naturalist narrative and to explore dangerous thematic possibilities. Stein uses American racial stereotyping both in the service of, and against the grain of, her ostensible naturalist story. As Conrad does in *The Nigger of the "Narcissus,"* she incorporates race into this fiction chaotically, undecidably.

Repeated passages of crude, profoundly offensive racial stereotyping should not be, but almost always are, overlooked by Stein critics.[9] I would guess that sequences such as the following, which comes right at the beginning of the novella, have kept "Melanctha" off numerous syllabi:

> Rose Johnson was a real black, tall, well built, sullen, stupid, childlike, good looking negress. She laughed when she was happy and grumbled and was sullen with everything that troubled. . . .
>
> Rose laughed when she was happy but she had not the wide, abandoned laughter that makes the warm broad glow of negro sunshine. Rose was never joyous with the earth-born, boundless joy of negroes. Hers was just ordinary, any sort of woman laughter.
>
> Rose Johnson was careless and was lazy, but she had been brought up by white folks and she needed decent comfort. Her white training had only made for habits, not for nature. Rose had the simple, promiscuous unmorality of the black people. (85–86)

The attributes of this repellent racial stereotyping that were liberating for Stein are apparent here: "*abandoned* laughter," "*earth-born, boundless* joy," "*promiscuous* unmorality."[10] Stein carefully distinguishes the "yellow," partly white, "complex and intelligent" Melanctha from the lazy, stupid, sullen, careless, black Rose, but it is Melanctha's "negro" qualities—her abandonment, her promiscuity, and her connection to the boundless joy of the earth (quite obviously, post-Cixous and Irigaray, maternal jouissance)—that excite Stein, quite literally, and unleash her new writing. It is Melanctha's "wandering," which summarizes and encodes the "negro" element of her racial identity, that necessitates the self-justifications that simultaneously confirm the naturalist narrative and carry Stein past the point of no return in acknowledging the excitement those "negro" qualities make her feel.

Racial stereotypes and counterstereotypes function in complex, undecidable concatenations throughout the text. It is worth noting that the only character conceived as a noncontradictory racial stereotype, the gambler Jem Richards (Melanctha's desperate last attempt to save herself through heterosexual involvement), is the least vividly realized character in the text. The rest of the characters simultaneously embody and contradict racial stereotypes. We have already seen that Rose Johnson is in a sense a classic stereotype, but Stein carefully counters that stereotype by making her an orphan who was raised by whites and who therefore "needed decent comfort." Also, having been raised by whites, she never laughed with the "wide, abandoned laughter that makes the warm broad glow of negro sunshine."

Rose's foil is Jane Harden, Melanctha's first (erotically cathected) woman ally and mentor (Rose is her last). Jane is, schematically, Rose's opposite: intelligent where Rose is stupid, reckless and generous where Rose is careful and shrewdly selfish. Again, Stein simultaneously employs and undercuts racist stereotype. Jane, like Melanctha, is intelligent and light-skinned, and the two qualities are linked: "Jane was a negress, but she was so white that hardly any one could guess it. Jane had had a good deal of education" (103). But, in spite of her "white" qualities, Jane is "bad" in a racially stereotyped way: "Jane Harden had many bad habits. She drank a great deal and she wandered widely" (104). The light-skinned, well-educated, intelligent woman suffers and dies from the "promiscuous unmorality of the black people," while the "sullen, stupid, childlike" black woman carefully marries and ensconces herself within a safe, bourgeois life.

Jeff Campbell is the most bourgeois, moralistic character in the novella; he has devoted his life to redeeming blacks from their "carelessness" and "simple promiscuous unmorality," or, as he would tellingly put it, their constant need for new "excitements." Before he becomes involved with and educated by Melanctha, he leads a life of narrow predictability and timidity. Stein assigns to him her own problem, as she had diagnosed it in *Q.E.D.*, of excessive intellection and concomitant blockage of emotion ("thinking rather than feeling"): evidently, sexual inhibition. But he is dark-skinned, more strongly identified with "the race" than Melanctha, both by the narrative and by his own concept of his mission in life (to save black people from themselves). Furthermore, he is described more frequently than any other character as laughing with the "wide, abandoned laughter that makes the warm broad glow of negro sunshine."

Melanctha herself constitutes the novella's most complex deployment of racist stereotype. The text makes it clear that her intelligence and general appeal are attributable to her light skin, the predominance of her "white blood": "Melanctha Herbert was a graceful, pale yellow, intelligent, attractive negress. She had not been raised like Rose by white folks but then she had been half made with real white blood" (86). However, the key characteristics that distinguish her from Jeff, and generate plot, are not her "white" intelligence, grace, and attractiveness but her need to "wander," which Jeff links to the need of "the negros" continually to seek new "excitements." Stein takes Melanctha's "wandering" much more seriously than either she or Jeff takes "negro excitements"—the former is at least in part an earnest desire for a deeper knowledge of life, while the latter is mere restless self-indulgence. Nonetheless, it is apparent that Melanctha's crucial "wandering," which thematizes the formal "wandering" of the text, at least partly falls into the category of, or looks like, the "simple promiscuous unmorality of the black people." The portion of the text devoted to viewing Melanctha's troubles from her own point of view constructs, as I have said, a persuasive rationalization of, or justification for, what Jeff Campbell considers her untrustworthy, shameful, "wandering" behavior, a justification that makes him the guilty party in his ungenerous inability to trust Melanctha: "I certainly am right the way I say it Jeff now to you. I certainly am right when I ask you for it now, to tell me what I ask you, about not trusting me more then again, Jeff, just like you never really knew me. You certainly never did trust me just then, Jeff, you hear me?" (157–58).

Melanctha is also characterized as strong and determined, with a "break-neck courage" and proud stoicism in the face of pain. She derives these positive attributes from her father, a very negative, harsh, violent character, whose blackness is always emphasized whenever he is mentioned: "Melanctha was pale yellow and mysterious and a little pleasant like her mother, but the real power in Melanctha's nature came through her robust and unpleasant and very unendurable black father.... Melanctha's father was a big black virile negro. . . . James Herbert was a common, decent enough, colored workman, brutal and rough to his one daughter"(90–91). James Herbert is another repellent racist stereotype, "big black virile" and also working class, who brutalizes his wife and daughter and has a knife fight in a bar. But he is the source of "the real power in Melanctha's nature," which encompasses a great deal more than courage, determination, and stoicism—it is an existential power, a force of being, much like James Wait's.

Class is a less overtly visible issue in "Melanctha" than it is in *The Nigger of the "Narcissus,"* but it functions undecidably along with race in Stein's dislocation of conventional naturalist narrative. The class status of each character is carefully, though unobtrusively, established. Melanctha, through her father, is working class; her association with the middle-class doctor Jeff Campbell is an important upward move for her. The educated Jane Harden provides Melanctha's initial access to middle-class possibilities. Rose offers a less upwardly mobile but stable version of bourgeois domesticity, though Melanctha's association with her is clearly a last step downward, just as much because her husband Sam is working class as because Rose herself is unworthy of Melanctha. Melanctha's last lover, Jem Richards, is a member of the quasi-criminal (non)class of reckless, rootless gamblers. Her move toward him abandons the class ladder in a gesture not of subversion but rather of hopelessness—upward mobility might not offer much, but it is the only game in town.

In this account, the class status of the characters accords with the naturalist antibildungsroman protagonist's trajectory of rise and fall through the class system (see, for example, *Sister Carrie*). But, again, the energizing, positively valued "wandering" that radicalizes this text, the source of its subversive power as an early modernist work, is just as much associated with lower-class status as it is with blackness. This empowered subversiveness disrupts the naturalist class trajectory. Jane Harden's positively valued "wandering," which gives her the "wisdom" that she imparts to Melanctha, is at odds with her middle-class educational attainments; in fact, it leads directly to her expulsion from college. Similarly, it is Melanctha's "wandering" that makes her relationship with Jeff, her move to the middle class, impossible, while, in the meantime, his contact with Melanctha's "wandering" broadens and deepens him. Her move downward here is not an inevitable outcome of the great impersonal social machine grinding down the helpless individual; it is rather the outcome of her magnetic "power," which is like (and is originally ignited by) Jane Harden's.

Similarly, it is not Rose Johnson's stupidity or laziness that hurts Melanctha, finally, but rather Rose's narrow bourgeois selfishness (her tenacity in clinging to her domestic security) that pushes Melanctha down the final step toward her ignominious death. And it is Melanctha's working-class black father, again, who gives her the strength of her nature without which there would be no story. In both of these instances, conventional assumptions about the impact of class status overtly endorsed by the text are overthrown.

Class functions much more overtly in *The Nigger of the "Narcissus,"* and, apparently, in the service of the ostensible narrative: Donkin, unlike Jimmy purely villainous, is both representative and self-appointed spokesman of the militant urban working class. Everything about him constitutes an overt attack on that class: he is "the independent offspring of the ignoble freedom of the slums full of disdain and hate for the austere servitude of the sea" (9). He is also, much more uncomplicatedly than Wait, a force of disruption in the sailors'-solidarity-in-toil plot, deliberately fomenting mutiny rather than passively functioning as a tantalizing existential abyss. At every opportunity, Conrad makes Donkin offensive, absurd, insidious, and evil, never inspiring sympathy despite his destitution. Unlike Jimmy, he has never been even "half a man," as Captain Allistoun puts it in explaining his act of sympathy (his irony heavy where Donkin is concerned, Conrad continually has him provoke the crew by insisting that he is the only real man on board). His opportunistically rabble-rousing harangues on the rights of the working man ("his filthy loquacity flowed like a troubled stream from a poisoned source" [78]) are always motivated by laziness, selfishness, envy, greed, and a simple desire to wreak havoc. As programmatically as can be, Donkin is Conrad's conservative condemnation of militant working class socialism and trade unionism, which he evidently finds not only destructive but ludicrous: "They [the near-mutinous crew] found comfort of a gloomy kind in an interminable and conscientious analysis of their unappreciated worth; and inspired by Donkin's hopeful doctrines they dreamed enthusiastically of the time when every lonely ship would travel over a serene sea, manned by a wealthy and well-fed crew of satisfied skippers" (80).

It is impossible to argue that Conrad's hatred of Donkin is in any way mitigated; it is tempting to argue that such unmitigated hatred bespeaks overcompensation—what potentiality does Donkin represent so threateningly attractive that Conrad must so violently repudiate it? Most of the language in the above passage does in fact support its ostensible point, the condemnation of what Donkin offers. The "wealthy and well-fed crew of satisfied skippers" is a violation of Conradian solidarity: skippers are lone men, like Captain Allistoun in the storm; solidarity comes from common toil and is disrupted by wealth, satisfaction, and skipperlike autonomy. Similarly, Donkin's motives constitute a violation of solidarity because they are inveterately selfish. But why do "Donkin's hopeful doctrines" inspire in the crew a vision of a "lonely ship" on a "serene sea"? The "serene sea" is an image of Conradian transcendence, though here of course also an image of group delusion. But the loneliness of the ship does not fit in this universe of willful self-deception. Why include in such a banal, sugarplum fantasy that off-note of the ship's loneliness, such a key motif in Conrad's fundamental vision of our existential condition? The loneliness of the ship *is* the loneliness of the human lot, for which human solidarity is the antidote, in literature as on the sea. The artist's appeal is to "the latent feeling of fellowship with all creation—and to the subtle but invincible conviction of solidarity that knits together the loneliness of innumerable hearts, to the solidarity in dreams, in joy, in sorrow, in aspirations, in illusions, in hope, in fear, which binds men to each other, which binds together all humanity—the dead to the living and the living to the unborn" (Preface to *The Nigger of the "Narcissus,"* viii).

This is just the kind of visionary language that might express what Conrad's defensive cynicism condemns in the crew's enthusiastic dreaming, and "solidarity" is, of course, a socialist word, an idea at the heart of the socialist vision.[11] It is the socialist vision that, more than any other in the bourgeois period, appeals to the desire to overcome isolation, atomism, and precisely the venal, destructive, craven self-serving that Conrad assigns to Donkin. Conrad's language in the Preface (the "solidarity" that "binds together all humanity") is, I would argue, influenced by precisely the "hopeful doctrine" of socialism that he must repudiate with excessive violence in the character of Donkin; excessive because the appeal of a subversive "doctrine" at odds with his professed conservatism is so strong.[12]

Solidarity "binds together all humanity—the dead to the living and the living to the unborn." In *The Nigger of the "Narcissus,"* the *Narcissus* gives birth to James Wait and is also the site of his death; Wait in himself binds together the dead, the living, and the unborn: "he had the secret of life, that confounded dying man" (30). Irigaray's ideas about the position of the repressed maternal origin in patriarchal representation have powerful implications for *The Nigger of the "Narcissus."* The *Narcissus* itself, wonderfully the actual name of the ship that inspired this story,[13] evokes both the destructive self-absorption that is the prime moral ill Conrad attacks in this novel, the antithesis of solidarity, and also that specularization in patriarchal representation by means of the endless reproduction of the selfsame that Irigaray attacks as the prime moral ill of Western culture. I will argue that the *Narcissus* is also the site of a (partial) return of the repressed maternal origin that invisibly underwrites the reproduction of the selfsame: a move toward entering it into representation.

During the remarkable Cape of Good Hope gale, the *Narcissus* becomes a woman in labor: "He [Captain Allistoun] kept his gaze riveted upon her as a loving man watches the unselfish toil of a delicate woman upon the slender thread of whose existence is hung the whole meaning and joy of the world" (39).[14] Under the extreme duress and life-death liminality of the gale, which images, I would argue, precisely the massive upheaval in culture that is the modernist historical moment, the ship whose name quite literally evokes the endless self-reflexivity of the masculine subject makes visible within itself the buried origin, the "secret of life" lodged within the threat of death: the maternal womb. The revelation of that womb at the center of the ship and the text occurs as the *Narcissus* reaches the climax of its "downward" (southern) journey *around Africa*: again, downwardness (here geographical, elsewhere social), darkness (the "dark continent" inhabited by black people), and the empowered maternal are conflated.[15]

The *Narcissus*, in the most remarkable sequence of the novel, gives birth to the black James Wait at the southern extremity of Africa, assisted by the crew in their finest moment of selfless solidarity-in-(superhumanly difficult) toil. Wait becomes imprisoned in his little cabin when the ship turns on its side, and a group of the crew's most sympathetic characters (including the narrator, whose position I will discuss later) defies death, gravity, and seemingly insuperable physical obstacles to rescue him. The imagery of this rescue is rife with suggestions of childbirth, as Albert Guerard makes clear (see n. 14), and echoes the difficulty and suspense of "the unselfish toil of a delicate woman upon the slender thread of whose existence is hung the whole meaning and joy of the world."

Jimmy is trapped on the other side of a bulkhead separating his cabin from the carpenter's shop. The position of the ship puts that shop beneath the crew, and Jimmy's cabin beneath the shop: a double downward encaving. This positioning is emphasized by Conrad's language, which also makes Jimmy's bulkhead-barrier very like a cervix: "The next door was that of the carpenter's shop. They lifted it, and looked down. The room seemed to have been devastated by an earthquake. Everything in it had tumbled on the bulkhead facing the door, and on the other side of that bulkhead there was Jimmy dead or alive"(51). We already know that this birth will be difficult, "the unselfish toil of a delicate woman." The "earthquake" brought on by this eruption from the womb-cave tumbles blocking obstacles onto the vaginal opening, making the birth even more difficult.

The obstacles are the dangerous contents of the carpenter's shop: "The bench, a half-finished meat safe, saws, chisels, wire rods, axes, crowbars, lay in a heap besprinkled with loose nails. A sharp adz stuck up with a shining edge that gleamed dangerously down there like a wicked smile" (51). What the earthquake explodes are the tools and materials of masculine (self-)construction. Exploded, those tools and materials become vaginal teeth: the potentially death-inflicting sharp edges "gleam[ing] dangerously down there like a wicked smile." That simile cannot, given everything else, be accidental. Masculine (self-)construction, undone here, reveals itself as constituting the "threat of castration" that masculine subjectivity has projected onto the all-powerful maternal, defining the maternal as deadly, its sharp "vaginal teeth" always gleaming in a wicked smile, the locus of death rather than life, because it is the unattainable locus of life.

The womb prevails as locus of life here, but, again, life and death are ultimately undecidable in this novel (as are light and dark), as in the ambiguity of the narrator's formulation "on the other side of that bulkhead there was Jimmy dead or alive." Ship and crew work together to give birth to a man essentially already dead, and at the penultimate moment of the rescue, the narrator announces Jimmy's sudden silence by saying, "He was as quiet as a dead man inside a grave; and, like men standing above a grave, we were on the verge of tears" (54). But Archie manages to rip a hole in the bulkhead, and Jimmy rushes it in another, and the most explicit, vaginal birth image: "he pressed his head to it, trying madly to get out through that opening one inch wide and three inches long" (54; he is "crowning"). Jimmy's final emergence completes this explicit birth metaphor, with the crew acting as midwives: "Suddenly Jimmy's head and shoulders appeared. He stuck halfway, and with rolling eyes foamed at our feet. We flew at him with brutal impatience, we tore the shirt off his back, we tugged at his ears, we panted over him; and all at once he came away in our hands as though somebody had let go his legs. With the same movement, without a pause, we swung him up. His breath whistled, he kicked our upturned faces"(55). As we have seen, it is James Wait who embodies the force that disrupts the ostensible seagoing tale of *The Nigger of the "Narcissus."* He also embodies the conflation of race, class (he is Donkin's familiar; Donkin is his privileged friend and wears his clothes), and the maternal in the textual dynamic of that disruption.[16] This textual dynamic corresponds of course to historical fact: colonialized nonwhites, the militant working class, and feminist women were the others disrupting white male bourgeois hegemony. They erupt together undecidably for Conrad in this early modernist narrative.

"Melanctha"opens with a childbirth episode. Like Conrad's, it emphasizes difficulty, torment, and life-death liminality. These are the opening paragraphs of "Melanctha":

> Rose Johnson made it very hard to bring her baby to its birth.
>
> Melanctha Herbert who was Rose Johnson's friend, did everything that any woman could. She tended Rose, and she was patient, submissive, soothing, and untiring, while the sullen, childish, cowardly, black Rosie grumbled and fussed and howled and made herself to be an abomination and like a simple beast.
>
> The child though it was healthy after it was born, did not live long. Rose Johnson was careless and negligent and selfish, and when Melanctha had to leave for a few days, the baby died. Rose Johnson had liked the baby well enough and perhaps she just forgot it for awhile, anyway the child was dead

and Rose and Sam her husband were very sorry but then these things came so often in the negro world in Bridgepoint, that they neither of them thought about it very long. (85)

The shocking aspects of this episode, particularly given its position as entry into the text, have been almost universally overlooked. The adjectival racism in the description of Rose is overshadowed by the blanket condemnation of "the negro world in Bridgepoint," in which the death of a baby is no big deal. And to open a novella so casually and nonjudgmentally with what amounts to infanticide, then to move on quickly to other matters as if it had not happened, is a drastic textual strategy indeed. There is something nightmarish in that quiet "perhaps she just forgot it for awhile." It introduces a world of unthinkable deprivation of nurturance and echoes the indifference of Melanctha's own mother toward her—Melanctha had, as a child, overheard her mother say that she wished Melanctha, the difficult daughter, had died instead of Melanctha's brother, the beloved son.

The painful, difficult birth-into-death of the black Johnson baby parallels James Wait's birth and death. Both are intimately implicated in the disruption of traditional narrative. Again, it is the "promiscuous unmorality of the black people" associated with the working-class Rose Johnson that constitutes the subversive force of "wandering," both thematically and, as we will see, formally in this novella. As in *The Nigger of the "Narcissus,"* the maternal in "Melanctha" is the locus of those powerful, dark forces that are just as compelling, and potentially liberating, as they are damned. The word Stein chooses to describe Melanctha's subversiveness, "wandering," suggests the classical notion that hysteria, the prime manifestation of thwarted female rebellion, is a "wandering womb": that dark cave that modernism partly brings to light. The new story is being born—the birth is painful and the progeny cannot yet live, but the process, as embedded in form, is irreversible.

The opening childbirth episode is characteristic of this text, with its disturbing, painful content covered over by understatement, by the cool detachment of the narrative tone and by the fatalistic stance Stein borrows from naturalism—life is cruel, "it is no one's fault," as in the Laforguian epigraph, and there is nothing to be done about it, since "these things came so often in the negro world in Bridgepoint."[17] It is also characteristic of the text in that the difficult birth of a black working-class baby can be seen as a metaphor of a new story not yet quite ready to be written.[18] The episode itself is much more important to the plot than it initially appears to be: we find out by the end of the story that Melanctha's involvement with Rose Johnson, emphasized in the opening of the narrative as Melanctha's kindness to Rose and the crucial importance of her presence and nurturance to the life of that baby, is her final attempt to save herself before she falls through the holes in the social order into death.

The baby is Melanctha's as much as it is Rose's, in that it depends on Melanctha for its life as much as it depended on Rose for its birth. Also, Melanctha dies shortly after the baby—their lives are linked. Coming at the beginning of the novella, the birth figures the painful, difficult eruption, out of a "darker" (race), "lower" (class) place, the mother's womb, of a new kind of narrative, figured also in the womblike "wandering" of Melanctha. As Melanctha wanders through the text, she disrupts its ostensible naturalism, but what she offers cannot yet form its own text.

I have been discussing disruption of conventional narrative in these two texts from the point of view of my Irigarayan paradigm, but it was a purely stylistic similarity that initially drew my attention to these two texts as early modernist narratives; I subsequently began to see the remarkable parallels between them in the importance of race, class, and the maternal as loci of disruption. The similarity in stylistic disruption resides in radical dislocation of narrative position.

The indeterminacy of narrative in The Nigger of the "Narcissus" is notorious—there is a first person narrator, but he has no consistency. At times he functions in actual positioning as an omniscient third narrator, as in the opening of the novel or in the sequences narrated from Wait's point of view and from the (impossible) point of view of an observer in Wait's cabin during his one-to-one deathbed encounters with Podmore and Donkin. At times he is a full-fledged first-person narrator, an embodied but unidentified crew member, as in the rescue of Wait during the gale, where, as participant, he gives a close-up, first-hand account. In most of the novel, he moves back and forth through various degrees of detachment and involvement, including frequent use of the first-person plural that seems to make him an embodiment of solidarity itself, a representation of the crew's group identity, more than an individual crew member.[19] Generally, the narrative occupies the detached position for the ostensible, masculine-heroic seagoing tale, while the first-person position appears in sequences where the narrative moves closest to the subversive, modernist Wait.

Very shortly after The Nigger of the "Narcissus," Conrad finds his great first-person narrator Marlow, who makes modernist narrative possible, as so many critical works have explained. The narrative position of The Nigger of the "Narcissus" is, as literally as can be, undecidable, in transition between traditional and modernist narrative. Narrative position in "Melanctha," technically omniscient third, shifts far more frequently than that in The Nigger of the "Narcissus." However, just like Conrad's, Stein's narrator moves back and forth through various degrees of closeness and distance. While the narrative inconsistencies of *The Nigger of the "Narcissus"* are famous, those of "Melanctha," more subtle though more radical, have been overlooked.[20]

Narrative position in "Melanctha"shifts in and out of characters' consciousnesses, sometimes located entirely within the consciousness of the character from whose point of view we are at that moment seeing the story, sometimes hovering just above that point of view, sometimes entirely outside it. Moreover, the detached narrative voice has various degrees of detachment. These complicated shifts can occur within the course of a short passage or even a single sentence:

> Melanctha sat there, by the fire, very quiet. The heat gave a pretty pink glow to her pale yellow and attractive face. Melanctha sat in a low chair, her hands, with their long, fluttering fingers, always ready to show her strong feeling, were lying quiet in her lap. Melanctha was very tired with her waiting for Jeff Campbell. She sat there very quiet and just watching. Jeff was a robust, dark, healthy, cheery negro. His hands were firm and kindly and unimpassioned. He touched women always with his big hands, like a brother. He always had a warm broad glow, like southern sunshine. He never had anything mysterious in him. He was open, he was pleasant, he was cheery and always he wanted, as Melanctha once had wanted, always now he too wanted really to understand. (137)

The first half of the above passage is narrated in relation to Melanctha, but the narrative position moves from outside to inside her consciousness. In the first three sentences, the narrator shows us Melanctha from Jeff's, and the text's, erotically desiring point of view: the "pretty pink glow" on her "pale yellow and attractive face," the hands "with their long, fluttering fingers, always ready to show her strong feeling." The next sentence moves suddenly to Melanctha's point of view: she "was very tired with her waiting for Jeff Campbell." That is Melanctha's language, her tone. "She sat there very quiet and just watching" next uses a language common to the narrator, Melanctha, and Jeff—like the "we" used by the narrator of *The Nigger of the "Narcissus,"* this language establishes a communal narrative voice. Although technically third person, the narrative that uses this group language is functionally positioned somewhere between third and first person, like the narrative of *The Nigger of the "Narcissus"* as a whole.

Then, suddenly, the narrative moves far outside and above the voices and consciousnesses of the characters: "Jeff was a robust, dark, healthy, cheery negro." From that sentence until the last half of the last sentence of the passage, we have a description of Jeff that combines a string of racist stereotypes with a denial of Jeff's erotic feeling for Melanctha: Jeff is a "robust, dark, healthy, cheery negro"—a recurring descriptive motif for him; "He always had a warm broad glow, like southern sunshine"—a recurring descriptive motif for "the negros." At the same time, "His hands were firm and kindly and unimpassioned. He touched women always with his big hands, like a brother. . . . He never had anything mysterious in him." This remarkably revealing juxtaposition of bland, sentimental (as opposed to contemptuous) racist stereotype with denial of eroticism is delivered in the most detached of the text's narrative voices. As in *The Nigger of the "Narcissus,"* narrative distance corresponds to adherence to the conventional story; in this case, an uncomplicated, uncontradicted racial stereotyping in conjunction with the denial of Melancthan subversive eroticism. The tone of this detached, distanced voice is the neutral, nonjudgmental, almost clinical tone of the naturalist narrative Stein is ostensibly writing.

In the middle of that last sentence, the narrative position shifts again, moving first partly, then entirely inside Jeff's consciousness: "and always he wanted, as Melanctha once had wanted, always now he too wanted really to understand." Jeff's wanting, "as Melanctha once had wanted," to "understand"—a word linked in this text to "wandering" and finding "wisdom"—signals the extent to which he has assimilated, and been affected by, what Melanctha represents. Narrative closeness to Jeff's point of view signals, similarly, the extent to which Melanctha has rewritten this text. (*Q.E.D.* was narrated consistently in detached omniscient third.)

Over against the remarkable parallels between these two early modernist texts is (among, of course, numerous others) the enormous difference, attributable to authorial gender, in predominant attitude toward the title character. As "nigger," James Wait is a destructive force in Conrad's conservative seagoing tale. Characteristically for male modernists, Conrad is attracted to what he overtly condemns: his ambivalence, and therefore the modernist elements of the text, emerge from the overly powerful attraction Wait's negative qualities exert. Melanctha, on the other hand, is the protagonist of Stein's ostensible naturalist story. Despite our irritation at her irresponsibility, we are made to want the best for her; despite the lengthy digression to Jeff's point of view in his affair with her (and despite the fact that it is Jeff's affair that reenacts Stein's with May Bookstaver, making Jeff the closest character in the novella to an authorial stand-in), it is Melanctha's story that this fiction tells. It is precisely Stein's attempt to *see* from Melanctha's point of view in order to justify it sufficiently for the requirements of naturalist "neutrality," to enter into the kind of consciousness that had eluded her while she was still at least emotionally and intellectually in the closet,[21] that leads her to wander well beyond the limits of the naturalist fiction she thought she was writing. She is a female modernist in this text; therefore her ambivalence stems from her fear of the rebellious freedom and eroticism to which she is attracted.

Both of these texts are certainly rich and strange, and Conrad's is set at sea, but water does not function in them as it does in most of the other texts treated in this study. At certain moments in *The Nigger of the "Narcissus,"* the language used to describe the ocean has the kind of feminine suggestiveness that appears so much more consistently in *Heart of Darkness* and *Lord Jim*. For example, members of the old generation, represented here by Singleton, are described as "the everlasting children of the mysterious sea" (20).[22] At the outset of the voyage the sea is described, in language suggestive of Irigaray's reading of Plotinus or Kristeva's account of "women's time," as "a great circular solitude," whose "smiling greatness ... dwarfed the extent of time."[23] Similar language appears at the end of the novel, when "Donkin chafed at the peace—at the ship—at the sea that, stretching away on all sides, merged into the illimitable silence of all creation" (113). But these are momentary alignments of the mighty ocean with the feminine (it is also the "sea of life" on the next to last page). These alignments have no consistent import in the thematic structure of the text. The sea is the power of the absolute in this text, and site of "good" where land (earth) is "evil." It is therefore more masculine logos, either violently punishing or serenely transcendent, than it is illimitable, silent, all-encompassing feminine matter.

Water as such hardly appears at all in "Melanctha." When it does, however, it is a "moistness" associated directly with the dangerously attractive feminine earthiness and life-force that Stein has projected onto "the negros": "Jeff always loved to watch everything as it was growing, and he loved all the colors in the trees and on the ground, and the little, new, bright colored bugs he found in the moist ground and in the grass he loved to lie on and in which he was always so busy searching"(149). Jeff's relation to nature provides a totally nonthreatening arena for the release of his erotic feeling, his connection to the maternal feminine. But when this feeling is allowed to include Melancthan human eroticism, it becomes dangerous:

> And they [Jeff and Melanctha] loved it always, more and more, together, with this new feeling they had now, in these long summer days so warm; they, always together now, just these two so dear, more and more to each other always, and the summer evenings when they *wandered*, and the noises in the full streets, and the music of the organs, and the dancing and the *warm smell of the people*, and of dogs and of the horses, and all the joy of the strong, sweet, pungent, *dirty, moist*, warm negro southern summer. (154, italics added)

When moist natural fecundity is expanded to include or acknowledge its human component, it suddenly becomes smelly, dirty, "negro," and associated with wandering. Although the overall tone of the above passage is very positive, it provides the setting for one of the crises of the novella. On the next page, Jeff, during one of these episodes of "warm wandering" (155) with Melanctha, suddenly becomes bitterly disgusted by what they are doing and turns against her, inflicting on her an irremediable injury and bringing about the (protracted but inevitable) decline and fall of their happy love for one another.

Water, as "moistness," is clearly gendered feminine and also functions as site of the ambivalence of "Melanctha" toward the subversive forces that disrupt its ostensible narrative structure. But since water makes only those two brief appearances, it cannot be considered an important element of the text. In Stein's later, more radical work *Tender Buttons*, language relating to water generates not just another representation of otherwise apparent gender-aligned thematic configurations, but the largest representation and constructor of the deliberately polysemous meanings of the text (see chapter 6).

Chapter 4

THE VAGINAL PASSAGE: *HEART OF DARKNESS*

AND *THE VOYAGE OUT*

IN "MELANCTHA" and *The Nigger of the "Narcissus,"* the birth sequences that mark the site of eruption of the transforming forces of cultural and narrative change are moments of the text whose importance and even existence are easy to miss. In *Heart of Darkness* and *The Voyage Out*, the site of eruption becomes the entire text.[1] Conrad and Woolf use the classical journey plot, the voyage of discovery, to reverse the parable of the cave, sending their protagonists not on the hero's journey to the underworld, requisite stage in the progress of his heroism, but on an antiheroic return to the terrifying heart of desire, the maternal origin of life that generates in these texts disillusionment and death. The metaphor and plot device of the voyage that dominates both texts does the work of inscribing into representation the Irigarayan vaginal passage, the possibility of link and movement back and forth between the masculine and the feminine that is the condition of the Kristevan impossible dialectic and of modernist *sous-rature*. Masculine and feminine, the two poles of the prime gendered cultural dualisms, constitute—fully represented as the massive cultural signifiers that they are—the organizing polarity of both texts.

Gender is an overt preoccupation of *The Voyage Out*, a female bildungsroman in which the young protagonist cannot pass alive the obstacle of marriage in a patriarchal culture.[2] The characters of the novel are very clearly positioned in relation to the late Victorian British sex-gender (as well as class) system. In *Heart of Darkness*, gender is, with a few notable exceptions, largely a suppressed preoccupation, not overtly treated but displaced onto Conrad's fabulously sex-rife imagery. In "The Return," a story Conrad finished between *The Nigger of the "Narcissus"* and *Heart of Darkness*,[3] Woolf's notion of the impossibility of marriage in late Victorian bourgeois London is dramatized overtly in a narrative sequence predictive of *Heart of Darkness*.

The title of "The Return" is applicable in an obvious way to the analysis I am about to offer for *Heart of Darkness*. As a title it is otherwise odd, highly ironic, since the story ends and the plot begins not with a return but with departures (the last line of the story is "he never returned"). It is, however, the return of Alvan Hervey's wife from her aborted flight to another man that brings about Hervey's shattering moment of revelation—a revelation not of "the horror!" but of what the horror compensates for and conceals: the wonder, the ultimate and absolute desirability of return to the mother.[4]

Upper-middle-class London is a graveyard in "The Return," just as bourgeois Brussels is a sepulchre in *Heart of Darkness*: London is a "billowy and motionless sea of tiles and bricks" (118); the "delightful world of crescents and squares" (124) the Herveys inhabit is really a "grim, impenetrable silence of miles of walls" (126); and, most explicitly, "on all sides of his [Hervey's] dwelling servile fears and servile hopes slept, dreaming of success, behind the severe discretion of doors as impenetrable to the truth within as the granite of tombstones" (165).

At the center of this city of the dead is its financial power. Hervey emerges appropriately, at the beginning of the story, from the "inner circle train from the City" (111): it is into the "inner circle" of social propriety, City wealth and ruling class hegemonic ideology that devastating modernist revelations intrude. "The inner circle train from the City rushed impetuously out of a black hole" (111) at the opening of the story; that black hole will reopen at the story's climax.

Hervey, his wife, their marriage, and every aspect of their lives constitute the relentless caricature of empty propriety and the false values of the bourgeoisie that was to become such a staple of the modernist vision. The men leaving the train with Hervey look "as if they had been wearing a uniform"; their faces are "indifferent" and "had all the same stare, concentrated and empty, satisfied and unthinking" (111; "I had not thought death had undone so many"). The Herveys

> moved in their enlarged world amongst perfectly delightful men and women who feared emotion, enthusiasm, or failure, more than fire, war, or mortal disease; who tolerated only the commonest formulas of commonest thoughts, and recognized only profitable facts. It was an extremely charming sphere, the abode of all the virtues, where nothing is realized and where all joys and sorrows are cautiously toned down into pleasures and annoyances. (113)

It is a "serene region . . . where noble sentiments are cultivated in sufficient profusion to conceal the pitiless materialism of thoughts and aspirations" (113): Conrad's attack on bourgeois ideology has Marxist bite.

Within this setting, just as Irigaray discovers, Alvan Hervey as haute-bourgeois everyman embodies a stereotypical—almost caricatured—and endlessly self-reproducing masculinity:

> He strode firmly. . . . he moved on in the rain with careless serenity, with the tranquil ease of someone successful and disdainful, very sure of himself—a man with lots of money and friends. He was tall, well set-up, good-looking and

healthy; and his clear pale face had under its commonplace refinement that slight tinge of overbearing brutality which is given by the possession of only partly difficult accomplishments; by excelling in games, or in the art of making money; by the easy mastery over animals and over needy men. (112)

(This passage might be cited against all who see Conrad as uncomplicatedly macho-conservative.)

Hervey arrives at home and enters the "dressing room," or bedroom: sexually fraught scene of the action of this story, the encounter between man and woman. The room is full of mirrors, and Hervey is reflected infinitely as he enters and moves about, becoming a neat objective correlative of Irigaray's thesis of the specularity of masculine self-generation over the abyss of the repressed maternal. Conrad makes it clear that these reflected Herveys reproduce the horde of City men who emerged from the train. Hervey's reflections are

a crowd of gentlemanly and slavish imitators, who were dressed exactly like himself; had the same restrained and rare guestures; who moved when he moved, stood still with him in an obsequious immobility, and had just such appearances of life and feeling as he thought it safe for any man to manifest. . . . And like the men he respected they could be trusted to do nothing individual, original, or startling—nothing unforeseen and nothing improper. (116–17)

Into this safe haven of masculine self-(re)production erupts a piece of writing, *written by a woman*—a piece of writing suggesting a feminine self-representation that might disrupt the cold perfection of this hall of mirrors. Appropriately, though somewhat inexplicably otherwise, Hervey considers this piece of writing indecent and outrageous in its very existence in this setting, before he even knows its contents (it is a note informing him that his wife has run off with a "literary man" Hervey has always disliked and considered not quite the thing but has cultivated for social-professional advancement). The contents of the note do not shatter Hervey's life irreparably—he might be able to find a way to preserve his facade by expunging his wife from his existence. What does shatter his life irreparably is her return (hopelessly conventional as she is, or perhaps because she realizes that what she is running to is no better than what she is running from, she has been unable to consummate her flight). Although she returns in cowardice, she had left because, as the gesture of writing makes tangible, the facade for her has shattered. She can no longer skim with Hervey "over the surface of life hand in hand . . . like two skilful skaters cutting figures on thick ice for the admiration of the beholders, and disdainfully ignoring the hidden stream, the stream restless and dark; the stream of life, profound and unfrozen"(115). That stream of life, hidden, restless, dark, profound and unfrozen, will lead to the heart of darkness. Here, the stream of life, though "dark" and associated with death, does not bespeak "the horror! the horror!" It is, at least in terms of the thematic structure of *this* story, unambiguously positive and desirable. It is everything real and valuable in life that is frozen over by the Herveys' existence; it is also quite simply the maternal.

The Herveys are childless, a fact that predicts the failure of the maternal in Mrs. Hervey. Hervey's revelation has two stages. First he sees that it is only through his wife that he might attain what is valuable in life, which he, in a characteristic Conradian displacement to moral abstraction, calls "faith and love": "She had the gift! She had the gift!" (163). Immediately after achieving this insight, he sees that this great "gift" is something she in particular, a betrayer, as opposed to she as Woman, is incapable of offering: "You haven't the gift" (163). She has demonstrated by the violation of writing that letter (Conrad makes it clear that the letter itself is the full extent of her actual transgression) that she hasn't the absolute, unconditional "faith and love" of the mother, extended, in Victorian gender ideology (an ideology periodically revived in our own century in times of antifeminist backlash, most notably the 1950s) to the wife's proper feeling toward her husband/master/son.

It is through "the gift" of sexual intercourse that the wife, by allowing the husband access to her body, gives him access to the "faith and love" of the maternal stream of life. What has happened between Alvan Hervey's discovery that "She had the gift!" and his terrible verdict that she hasn't the gift is that she has denied him that access. When she realizes what he wants ("in all the world she was the only human being that could surrender it [the gift] to his immense desire. He made a step forward, putting his arms out, as if to take her to his breast"), she runs from him in "undisguised panic," "showing her teeth" (163).[5] They are the same teeth, I would argue, that, in the form of sharp adz and carpenter's nails, block Jimmy Wait's birth canal in *The Nigger of the "Narcissus,"* denying the rescuers access to the maternal womb Wait occupies and represents.

After this scene of sexual rejection, which takes place on the landing outside the drawing room, Mrs. Hervey retreats upstairs to "their room"; eventually Alvan follows her. As he is about to enter that ominous chamber—his arm is actually raised to open the door—he sees the maid who has been locking up the house ascending toward him on the stairs. He tells himself he will wait until she has passed and hides behind some drapery. As he watches her, the story's final revelation comes to him, and he decides he cannot any longer share a deceitful life with a "woman of marble" (his wife becomes for him one of their tasteless pieces of Victorian bric-a-brac). He leaves, never to return. Conrad's narration of the maid's ascent warrants full citation:

He saw her come up gradually, as if ascending from a well. At every step the feeble flame of the candle swayed before her tired, young face, and the darkness of the hall seemed to cling to her black skirt, followed her, rising like a silent flood, as though the great night of the world had broken through the discreet reserve of walls, of closed doors, of curtained windows. It rose over the steps, it leaped up the walls like an angry wave. . . . It flowed from outside—it rose higher, in a destructive silence. And, above it, the woman of marble, composed and blind on the high pedestal, seemed to ward off the devouring night with a cluster of lights. . . . The girl ascended facing him. . . . And on her track the flowing tide of a tenebrous sea filled the house, seemed to swirl about his feet and rising unchecked, closed silently above his head. . . . He stepped out, with a rebelling heart, into the darkness of the house. It was the abode of an impenetrable night. . . . And looming vaguely below the woman of marble, livid and still like a patient phantom, held out in the night a cluster of extinguished lights. (166–67)

The upper-middle-class wife does not have the gift—she is a statue of marble, holding out only a cluster of extinguished lights.[6] She cannot give the masculine subject access to the maternal stream of life, which, precisely as in *Heart of Darkness*, is also the dark flood of death: it "closed silently above his head." Such access can come only from a place both darker and lower down: again, as in *The Nigger of the "Narcissus,"* the darkness and "down-there-ness" of the maternal womb (the Platonic cave) is conflated with the lower classes (here the darkness is not racial but is displaced onto the darkness of the maid's dress and of the flooding or streaming water itself; the sympathy and sexual accessibility accorded by her youth and lower social status is emphasized by "her tired, young face").

The well, deep and dark, will become a crucial figure of the maternal feminine in *Lord Jim*. But more obviously, the liquid "great night of the world" that, rising in flood, has "broken through the discreet reserve of walls," those granite tombstones, and "leaped up the walls like an angry wave," the "devouring night," the "rising tide of impenetrable gloom," are all figures that predict the representation that we will see in *Heart of Darkness* of the maternal feminine as dark stream of both life and death, and also carrier of the truth suppressed by the civilization of Herveys.

The river of life that is purely figural in "The Return" becomes the (unnamed) Congo in *Heart of Darkness*, and the river journey sequence in *The Voyage Out* is obviously inspired by the Conrad text.[7] The river journey occupies most of *Heart of Darkness* and only a short segment of *The Voyage Out*, but the parallels between the two texts, structural and stylistic as well as thematic, are much more extensive than that disproportion suggests. As with "Melanctha" and *The Nigger of the "Narcissus,"* those parallels, apart from Woolf's Conradian river journey itself, are not particularly evident at first glance. *Heart of Darkness* is a novella, *The Voyage Out* a full-length novel; *Heart of Darkness* is as commonly read and well known a work as any in the Anglo-American fictional Great Tradition (*pace* Leavis's reservations about it) and almost universally considered one of Conrad's greatest works, while *The Voyage Out* is obscure, little read, Woolf's first novel, her *Almayer's Folly*.

Nonetheless, the overall structure of each narrative is much the same. An opening section set in London and dominated by the Thames introduces an ocean voyage to the third world, a second section (much longer and more important in *The Voyage Out*) narrates the ocean voyage, a third section establishes the colonial setting and relationships between the protagonist and secondary characters, a fourth section narrates the river passage, with its climactic episode of arrival at the up-river destination, and a final section of return and its aftermath is marked by death and failed marriage.

In each text, the opening section posits hegemonic gender, economic and narrative structures, emphasizing the malaise they have generated. The first page of *The Voyage Out* establishes a nexus of marriage, the social dominance of the middle class and the gender dominance of the male, conventional realist narrative, and sorrow. The setting for this nexus is Thameside London. As protagonists of bourgeois-realist narrative, Ridley and Helen Ambrose tower above the "lawyers' clerks" and "young lady typists," the "small, agitated figures—for in comparison with this couple most people looked small—decorated with fountain pens, and burdened with despatch-boxes" who "had appointments to keep, and drew a weekly salary" (9). But this towering and the marriage that supports it are immediately made problematical: the first sentence tells us that the Embankment streets are too narrow for the Ambroses to be able to walk arm-in-arm, an obvious symbol of their married state, without antagonizing the trivial people over whom they tower, whose "angry glances struck their backs" (9).

The narrative point of view latches quickly onto Helen Ambrose's "sorrow," a sorrow that seems to emerge directly from the Ambroses' precarious position in non-West End London and in a novel that will try to escape the confines of both Londons: "It was only by scorning all she met that she kept herself from tears, and the friction of people brushing past her was evidently painful" (9). But the source of her sorrow shifts from the dissonance of her immediate setting to the fact that she is about to leave her children for a long period of time: the tears finally flow as she thinks of her children. The novel that introduces her as a figure of a social and fictional world at odds with contemporary reality (the modernist urban [un]reality of mean commercial streets to be definitively represented by Eliot) merges the precariousness of her position in that reality with maternal guilt and loss.

Ridley and Helen Ambrose play stereotypical gender roles in relation to one another in this opening scene. He paces back and forth over Waterloo Bridge lost in thought, totally ineffectual in the face of her sorrow and muttering verse to himself out loud as Mr. Ramsay will and as Leslie Stephen did, while she cries into the Thames and then stops crying when Ridley silently demands it, capitulating to his need as Mrs. Ramsay will and Julia Stephen did. Helen adds her tears to the water of the Thames— she is deeply connected to the maternal and its sorrow in patriarchal culture. She is a bad mother, however, locked into that culture, ultimately its enforcer: she does not *see* the Thames. "It is always worth while to look down and see what is happening. But this lady looked neither up nor down" (10). When she does look down at the water, she sees "a circular iridescent patch slowly floating past with a straw in the middle of it" (10), a blank, impenetrable figure to her—it will not be given to Helen Ambrose to see this novel's truth, though she is a crucial component of it— but a figure suggestive of the maternal: a womb with an umbilical cord.

As it is for Conrad, London is for Woolf here a smothering darkness, a blot, a "vast black cloak" (12). It is also, for Woolf, home of "the poor who were unhappy and rightly malignant" (11). Helen's sense of her alienation from this London, and of its awfulness, focuses on class: "the skeleton beneath" the "beauty that clothed things" (12) is poverty—"tattered old men and women were nodding off to sleep upon the seats" (11). London is "a great manufacturing place," a vast factory of which the relatively tiny West End is the "finished work. It appeared to her a very small bit of work for such an enormous factory to have made. For some reason it appeared to her as a small golden tassel on the edge of a vast black cloak" (12). Helen sees the evil of this social order but sees it as she enacts it, wrapping herself in the cloak of her privilege (she gets Ridley to hail a cab), just as she continually evades Ridley himself but not her marriage to him. Woolf uses Helen here to establish the link between moribund, pernicious regimes of class and of gender: Helen simultaneously represents and is alienated by those regimes. Again, the scene is organized around the motif of her sorrow. Through her we see why fiction must voyage out of its old world.

Like Woolf's, Conrad's opening section is dominated by an ominous gender polarity, by the gloom (Woolf's sorrow is Conrad's gloom) of turn-of-the-century urban capitalism, and by the ambiguous mysteriousness of the Thames. The differences between the two texts are, of course, much more apparent than these similarities. In addition to the obvious differences of style, character, and setting, Woolf's opening is a very brief prologue, a five-page scene on the Thames Embankment, introducing us to unchanging figures of the old order before we meet the out-voyaging, bildungsroman protagonist Rachel. By contrast, Conrad's extended introduction to Marlow's journey focuses almost immediately on the true protagonist, encompassing not only his present-time reactions to London and the Thames, but also his childhood and adult motivations, his meditations on ancient history, and his densely symbolic preliminary journey to the sepulchral imperialist city of Brussels.

Heart of Darkness opens with an ironic contrast between the framing narrator's Thames fantasy and Marlow's. The first narrator, opening the text (however briefly) entirely within the domain of nonmodernist narrative, presents a traditional light/dark dualism, identical to the one that governs the official narrative of *The Nigger of the "Narcissus,"* a dualism of benign and great nature (water/sky, just as in *The Nigger of the "Narcissus"*) versus blighted culture (city):

> The day was ending in a serenity of still and exquisite brilliance. The water shone pacifically; the sky, without a speck, was a benign immensity of unstained light; the very mist on the Essex marshes was like a gauzy and radiant fabric, hung from the wooded rises inland, and draping the low shores in diaphanous folds. Only the gloom to the west, brooding over the upper reaches, became more sombre every minute, as if angered by the approach of the sun. . . . that gloom brooding over a crowd of men. (28)

The "gloom to the west" is, of course, London. The contrasting "gauzy and radiant fabric" of the mist suggests feminine gendering, which connects importantly to the imagery in the narrator's description of the *different* kind of story Marlow tells:

> The yarns of seamen have a direct simplicity, the whole meaning of which lies within the shell of a cracked nut. But Marlow was not typical (if his propensity to spin yarns be excepted), and to him the meaning of an episode was not inside like a kernel but outside, enveloping the tale which brought it out only as a glow brings out a haze, in the likeness of one of these misty halos that sometimes are made visible by the spectral illumination of moonshine. (30)[8]

It is crucial that the "meaning" of Marlow's tale resides in the realm of the feminine ("enveloping . . . misty . . . moonshine"). The framing narrator, from within the boundaries of premodernist narrative, points to the place where the difference of modernist narrative lies.

The framing narrator does not see the implications of his own remarks. His self-aggrandizing reverie about the Thames ("nothing is easier for a man who has, as the phrase goes, 'followed the sea' with reverence and affection, than to evoke the great spirit of the past upon the lower reaches of the Thames") focuses on the Elizabethan golden age of English exploration, the masculine "origin" of turn-of-the-century imperialism, with its "great knights-errant of the sea" who sailed to glory out of England on "that stream." These "great knights-errant" evoke the masculine myth Marlow's story will appropriate and rewrite. The framing narrator elaborates the knights-errant idea into a formulation of the sentimental ideology of imperialism, the ideology that Conrad is about to demystify in this text: "Hunters for gold or pursuers of fame, they all had gone out on that stream, bearing the sword, and often the torch, messengers of the might within the land, bearers of a spark from the sacred fire. What greatness had not floated on the ebb of that river into the mystery of an unknown earth! . . .The dreams of men, the seed of commonwealths, the germs of empires"(29). Note how extensively imperialism is associated with the phallic (the sword, the torch) and with masculine might and generativity (the seed).

Enter Marlow and his famous opening, " 'And this also,' said Marlow suddenly, 'has been one of the dark places of the earth' " (29). The first narrator's neat, comfortable dualism, separating the gloom of modern London from the shining heroic past of British might, is collapsed in a stroke, as we move through Marlow into modernist narrative. Marlow insists that the darkness is always already part of the solar logocentric might of Brittania. His historical imagination carries him back not to Elizabethan glory days but to the Thames's ignominious, squalid, Western-cultural origin as colonized rather than colonizing river. This Thames is barely distinguishable from the Congo, and pre-urban London is just as much a "dark place" as the Congo jungle:

> To the exiled Roman conqueror, the Thames was the very end of the world, a sea the colour of lead, a sky the colour of smoke. . . . Sand-banks, marshes, forests, savages,—precious little to eat fit for a civilized man, nothing but Thames water to drink. . . . cold, fog, tempests, disease, exile, and death— death skulking in the air, in the water, in the bush. . . . They were men enough to face the darkness. (30–31)

Marlow then links his Thames fantasy more overtly to his Congo memory, as he evokes as setting for his Roman conqueror

> all that mysterious life of the wilderness that stirs in the forest, in the jungles, in the hearts of wild men. There's no initiation either into such mysteries. He [Marlow's hypothetical Roman] has to live in the midst of the incomprehensible, which is also detestable. And it has a fascination, too, that goes to work upon him. The fascination of the abomination—you know, imagine the growing regrets, the longing to escape, the powerless disgust, the surrender, the hate. (31)

I quote this section at length, beyond what is necessary to make the point, in order to accumulate sufficient detail to argue that from the beginning, the feminine place of darkness in this text is eroticized.[9] In this opening section, the wilderness is solely fearful and dangerous in its seductiveness: "fascination of the abomination . . . growing regrets, the longing to escape, the powerless disgust, the surrender, the hate."

Marlow's account of how he came to make the journey up the Congo, the passage into and out of the heart of darkness, reinforces patriarchal gender ideology, linking it to imperialism, at the same time that it shows us the alienation generated by the systems of economy and gender underlying that ideology. This configuration is identical to Woolf's linkage of Helen Ambrose's sorrow in "manufacturing" non-West End London with Mrs. Ambrose's status as conventional bourgeois wife and mother.

In his meditation on that hypothetical Roman colonizer, Marlow insists on making him not a colonizer at all, but rather a mere "conqueror," differentiating the pure rapacity of his motives from those of modern imperialists, whose practice is "redeemed" if it has "an idea at the back of it; not a sentimental pretence but an idea; and an unselfish belief in the idea—something you can set up, and bow down before, and offer a sacrifice to" (32). In light of the story he is about to tell, Marlow's insistence here on the virtue of the "idea at the back of" imperialism is highly ironic, and even in this passage that insistence is radically undercut.[10]

Marlow describes the Romans as "those who tackle a darkness," which in fact all colonizers, however genuinely idealistic, do: "It was just robbery with violence, aggravated murder on a great scale, and men going at it blind—as is very proper for those who tackle a darkness. The conquest of the earth, which mostly means the taking it away from those who have a different complexion or slightly flatter noses than ourselves, is not a pretty thing when you look into it too much" (31–32). After this pungent and oft-quoted, near blanket condemnation of all imperialism (the "mostly" is a weak enough gesture toward excepting the British),[11] the assertion of a redeeming "unselfish belief in the idea" has little force, a force that is further weakened by the ironic tone of "set up, and bow down before, and offer a sacrifice to." That formulation makes it seem as if (which is the case) this "unselfish idea" proves to be yet another version of the golden calf, antithesis of the logocentric "idea" or patriarchal Mosaic abstraction.

Nonetheless, this "idea" must be asserted, however unconvincingly, at this point in the text. It is more than a mere sop to Conrad's defensively overdone Britishness. It is, in fact, an assertion of the validity of the masculine pole of culture: precisely of logocentric abstraction, of altruistic superego, of the law of the father. If that cultural mode had no value, if it were merely bankrupt and oppressive, there would be no story to write here, both because there would be no opening of a passage between the father and the mother without the assertion of the father's law, and also because modernist narrative depends on a retention of signal elements of conventional fiction associated with the rule of the father even as it undercuts and rewrites them.[12] Again, the opening section establishes the terms of the hegemonic, hierarchical, misogynist gender polarity that the rest of the text will rewrite as impossible dialectic. Here the abstract and purely moral light of the law of the father (even though undercut from the outset) is opposed to the evil, abominable, rapacious, and deadly darkness of the chaos of the mother.

A hint of the passage that will open up and alter these relations between father and mother is given in Marlow's wonderful description of his original motivation for his journey. He explains that as a boy he always put his finger on the "many blank spaces on the earth" on the map of the world and said "When I grow up I will go there": a pure Oedipal fantasy. When he actually grew up, most of those blank spaces had been filled—a wonderful conflation of the historical progress of imperialism with the shift from unfettered childhood fantasy to constricted adult reality. "But there was one yet—the biggest, the most blank, so to speak— that I had a hankering after" (33): the Congo ("hankering" is the perfect word here). Conrad links Marlow's adult Congo-obsession to his overtly sexual childhood Oedipal fantasies. That link is brilliantly developed in Marlow's famous snake simile:

> It had ceased to be a blank space of delightful mystery—a white patch for a boy to dream gloriously over. It had become a place of darkness. But there was in it one river especially, a mighty big river, that you could see on the map, an immense snake uncoiled, with its head in the sea, its body at rest curving afar over a vast country, and its tail lost in the depths of the land. And as I looked at the map of it in a shop-window, it fascinated me as a snake would a bird—a silly little bird. (33)

Marlow's initiation into fallen adult sexuality has made the liberating feminine, the "blank space of delightful mystery—a white patch for a boy to dream gloriously over" into a deadly, ominous "place of darkness." This figure confirms the story of patriarchal gender relations. But the next sequence, elaborating the figure of the "immense snake uncoiled," begins to deconstruct those relations even as it asserts them.

Marlow's obviously phallic snake is an initial version of Conrad's representation of the Irigarayan vaginal passage. In his reverse birth, his ambivalent return to and reinscription of the repressed maternal womb, Marlow will enter that vaginal passage at its mouth, and journey up, with great difficulty, its increasingly narrow course to arrive at the tail of the snake lost in the depths of the land. "The snake had charmed me": the great, strong, phallic-paternal river occupies and appropriates the mother's vagina and marks with its tail the womb, the lost site of maternal origin. As snake, serpent, it represents the sexual fall that has made the delightful white patch an alienated place of darkness—Eve-like, Marlow is tempted by the serpent to guilty knowledge—at the same time that it represents the occupying paternal phallus that prevents the Oedipal son from reclaiming the mother's womb. As Oedipal son, Marlow also identifies with and is challenged by that paternal phallus, desiring to displace it by engaging in the masculine endeavor of exploration, which he finds he can do only under the aegis of European imperialism.

The result, however, is no standard masculine or realist narrative, because Marlow's object is not simply to become or replace the phallus, occupying the vaginal passage and maintaining the invisibility of the site of origin. Instead, by means of a deliberately antirealist narrative repeatedly allied to the dream, the Freudian unconscious and its revelation of the overdetermination of language, Conrad, enabled by his own invention of modernist narrative, will place Marlow at last on shore. He is to find and represent not the snake's tail—having done its work of charming Marlow, the snake will disappear, revealing the repressed vaginal passage, the route of access to and release from the womb the snake occupies and conceals. This two-way passage, this bringing to representation of a linkage of the bankrupt but potentially idealistic order of the father with the liberating but deadly maternal heart of darkness, is represented in all its ambiguity for a patriarchal imperialist culture coming apart at the seams, hating the old cloth but terrified of what those rupturing seams will release.

The location of the map of the Congo in a "shop-window" suggests that Marlow's experience is framed and controlled by commercial culture. This theme dominates the Brussels sequence, in conjunction with a heightened emphasis on conventionally misogynist gender polarity (again, as in *The Voyage Out*, conventional gender roles are linked to the European capitalist setting). Marlow's enterprise is compromised from its inception—he gets the job by "worrying" his relatives, "already a fresh departure for me. I was not used to get things that way" (33). Again, the ethos of the "shop-window" governs his experience.

His male relatives "said 'My dear fellow,' and did nothing. Then— would you believe it?—I tried the women. I, Charlie Marlow, set the women to work—to get a job" (34). In the world of the shop-window, relatives are strictly divided into male and female, and one (masculine subject) compromises oneself shockingly by appealing to the latter for a job. His "excellent aunt" gets him the job by representing him to her influential friends not only as "an exceptional and gifted creature" (38), embarrassing enough, but, worse still, as one of the Workers, with a capital—you know. Something like an emissary of light, something like a lower sort of apostle. There had been a lot of such rot let loose in print and talk just about that time, and the excellent woman, living right in the rush of all that humbug, got carried off her feet. She talked about "weaning those ignorant millions from their horrid ways," till upon my word, she made me quite uncomfortable. I ventured to hint that the Company was run for profit. (39)

What does this make of "the unselfish belief in the idea"? Already, the notion of an "emissary of light," torch-bearer of the paternal logos, is extinguished by dripping irony. The redeeming idea of "weaning those ignorant millions from their horrid ways" is merely ideological "rot" and "humbug." In fact, like all imperialist ventures, "the Company was run for profit." This encounter prepares us for the transformation of "run for profit," in combination with its covering ideology of the white man's burden, into "the horror! the horror!"

Furthermore, the abstract and superegotistical masculine idea is reassigned, as bankrupt sentiment, to women. It is the "excellent aunt" who is the spokeswoman of this ideological "rot" and "humbug," prey to what is "let loose in print and talk." In the deforming world of misogynist imperialism, the masculine idea is alienated as feminine idealism, an ideological mode of self-deception: "It's queer how out of touch with truth women are. They live in a world of their own, and there had never been anything like it, and never can be. It is too beautiful altogether, and if they were to set it up it would go to pieces before the first sunset. Some confounded fact we men have been living contentedly with ever since the day of creation would start up and knock the whole thing over" (39).

In this passage Marlow puts under erasure his own scorn of women. The segregation and suppression of women demanded by hierarchical gender polarity has produced a "world of their own" that is as fragile as a house of cards, a world that will "go to pieces" in the strong paternal light of the sun, when the phallogocentric "truth," the masculine hegemony established tellingly "since the day of creation," that usurping masculine myth, violently "start[s] up and knock[s] the whole thing over." But the power of woman reemerges in her appropriation and debasement of the masculine idea, the redeeming idea that makes the colonizing venture more than mere rapacity. The signifier "truth" has slipped from what we would expect to be its association with the logos—the idea that you can "set up, and bow down before, and offer a sacrifice to"—to an association with the "confounded fact" of the profit motive. That is what Marlow must chiefly mean by the "truth" that women are "out of touch with," thereby (by being out of touch) playing out for patriarchal imperialist culture its own need to dissociate itself from the "truth" that it is "run for profit." In discrediting his own account of the redeeming idea at the back of imperialism by imprisoning it within the feminine house of cards, Marlow represents the contradictions of the economic-gender system whose repression of the maternal he is about to undo.

Back in the sepulchral city, before Marlow marks his departure for Africa with the above meditation on femininity, he tells three stories to make sure we get the point about both the journey he is about to undertake and also the culture it ostensibly serves. The third story, about his comical visit to the doctor-phrenologist who measures his skull to find out why anyone would want to do what Marlow is about to do, and admonishes him to "avoid irritation more than exposure to the sun. . . . Du calme, du calme" (38), relieves the dead-heavy atmosphere established by the second story, the famous visit to the Company offices.

The first, introductory story concerns the murder of Fresleven, the Danish captain Marlow is about to replace, as a result of a quarrel arising "from a misunderstanding about some hens. Yes, two black hens" (34). This quarrel causes Fresleven to "hammer the chief of the village with a stick," having gone berserk after "a couple of years already out there engaged in the noble cause" (34). The chief's son then kills Fresleven, and his people flee in panic, never to return, as does Fresleven's steamer. This is our first view of the fruits of "the cause of progress." Marlow says explicitly that he "stepped into his [Fresleven's] shoes" and makes a point of noting his subsequent discovery of Fresleven's bones, still intact though covered by the tall grass of the jungle.

The two absurd black hens, source of this disaster, are transmogrified, I would argue, into the two famous women knitting black wool, guarding the portals of the Company and "piloting over" the young men with "foolish and cheery countenances" into the "unknown." Marlow's description of the neighborhood of the Company offices in Brussels, the "whited sepulchre," explicitly echoes his description of Fresleven's bones: "a dead silence, grass sprouting between the stones" (35). "Stones" echoes "bones," and the grass grows up between them just as "the grass growing through his [Fresleven's] ribs was tall enough to hide his bones" (35, immediately preceding paragraph). The ominous women, like the death-dealing hens, bespeak the deadly power of the feminine within the heart of darkness, obverse of the futility of excellent, idealistic women like Marlow's aunt in their houses of cards. The two knitting everywomen—one thin and young, one fat and old—know about the profit motive, and they signal death, "uncanny and fateful" (37) in their impassive watching and "piloting." They are quite literally "guarding the door of Darkness" (37), marking the point of entry into a different order of gender relations, where the power of the maternal is de-repressed, at the same time that they represent, in the horror they inspire (here they function as obverse not of the aunt but of Kurtz's jungle woman), the link between the profit motive and the alienation of the feminine in patriarchal imperialist culture.

Where Marlow is "piloted across" by an ominously knitting woman, Helen and Ridley Ambrose are, more literally, piloted by a Thames boatman, who is benign rather than ominous, gathering them up protectively and guiding them out of the old world Woolf is only too eager to disempower and quit:

> From a world exclusively occupied in feeding waggons with sacks, half obliterated too in a fine yellow fog, they got neither help nor attention. It seemed a miracle when an old man approached, guessed their condition, and proposed to row them out to their ship in the little boat which he kept moored at the bottom of a flight of steps. With some hesitation they trusted themselves to his care, took their places, and were soon waving up and down upon the water, London having shrunk to two lines of buildings on either side of them, square buildings and oblong buildings placed in rows like a child's avenue of bricks. (13)

In *The Voyage Out*, as the title indicates, the main idea is to get out of the old order, rather than to get (yet) to another. The Stygian ferryman becomes a savior in whose care the "enormous factory" of London is made to shrink to child's play, with Helen and Ridley, restored to a childlike omnipotence, at its center ("on either side of them") rather than relegated to the "small golden tassel." In *Heart of Darkness*, Conrad is much more concerned with what he is voyaging to: "I felt as though, instead of going to the centre of a continent, I were about to set off for the centre of the earth" (39): the maternal origin. Accordingly, Conrad gets us there quickly—his ocean voyage to the mouth of the river takes two pages—while Woolf's ocean voyage occupies six chapters. Both voyages accomplish the disengagement of the protagonist from the Old World, the old order, and innocence.

Marlow's description of Africa is negative from the outset. Its coast is "featureless . . . with an aspect of monotonous grimness. . . . a God-forsaken wilderness . . . we passed various places—trading places—with names . . . that seemed to belong to some sordid farce acted in front of a sinister back-cloth" (40). Within this setting, Marlow is in "isolation amongst all these men with whom I had no point of contact," entirely detached from his familiar world. Moreover, Africa "seemed to keep me away from the truth of things, within the toil of a mournful and senseless delusion" (40). Marlow is now himself entering the position he so blithely assigned to women before he left for Africa, the position of separation from "the truth of things." The state of delusion, now that he is in it, is no longer "too beautiful altogether" but is rather "mournful and senseless."

Marlow's horrified language escalates after he encounters a French man-of-war firing blindly at the coast. The ship's "ensign dropped limp like a rag," and her "thin masts" swayed on the "greasy, slimy swell. . . . there she was, incomprehensible, firing into a continent. Pop, would go one of the six-inch guns; a small flame would dart and vanish, a little white smoke would disappear, a tiny projectile would give a feeble screech—and nothing happened. Nothing could happen" (41). European military-phallic power is ludicrously impotent here, in the realm ruled by the power of the mother.

Immediately after he recounts this episode, Marlow's description of Africa becomes thematically and imagistically focused and explicit:

> We called at some more places with farcical names, where the merry dance of death and trade goes on in a still and earthy atmosphere as of an overheated catacomb; all along the formless coast bordered by dangerous surf, as if Nature herself had tried to ward off intruders; in and out of rivers, streams of death in life, whose banks were rotting into mud, whose waters, thickened into slime, invaded the contorted mangroves, that seemed to writhe at us in the extremity of an impotent despair. (41)

The maternal, "Nature herself," invaded by "trade," is the horrific, slimy site of emasculation and death, more powerful than it is in Europe but still entirely alienated from the masculine subjectivity of the text.

The dominant tone of the ocean voyage in *The Voyage Out* is opposite to that of Marlow's brief journey: Woolf seems exuberant, triumphant, at leaving England behind. The ship on which this novel voyages out is called the *Euphrosyne*, the Grace of joyfulness. But, tellingly, the *Euphrosyne* is not really meant to carry passengers and only takes them "by special arrangement." It is "primarily a cargo boat . . . her business being to carry dry goods to the Amazons, and rubber home again" (40). Rachel Vinrace's father, Willoughby, owner of the ship, is engaged in the same endeavor as Marlow's detestable Company, and Woolf's voyage out is just as much contaminated by the profit motive as is Conrad's voyage in. Accordingly, the liberating ocean contains psychic and political monsters, monsters associated with the Old World economic and gender systems that it is impossible for Woolf to leave behind.

As they will be on the Amazon passage, the bourgeois proprieties are very much preserved aboard the *Euphrosyne*. When the ship departs, the passengers, rather than watching from the deck, are in the "saloon," eating a proper dinner while engaging in proper conversation: "Each of the ladies, being after the fashion of their sex, highly trained in promoting men's talk without listening to it, could think—about the education of children, about the use of fog sirens in an opera—without betraying herself" (17). The bastion of propriety is gender polarity, marked by male dominance ("highly trained in promoting men's talk") with an accompanying subversive female privacy ("without listening to it").

The ocean, and the distance from this civilization it provides, begins to make this highly conventionalized gender behavior seem arbitrary and strange to Rachel, initiating the process of her detachment from the dominant system without beginning to give her any defense against it:

> Why did they [her aunts] do the things they did, and what did they feel, and what was it all about? Again she heard Aunt Lucy talking to Aunt Eleanor. . . . How odd! How unspeakably odd! But she could not explain to herself why suddenly as her aunt [Helen Ambrose] spoke the whole system in which they lived had appeared before her eyes as something quite unfamiliar and inexplicable, and themselves as chairs or umbrellas dropped about here and there without any reason. (36)

Her sense of alienation from "the whole system in which they lived" turns immediately back on herself, making her feel like a dropped object, a chair or umbrella, something to be sat upon or forced open for shelter.

The space opened up by the ocean between "civilization," particularly English civilization, and her novel is clearly a space of freedom for Woolf (as it is for Conrad in *The Nigger of the "Narcissus"*), while in *Heart of Darkness* it is a space of alienation and fear. While "darkness" is overwhelmingly deadly and ominous in the first part of *Heart of Darkness*, it presents itself in *The Voyage Out* as a relief from the blazing, unextinguishable light of London, of logos, as the *Euphrosyne* moves "steadily down the river":

> London was a swarm of lights . . . the lights of the great theatres, the lights of the long streets, lights that indicated huge squares of domestic comfort, lights that hung high in air. No darkness would ever settle upon those lamps, as no darkness had settled upon them for hundreds of years. It seemed dreadful that the town should blaze for ever in the same spot; dreadful at least to people going away to adventure upon the sea, and beholding it as a circumscribed mound, eternally burnt, eternally scarred. From the deck of the ship the great city appeared a crouched and cowardly figure, a sedentary miser. (17–18)

The eternally, indomitably blazing light of logos is lodged for Woolf, along with modern capitalism, in the city of London, a "circumscribed mound, eternally burnt, eternally scarred"—the opposite of a shining torch unto the nations; a "crouched and cowardly figure" hoarding its filthy lucre rather than the glorious golden inseminator of the world imagined by Conrad's opening narrator. The ocean, again, frees the novel from this self-consuming blaze of money and "domestic comfort": "All the smoke and the houses had disappeared, and the ship was out in a wide space of sea very fresh and clear though pale in the early light.

They had left London sitting on its mud. . . . They were free of roads, free of mankind, and the same exhilaration at their freedom ran through them all" (27).

Completely out of sight of the cultural prison of England, a majestic apotheosis makes the *Euphrosyne* a personification for Woolf of a utopian fantasy of female freedom, power, and autonomy (she uses to great advantage the conventional gendering of ships as female):

> an immense dignity had descended upon her [the ship]; she was an inhabitant of the great world, which has so few inhabitants, travelling all day across an empty universe, with veils drawn before her and behind. She was more lonely than the caravan crossing the desert; she was infinitely more mysterious, moving by her own power and sustained by her own resources. The sea might give her death or some unexampled joy, and none would know of it. She was a bride going forth to her husband, a virgin unknown of men; in her vigour and purity she might be likened to all beautiful things, worshipped and felt as a symbol. (32)[13]

This fantasy is disrupted by the insertion of Mr. and Mrs. Richard Dalloway into the shipboard company. Richard is a Conservative politician "who thinks that because he was once a member of Parliament, and his wife's the daughter of a peer, they can have what they like for the asking" (39). Clarissa is a beautiful, somewhat brittle socialite, an entirely conventional woman. When the Dalloways come aboard in Portugal, the dimensions of the gender system become more explicitly political.[14] We are made to wince through an appalling (and no doubt historically accurate) discussion of the suffrage movement, as Richard's convictions erupt: " 'Nobody can condemn the utter folly and futility of such behaviour more than I do; and as for the whole agitation, well! may I be in my grave before a woman has the right to vote in England! That's all I say.' The solemnity of her husband's assertion made Clarissa grave" (43). Much as Clarissa agrees with her husband and is if anything more indignant than he at the suffragists, the ironic echo of "grave" is telling (perhaps subliminally reminding us of London as "circumscribed mound").

The politics of gender are linked in the person of Richard Dalloway to the politics of capitalism and imperialism. He embodies the male dominance and aggressive sexuality of phallic industrialism: "He seemed to come from the humming oily centre of the machine where the polished rods are sliding, and the pistons thumping; he grasped things so firmly but so loosely; he made the others appear like old maids cheapening remnants" (47). "Old maids cheapening remnants" wonderfully encapsulates the position of unmarried women in Dallowayan England. And if she declines the status of "old maid," Rachel can only follow "in the wake of the matrons, as if in a trance" (47).

Imperialism, linked to patrilineality and (as for Conrad's opening narrator) virile potency, is as important a component of Dallowayan masculine supremacism as is industrialism, as is evident in the following touching connubial chat between Richard and Clarissa. I will quote it in full because it moves so beautifully from premise to premise, delivering finally the whole package of ideology that Woolf's entire career will attempt to explode and replace. Clarissa opens the conversation with the founding nugget of gender ideology:

> "The men always *are* so much better than the women."
>
> "One always has something to say to a man certainly," said Richard. "But I've no doubt you'll chatter away fast enough about the babies, Clarice."
>
> "Has she got children? She doesn't look like it somehow" [tellingly, they are discussing Helen].
>
> "Two. A boy and girl."
>
> A pang of envy shot through Mrs. Dalloway's heart.
>
> "We *must* have a son, Dick," she said.
>
> "Good Lord, what opportunities there are now for young men!" said Dalloway, for his talk had set him thinking. "I don't suppose there's been so good an opening since the days of Pitt. . . . To be a leader of men," Richard soliloquised. "It's a fine career. My God—what a career!"
>
> The chest slowly curved beneath his waistcoat.
>
> "D'you know, Dick, I can't help thinking of England," said his wife meditatively, leaning her head against his chest. "Being on this ship seems to make it so much more vivid—what it means to be English. One thinks of all we've done, and our navies, and the people in India and Africa, and how we've gone on century after century, sending out boys from little country villages—and of men like you, Dick, and it makes one feel as if one couldn't bear *not* to be English! . . .
>
> "It's the continuity," said Richard sententiously. A vision of English history, King following King, Prime Minister Prime Minister, and Law Law had come over him while his wife spoke. He ran his mind along the line of conservative policy, which went steadily from Lord Salisbury to Alfred, and gradually enclosed, as though it were a lasso that opened and caught things, enormous chunks of the habitable globe.
>
> "It's taken a long time, but we've pretty nearly done it," he said; "it remains to consolidate." (50–51)

Woolf's "Law Law" makes one think of Kurtz's "the horror! the horror!": two expressions of extreme alienation from either pole of the Western gendered dualism.[15]

This Dallowayan paternalism is definitively left behind on this voyage out, but the maternal offers no uncomplicated alternative. Woolf is ambivalent not only toward the maternal in general, as we will see, but toward Helen Ambrose, Rachel's substitute mother, in particular. Helen's destructiveness is as great as her allure. She is detached and harsh, expressing initially indifference toward, and even suspicion of, Rachel, thinking for example that "when you said something to her [Rachel] it would make no more lasting impression than the stroke of a stick upon water" (20). She is no "grave" conventional Clarissa Dalloway, however. Like the ocean, which might bring death or some unexampled joy, she is an ambiguous figure of female power, granting insight into, and detachment from, the dull, crippling, deathly gender-economic system of London even as she lures Rachel to a different kind of death.

Helen has, literally, designs for (on) Rachel. Immediately following the fantasy of the *Euphrosyne* as puissant virgin, we see Helen sitting on deck with her embroidery frame and her "black volume of philosophy"—a symbolical tableau indeed—especially when we find out what she is embroidering:

> She chose a thread from the vari-coloured tangle that lay in her lap, and sewed red into the bark of a tree, or yellow into the river torrent. She was working at a great design of a tropical river running through a tropical forest, where spotted deer would eventually browse upon masses of fruit, bananas, oranges, and giant pomegranates, while a troop of naked natives whirled darts into the air. Between the stitches she looked to one side and read a sentence about the Reality of Matter, or the Nature of Good. (33)

Helen is the antithesis here of Conrad's two women knitting black wool. Where they signal the ominous threat to the masculine modernist of the liberating female heart of darkness, Helen's great design of a tropical river, in its "vari-coloured tangle" of lush and verdant life, signals the promise to the feminine modernist of the passage to the maternal womb. In fact, in convincing Rachel to stay with her in the coastal South American colonial settlement instead of going on up the river with her father, Helen "promised a river"—precisely the river she has created in her embroidery: "Visions of a great river, now blue, now yellow in the tropical sun and crossed by bright birds, now white in the moon, now deep in shade with moving trees and canoes sliding out from the tangled banks, beset [Rachel]" (86).

To the extent, however, that Helen is a bad mother, literally the wrong passage, Woolf makes her sinister and cold.[16] Here her ominous allegiance to patriarchy is made apparent by the way she divides her attention equally between her magnificent embroidery and the "black volume of [masculine] philosophy"—death sentences[17] about those prime Irigarayan-Plotinian abstractions of the ultimate Western gendered dualism, the Reality of Matter and the Nature of Good.

Because this is a modernist narrative, its most important figuration concerns what is under the surface of the ocean, of consciousness, within the maternal. At the end of the first chapter, Mr. Pepper, one of the eccentric minor characters, launches a "discourse . . . upon the unplumbed depths of ocean," specifically "the great white monsters of the lower waters" (22)—"white, hairless, blind monsters lying curled on the ridges of sand at the bottom of the sea, which would explode if you brought them to the surface, their sides bursting asunder and scattering entrails to the winds when released from pressure" (23). I would argue that these "monsters" are simultaneously fetal images and a repressed desire for autonomy; the ocean at once the womb and the unconscious; and the violent, explosive bringing of the monsters to the surface a figure simultaneously of release of repressed desire and a horrific birth image. The de-repression of the maternal is a terrifying prospect for Mr. Pepper, much as he wishes one of Ridley's ships would undertake it.

A few pages later Rachel herself looks down into the ocean, "into the depth of the sea" (27). What she sees is mysterious and alluring rather than terrifying: "it was green and dim, and it grew dimmer and dimmer until the sand at the bottom was only a pale blur. One could scarcely see the black ribs of wrecked ships, or the spiral towers made by the burrowings of great eels, or the smooth green-sided monsters who came by flickering this way and that" (27–28). This passage is clearly linked to the previous one by the invocation of the sand at the bottom, the echoing of "ridges" in "ribs," and the use of the word "monsters." For Rachel, the maternal-unconscious is not violent and terrifying, but rather unknown, alluring, dimly seen, its potential or promise just as magical as it is violent.

Mr. Grice, a shipboard eccentric, has a collection of sea treasures that he keeps in glass jars: "here were the treasures which the great ocean had bestowed upon him—pale fish in greenish liquids, blobs of jelly with streaming tresses, fish with lights in their heads, they lived so deep" (54). When Clarissa Dalloway remarks that "they have swum among bones," Mr. Grice feels compelled to recite, "in an emphatic nasal voice," "Full fathom five thy father lies" and then to remark sententiously, "a grand fellow, Shakespeare" (54). Again, much as he *appreciates* the ocean deep, Mr. Grice ruins Ariel's magical poetry of sea-change just as he controls the maternal by collecting dead, and explicitly feminine ("tresses"), sea riches in glass jars.

The culmination and synthesis of this sequence of ocean figuration is the dream Rachel has after Richard Dalloway kisses her:

> She dreamt that she was walking down a long tunnel, which grew so narrow by degrees that she could touch the damp bricks on either side. At length the tunnel opened and became a vault; she found herself trapped in it, bricks meeting her wherever she turned, alone with a little deformed man who squatted on the floor gibbering, with long nails. His face was pitted and like the face of an animal. The wall behind him oozed with damp, which collected into drops and slid down. (77)

This dream-vision is much like Marlow's offshore vision of Africa: the maternal as deathly and terrifying trap. The tunnel and vault figure vagina and womb, the vault also literally a vault, a grave. The deformed man with long nails is, I would argue, a figure of the distortion of the female in patriarchal culture: as Freud reveals, woman in patriarchy can only be visible or explicable as a "deformed man." After her violation by Richard and all he represents, as Woolf so painstakingly constructs it, Rachel can no longer find the ocean depths mysterious, magical, and alluring (after the kiss, Richard, eating beef, tells "wonderful masculine stories . . . about Bright and Disraeli and coalition governments"). The "deformed man" with "*pitted* face" who "*squatted* on the floor" is also reminiscent of the vision of "eternally *scarred*" London as "a *crouched* and cowardly figure": London and its Dallowayan economic-gender system cannot be left behind; in the persons of the Dalloways, it boarded the ship in Portugal, the last stop in Europe. The maternal ocean has become the site of patriarchal suppression, distortion, and occupation of the feminine.

The long middle section of *The Voyage Out*, set in the British colonial enclave where Rachel, Helen, and Ridley settle in, investigates alternatives to the social order whose oppressive dimensions the ocean voyage has revealed. Helen and Rachel become close, after a fashion, though an unbridgeable gulf opens between them toward the end of this section— there is a point at which Helen, though in many ways free of feminine constraints (her mind is relatively unfettered), cannot lead Rachel any farther out of cultural entrapment.

Helen and Rachel meet St. John Hirst and Terence Hewet, composites of Virginia's brother, Thoby Stephen, and the other "Bloomsbury" men, Cambridge Saints (primarily Lytton Strachey and Clive Bell) who had become so important to Virginia's own ambivalent liberation. The British colony recreates bourgeois propriety (the secondary characters are all staying in a local hotel) in a way that makes its ludicrousness as clear to the reader as to Rachel. But, at the same time, the colony's distance and difference from London allow Rachel and Terence to pursue their ideas about a more authentic, honest, gender-egalitarian way of life. The issue of class, though not treated explicitly again after its prominence in the opening section, functions silently as a central premise of the novel: the oppressive inadequacy of the minor characters' way of life, which provides a contrast to the attempts of Helen, St. John, Terence, and Rachel to forge an alternative, is an acting out of the obsolescence of the bourgeois culture of which the old text that Woolf must rewrite is the prime representation. Helen establishes the third-world setting of the middle section as an alternative to classbound London early in that section in a letter home mentioning the absence of aristocracy and the nonservility of the native servants—"here the servants are human beings" (96).

Woolf's overt anger, however, is directed primarily against the ignorance in which girls like Rachel are raised, an ignorance that is universal but particularly pernicious in its denial of the facts of sexuality. All four major characters have in mind differently inflected versions of a world in which women and men would be intellectual equals and therefore, subsequently, equals in every other way (Woolf always placed education first in her feminist program—see *A Room of One's Own* and particularly *Three Guineas*).

Toward the end of this section, as Rachel draws away from Helen, she draws closer to Terence Hewet. He is delineated very sympathetically in this part of the novel, given warmth of feeling as well as power of intellect, while Hirst, the genius, based on Lytton Strachey, is vitriolic and cold. Hewet gives a long feminist speech during an important courtship scene with Rachel in which he "instinctively adopt[s] the feminine point of view" (213). His speech is a clear counterpoint to Richard Dalloway's shipboard disquisitions. Hewet's speech culminates in the exclamation: "Doesn't it make your blood boil? . . . I'm sure if I were a woman I'd blow someone's brains out" (215). If egalitarian marriage, marriage that defied and transcended the Dallowayan system, were possible with anyone anywhere, it should be possible with Hewet here.

But Hewet cannot free Rachel. He is a novelist who wants to write a book about "Silence . . . the things people don't say" (216). This is at once an admirable project, intimating revelation of the truth beneath culture's lies, and also a defeated project, intimating that the truth is unspeakable, a blank, a death—Rachel calls life "the short season between two silences" (82). Hewet at this point in the novel is as good as a man can be, but that is simply not good enough—his text is a dead end for the feminist modernist.

At the very end of the middle section, Rachel moves through the hotel from one to another of the secondary characters, finding them each in turn inadequate and stifling. The last character she encounters is Mrs. Paley, a tyrannical, deaf old woman in a wheelchair attended by her niece, the niece a classically conventional, repressed and oppressed woman. As a pair they are the dark double of Helen and Rachel. Mrs.

Paley is the ultimate bad mother. Her inability to hear or understand what a third character says to her, as the three (Miss Allan, Rachel, and Mrs. Paley) confront one another in the hotel corridor, results in "a complete block in the passage": "this misunderstanding, which involved a complete block in the passage, seemed to her [Rachel] unbearable. She walked quickly and blindly in the opposite direction, and found herself at the end of a *cul de sac*" (257). At the end of the cul-de-sac she finds a table on which is "a rusty inkstand ... and a pen with a broken nib" (257). Running away from the passage completely blocked by the horrific mother only leads her to a dead end containing the defunct, no longer usable implements for writing the old text. On the next page "she had now reached one of those eminences, the result of some crisis, from which the world is finally displayed in its true proportions. She disliked the look of it immensely—churches, politicians, misfits, and huge imposters—men like Mr. Dalloway ... Mrs. Paley blocking up the passage"(258). The only alternative to the obstruction of Mrs. Paley on one side and the old text of Mr. Dalloway on the other is, again, for Rachel to attempt to open the blocked passage. How interesting and perfectly apt that for Marlow the passage is occupied by the phallic snake, while for Rachel it is blocked by the totally demanding, totally uncomprehending, useless hulk of the mother.

This section of the novel suppresses, for the most part, the third-world colonial setting. We feel that this group of privileged English people has been transported to another planet, or to a fictive space in which setting serves only to detach the characters from the context in which their behavior appears normal and inevitable. In the next section, setting will become crucial, as the group undertakes a pleasure excursion up the Amazon, enabling Rachel's attempt at opening the passage. In Conrad's third section, Marlow's arrival and pre-river-passage sojourn in Africa, setting is heightened as much as it is suppressed in Woolf's. At the first Company station, we see immediately and unequivocally the truth of imperialism. All pretense of a "redeeming idea" is shattered by the horror of the hypocrisy, exploitation, and suffering Marlow encounters there, all for the "precious trickle of ivory" (46). As the miraculously starched and snowy-white Company chief accountant says, within sight of the appalling "grove of death," "When one has got to make correct entries, one comes to hate those savages—hate them to the death"(47).

It is after Marlow's two-hundred-mile tramp through the interior to the Central Station, where he finds his steamer "at the bottom of the river," that Conrad's descriptions of the jungle "darkness" change utterly. The crucial terms "fact" and "truth" shift again, this time from connection to the profit motive to connection to the heart of darkness itself. The feminine "wilderness" is now the locus of fact and truth, while the male European emissaries of profit construct the world of illusion:

> I went to work the next day, turning, so to speak, my back on that station. In that way only it seemed to me I could keep my hold on the *redeeming facts of life*. Still, one must look about sometimes; and then I saw this station, these men strolling aimlessly about in the sunshine of the yard. I asked myself sometimes what it all meant. They wandered here and there with their absurd long staves in their hands, like a lot of faithless pilgrims bewitched inside a rotten fence. The word "ivory" rang in the air, was whispered, was sighed. You would think they were praying to it. A taint of imbecile rapacity blew through it all, like a whiff from some corpse. By Jove! I've never seen anything so *unreal* in my life. And outside, the silent wilderness surrounding this cleared speck on the earth struck me as something great and invincible, *like evil or truth*, waiting patiently for the passing away of this fantastic invasion. (52, italics added)

And a few pages later, even more explicitly: "There was an air of plotting about that station, but nothing came of it, of course. It was as unreal as everything else—as the philanthropic pretence of the whole concern" (54).

The reversal of Marlow's prevoyage position is absolute. The profit motive, instead of constituting a reassuringly solid, masculine "fact," to hold up against the rot of sentimental feminine imperialist ideology, is now "imbecile rapacity," with a stink of death upon it, worshiped obscenely by faithless pilgrims with useless phallic staves—a parody of the phallogocentric "idea" behind imperialism that one might bow down before, now become very explicitly a "philanthropic pretence." The profiteers' world is a world of unreality, while profound (if also "evil")[18] truth resides in the empowered feminine of the wilderness. This wilderness is a far cry from the alien, emasculating, death-dealing jungle, swallowing up the helpless mangroves, that Marlow saw from the ocean shore. It is "waiting patiently for the passing away of this fantastic invasion" rather than violently annihilating it. In the face of the pernicious bankruptcy of the "confounded fact" of imperialism, Marlow has shifted his allegiance from the order of the European father to the wilderness of the African mother.

Immediately after this passage, Conrad emphasizes the contrast between the evil of imperialism and the maternal aspect of the African wilderness. A cruelly beaten African, after suffering "for several days, sitting in a bit of shade looking very sick and trying to recover himself" (reminiscent of the denizens of the grove of death), "arose and went out—and the wilderness without a sound took him into its bosom again" (53). This far into the wilderness, the Africans, helpless at the first Company station, have access to the jungle's bosom.

Marlow's steamer is hauled out from its immersion in the vaginal river "like a carcass of some big river animal" (56); the steamer's immersion is a figure of Marlow's own transformation, his initiation into the mystery of the passage to the womb. As he works on the steamer, making it ready for that passage, his allegiance to the river is complete—the work gives him his only sense of reality, and he lives aboard the steamer rather than contaminating himself by association with the faithless pilgrims. Yet the work is a string of frustrations, and the river is treacherous. And if we return to the passage about the faithless pilgrims with their imbecile rapacity, we will see that the dualism of positive feminine wilderness versus negative male imperialism is not at all as clear-cut as it at first appears. The pilgrims are "bewitched," an important word, by the ivory that comes from the jungle. Moreover, the ivory produces "a taint of imbecile rapacity . . . like a whiff from some corpse." These formulations all suggest the association of the maternal with witchcraft, emasculation (the "absurd long staves"), and death. The ivory that is the "confounded fact" behind the whole operation is at times made to appear a trap deliberately set for the hapless European male by the African mother-witch.

The ten-page sequence in which Marlow works on the steamer is dense with important figuration of the absolute ambiguity for Conrad of the maternal heart of darkness. As Marlow listens to the self-important assistant manager, the "papier-mâché Mephistopheles," dilate upon his ambitions (Marlow has his "shoulders against the wreck of [his] steamer"), he is moved to a vision of the jungle that is such an excellent illustration of my arguments, as if made to order, that I will quote it in full:

> The smell of mud, of primeval mud, was in my nostrils, the high stillness of primeval forest was before my eyes; there were shiny patches on the black creek. The moon had spread over everything a thin layer of silver—over the rank grass, over the mud, upon the wall of matted vegetation standing higher than the wall of a temple, over the great river I could see through a sombre gap glittering, glittering, as it flowed broadly by without a murmur. All this was great, expectant, mute, while the man jabbered about himself. I wondered whether the stillness on the face of the immensity looking at us two were meant as an appeal or as a menace. What were we who had strayed in here? Could we handle that dumb thing, or would it handle us? I felt how big, how confoundedly big, was that thing that couldn't talk, and perhaps was deaf as well. What was in there? I could see a little ivory coming out from there, and I had heard Mr. Kurtz was in there. I had heard enough about it, too—God knows! Yet somehow it didn't bring any image with it—no more than if I had been told an angel or a fiend was in there. . . . It seems to me I am trying to tell you a dream—making a vain attempt, because no relation of a dream can convey the dream-sensation. (56–57)

This passage strikes me as self-explanatory in light of my reading, but perhaps I should make clear how: the description of the river and the surrounding vegetation in the first part of the passage is not only feminine and explicitly vaginal, but also suggestive of the Irigarayan maternal origin, with its primeval mud, its moonlight, its rank grass, and its "wall of matted vegetation standing higher than the wall of a temple"—we are in the domain of the empowered mother ("higher than the wall of a temple" has a note of genuine awe missing from Marlow's earlier formulations of worship—the "unselfish idea" one can "set up, and bow down before, and offer a sacrifice to," and, of course, the ivory that the faithless pilgrims pray to). "It didn't bring any image with it"—while not the formless void of nonbeing of Plotinian misogyny, since it *is* the jungle, it is accorded the terror "nonbeing" really inspires, a terror recast in patriarchy as scorn. The connection of the de-repressed maternal with the dream and of both with modernist narrative (this story) are also established here: again, as Irigaray argues, the dream is the terrain on which that de-repression can be transacted, and at the same time, as we saw in "The Yellow Wallpaper," it provides an alternative mode of representation, a substitute for realism's logocentric, linear logic of causal relations. The greatness of the river and surrounding jungle—they are "big, confoundedly big"—is contrasted to the puniness and insignificance of the ambitious imperialist man jabbering on about himself: the governing European hierarchies are reversed.

Another passage five pages later emphasizes precisely the same qualities of the wilderness: the vaginal imagery, the immensity, the silence and stillness, the moonlight, the contrasting puniness of the invading men, and also adds the elements of almost limitless, overwhelming fecundity, and the related image of drowning that will be reiterated just as Marlow is about to set out up the river ("In a few days the Eldorado Expedition went into the patient wilderness, that closed upon it as the sea closes over a diver" [66]):

> We stopped, and the silence driven away by the stamping of our feet flowed back again from the recesses of the land. The great wall of vegetation, an exuberant and entangled mass of trunks, branches, leaves, boughs, festoons, motionless in the moonlight, was like a rioting invasion of soundless life, a rolling wave of plants, piled up, crested, ready to topple over the creek, to sweep every little man of us out of his little existence. And it moved not. (60–61)

Yet this great maternal power does not, to Marlow, offer the benign bosom that shelters the beaten African; again, its "stillness" might portend "an appeal or . . . a menace," and it might harbor "an angel or a fiend." It is an enormous power that these men might not be able to "handle"—it might, with a rather explicit sexual threat, "handle" them.

These are the familiar formulations of irresolvable ambiguity, of *sous-rature*. A few pages later, just before Marlow embarks on the passage itself, the threatening potentiality of the maternal is emphasized: Marlow refers to "the lurking death, the hidden evil . . . the profound darkness of its heart. . . . The high stillness confronted these two figures [the manager and his nephew] with its ominous patience, waiting for the passing away of a fantastic invasion" (65). While Marlow deliberately distances himself from these crass imperialists, his position in relation to the heart of darkness is still inevitably that of a white European man. In fact, in discussing the awe-inspiring immensity of the wilderness, he associates himself with the papier-mâché Mephistopheles he otherwise so carefully distances himself from: "I wondered whether the stillness on the face of the immensity looking at *us two* were meant as an appeal or as a menace. What were *we* who had strayed in here? Could *we* handle that dumb thing, or would it handle *us*?" (56, italics added).

The maternal origin is always described as silent and still—"mute," "dumb," a "thing that couldn't talk, and perhaps was deaf as well" (remember Mrs. Paley's infuriating deafness). Note the tone of contempt, almost irritation, in these descriptions, paralleling Rachel's desperate impatience with Mrs. Paley's inability to hear as she blocks the passage. Marlow's irritation erupts, immediately following "perhaps was deaf as well," in "What was in there? I could see a little ivory coming out from there, and I had heard Mr. Kurtz was in there." I read this deaf-muteness not as the oppressed silence of the feminine in patriarchal culture but rather as an aspect of the ominous power of the maternal in these modernist texts.[19] It is the impenetrable, uncommunicating power of the buried origin that contains something of immense value. The silence of the heart of darkness is part of its concealment. Marlow, however, knows that precious/evil ivory trickles out. The ivory functions partly as vaginal teeth, like the carpenter's nails and the sharp adz blocking Wait's birth passage in *The Nigger of the "Narcissus."* And just as the perfectly ambiguous Wait is lodged in the uterine compartment of the *Narcissus*, the heart of darkness contains Mr. Kurtz.

Marlow's first clue to Kurtz comes from the painting Kurtz somehow managed to execute in oils in the middle of the jungle and then left behind him at the Central Station; a painting which leads Marlow to ask, "Who is this Mr. Kurtz?" and to say, at the end of the narrative, that he had always assumed Kurtz was an artist: "I noticed a small sketch in oils, on a panel, representing a woman, draped and blindfolded, carrying a lighted torch. The background was sombre—almost black. The movement of the woman was stately, and the effect of the torch-light on the face was sinister" (54). This painting immediately recalls the lamp-statue of "The Return," a figure of the betrayal of the feminine-maternal gift experienced by Alvan Hervey. It recalls the image of Britannia as the torch unto the nations that opened the narrative, recast here in a literally "sinister" light, or darkness. It also foreshadows the reiterated gesture of arms outstretched of the jungle woman and of the Intended, though their arms, abandoned by Kurtz, are empty. What is most important about this painting is the way it connects Kurtz, in our crucial first impression, with both the power and the danger of the feminine.[20]

Kurtz and the maternal heart of darkness are allied mysteries, but, I will argue, crucially differentiated in the accumulations of meaning they accrue by the end of the text. Since I am reading *Heart of Darkness* as an opening of the vaginal passage to the womb, I see Kurtz and the maternal jungle as unified at this point in the text just as the mother and the fetus are one organism before the mother gives birth.

During Marlow's ruminations on his experience of the jungle as he prepares to set off up the river, he initiates the important association of Kurtz with lying, suggested also by the painted woman's blindfold: in addition to the figure of blind justice holding the scales, the blindfold suggests that the woman cannot see the truth her torch presumably illumines. Marlow informs us that "I would not have gone so far as to fight for Kurtz, but I went for him near enough to a lie" (57). In going near enough to Kurtz, Marlow goes near enough to Kurtz's lie, which is, quite explicitly, the ideology of imperialism.[21] The ambitious manager quotes Kurtz with disgust: " 'Each station should be like a beacon on the road towards better things, a centre for trade of course, but also for humanizing, improving, instructing.' Conceive you—that ass!" (65). The manager proves to be right about Kurtz's hypocrisy. Marlow insists, in a famous passage: "You know I hate, detest, and can't bear a lie, not because I am straighter than the rest of us, but simply because it appals me. There is a taint of death, a flavour of mortality in lies—which is exactly what I hate and detest in the world—what I want to forget. It makes me miserable and sick, like biting something rotten would do" (57). I would suggest that lying, untruth, comes to be the province of Kurtz, and Marlow becomes implicated in lying, death, and "biting something rotten"—the links in the chain of association he establishes in the above passage—to the (rather large) extent that he identifies with Kurtz. Through Kurtz he comes as near to death as to a lie.[22] But, as we will see, the text carefully maintains distinctions between Marlow, Kurtz, and the heart of darkness.

The climactic journey up the river to the aptly named Inner Station is initiated by Marlow with imagery that by this point in my reading seems to announce itself as clearly as can be, just short of using Irigaray's terminology, as a passage to the maternal origin: "Going up that river was like travelling back to the earliest beginnings of the world, when vegetation rioted on the earth. . . . An empty stream, a great silence, an impenetrable forest. The air was warm, thick, heavy, sluggish" (66). During the journey "one" feels "bewitched," and "there were moments when one's past came back to one . . . in the shape of an unrestful and noisy dream" in "this strange world of plants, and water, and silence" (66). I would argue that the "unrestful and noisy dream" is simultaneously modernist narrative and troubled pre-Oedipal memory. The implacable silence of the wilderness will become filled near the Inner Station with an external correlative of that noisy dream: the speech, incomprehensible to this text, of the denizens of the heart of darkness.

In the first few pages of the passage up the river, Marlow establishes the crucial dynamic of the new relationship between the masculine and feminine, paternal and maternal, poles of culture Conrad is in the process of forging in this text. Ultimately, again, Marlow is a European man. Although he distances himself decisively from the "pilgrims" of phallo-imperialist Western culture, and although it is he who opens the passage to the maternal origin, his relation to that heart of darkness is, like Conrad's, inevitably ambivalent, his positive attachment to it coexisting with fear and "horror."

Throughout the passage to the Inner Station, the confrontation with Kurtz and his "savages," and the quick return, Marlow oscillates between identification with the heart of darkness and assertion of an alternative paternal principle: precisely Kristeva's "constant alternation, never the one without the other." As the midwife who delivers Kurtz from the mother's womb but delivers him to his death, just as the narrator in *The Nigger of the "Narcissus"* helps to deliver Wait but, again, delivers him to his death, Marlow is the agent of the evacuation of deceit, death, and alienated, rapacious, violent orality—Kurtz's metonymic chain—from the maternal that has been "invaded," as Marlow says again and again, by the phallo-imperialist ideology Kurtz represents.

Kurtz is, of course, the ultimate imperialist. His acquisition of ivory is as legendary as his noble idealism. "All Europe contributed" to his making. He spouts tommyrot sentiment in his pamphlet for the "International Society for the Suppression of Savage Customs," "a beautiful piece of writing," then scrawls at the bottom of the last page, "Exterminate all the brutes!" (86–87). Meanwhile he holds Africans in thrall, murders "rebels" and puts their heads on stakes around his house, and plunders ivory on a massive scale. He represents, as we will see, the bankrupt relationship of representation to gender and history embodied in premodernist narrative. He is the phallic snake that charmed Marlow; his invasion of the maternal was, literally and admittedly, in the interest of "suppression": simultaneously the suppression of the maternal and the suppression of African people in the name of white Western male supremacy and profit. He is a horrific and powerful version of the ludicrous Richard Dalloway, complete with hollow and interminable "eloquence."

Concomitantly, his story is a typical example of one mode of what I have been calling "the old text": an action-packed adventure tale, rounded out with a love interest. The charismatic hero, a multi-talented loner, conquers the wilderness, "the horror, the horror" of which can be made visible only in a modernist text that has opened a passage to the mother. It is made visible through Marlow's dangerous identification with Kurtz. Through his fascination with Kurtz, Marlow comes closest to the heart of darkness. The opening of the vaginal passage *is* for Marlow an attempt to reach Kurtz: he says "for me it [the steamer] crawled towards Kurtz—exclusively" (68). At the same time, through his association with Kurtz Marlow comes to repudiate what Kurtz represents, forging instead an alternative, new story of gender and race relations, narrated in the impossible dialectic of modernist form.

Kurtz's famous eloquence is, I would argue, associated for Conrad with the bankruptcy of the old text that is part of what Kurtz represents (since this is a modernist text, everything important in it is overdetermined). Conrad's ambivalence toward Kurtz—Marlow's fascinated identification over against the reader's revulsion; Kurtz's great power and his ultimate hollowness ("he was hollow at the core" [97])—is a representation of the conflict between Conrad's attachment to the old or conventional text, the adventure tale with heroic hero, and his agonized sense of its insufficiency to the truth. Hence Kurtz's fabulous eloquence matched by his fabulous exploits, and the evil emptiness of both.

The old phallocratic text, the immense snake uncoiled, has become impotent. *Kurtz* of course means short—the immense snake turns out to be rather tiny when one actually finds out what it is. But Kurtz is not as tiny as the joke of his name suggests; the truth is more painful than that: "Kurtz—Kurtz—that means short in German—don't it? Well, the name was as true as everything else in his life—and death. He looked at least seven feet long" (99). But the seven feet do not do him or his bankrupt social text any good: "His covering had fallen off, and his body emerged from it pitiful and appalling as from a winding-sheet. I could see the cage of his ribs all astir, the bones of his arm waving" (99). He is pathetically moribund, a "pitiful Jupiter" (100), a dead god to begin with, his great length only emphasizing his helplessness.

Kurtz, the dying father, is at the same time the heart of darkness's baby. Like a baby, he is "impressively bald" (84). Just after Marlow describes his "pitiful and appalling" body, he goes on to describe his infantile orality: "I saw him open his mouth wide—it gave him a weirdly voracious aspect, as though he had wanted to swallow all the air, all the earth, all the men before him" (99). In Kurtz's attempt to escape from the steamer he crawls like a baby on all fours, and "the wilderness . . . seemed to draw him to its pitiless breast" (107). Marlow wonders at his exhaustion after carrying Kurtz back to the steamer, since Kurtz "was not much heavier than a child" (108).

Marlow must find, in the context of the vaginal passage to the maternal womb, an alternative to Kurtz, a masculine-paternal principle he can believe in and enunciate in order to avoid both Kurtz's fate and the silence or pre-Oedipal babble of the mother. Marlow opens the passage not just *to* the mother but back and forth between the maternal and the paternal. Having chosen his own nightmare, the horrific dream-truth of this narrative, Marlow must continue to have a language in which to narrate it.

Again, the heart of darkness itself, though it remains ambiguous, a locus of mysterious, sometimes terrifying danger, becomes primarily positive for Marlow as he opens the passage. The experience of returning to the womb "between the high walls of our winding way . . . made you feel very small, very lost, and yet it was not altogether depressing, that feeling" (68). Furthermore, the heart of darkness is not really silent. It contains an exciting human noise:

> We are accustomed to look upon the shackled form of a conquered monster, but there—there you could look at a thing monstrous and free. . . . what thrilled you was just the thought of their humanity—like yours—the thought of your remote kinship with this wild and passionate uproar. . . . if you were man enough you would admit to yourself that there was in you just the faintest trace of a response to the terrible frankness of that noise, a dim suspicion of there being a meaning in it which you—you so remote from the night of first ages—could comprehend. . . . truth—truth stripped of its cloak of time. (69)[23]

The maternal origin, unshackled, "monstrous and free," harbors, in the speech of the colonized, the terrifying but thrilling pre-Oedipal noises of truth, antithesis of Kurtz's lying imperialist eloquence. "Truth stripped of the cloak of time" is precisely the Kristevan feminine;[24] it is also the truth of African culture stripped of the imperialist invasion.

This full acknowledgment of the power of the mother is met immediately in Marlow by an enunciation of a paternal principle uncontaminated by the drive to invasion and suppression of the maternal and its allied dark-skinned people:

> Let the fool gape and shudder—the man knows, and can look on without a wink. But he must meet that truth with his own true stuff—with his own inborn strength. Principles won't do. Acquisitions, clothes, pretty rags—rags that would fly off at the first good shake. No; you want a deliberate belief. An appeal to me in this fiendish row—is there? Very well; I hear; I admit, but

I have a voice, too, and for good or evil mine is the speech that cannot be silenced. Of course, a fool, what with sheer fright and fine sentiments, is always safe. (69)

This passage is often taken as yet another Conradian enunciation of (British) imperialist ideology, but I read it differently. The distinction Marlow makes here is not between man and savage or man and woman but between man and "fool"—the fool who has acquired principles that are no better than pretty rags, "fine sentiments" covering "sheer fright" (obviously he has in mind the "pilgrims"). It is crucial that Marlow has "a voice, too, and for good or evil [his] is the speech that cannot be silenced." His voice speaks "deliberate principle" rather than the "fine sentiments" of the imperialist ideology the pilgrims bow down before; it emanates from "his own true stuff," "his own inborn strength." Marlow, a European man feminized by his association, as Buddha, with the East (see chapter 5), can also speak a truth uncontaminated by invasion, possession, suppression.

Immediately after this crucial avowal, Marlow's steamer comes upon the Russian sailor's hut. The Russian sailor, the harlequin, is what might be called Kurtz's bright double. He is incapable of either "fine sentiments" or "sheer fright." Although he wears rags, they are durable—they not only refuse to "fly off at the first good shake," they, like their wearer, seem invulnerable. He is a "fool," but a holy fool. In his hut Marlow finds the book that seems an objective correlative of his credo of the unsilenceable voice that speaks "true stuff," "inborn strength," and "deliberate belief." It is, inevitably for Conrad, a book on seamanship:

Not a very enthralling book; but at the first glance you could see there a singleness of intention, an honest concern for the right way of going to work, which made these humble pages . . . luminous with another than a professional light. The simple old sailor, with his talk of chains and purchases, made me forget the jungle and the pilgrims in a delicious sensation of having come upon something unmistakably real. (71)

The book is an alternative to *both* the jungle and the pilgrims, the mother and the invading male Europeans. The book is not very enthralling, however, and Conrad wants his fiction to be enthralling. Modernist fiction, unlike a manual on seamanship, cannot exclude either the bankrupt old text of the pilgrims or the enabling new text of the jungle. In fact, the old text invades even Marlow's reference to the seamanship manual, in the "talk of chains and purchases": the talk of the imperialism in the service of which that noble seamanship was, in Conrad's experience, deformed. But the sailor's manual does give Marlow, as Conrad's modernist voice, a position from which it is possible, if not entirely safe, to open the pas-

sage to the mother without being swallowed up, to go ashore at the Inner
Station without being part of the pilgrims' invasion.

Having enunciated his credo and found it confirmed, more or less, in
An Inquiry into some Points of Seamanship, Marlow is ready to meet
Kurtz. In the sequence immediately preceding the arrival at the Inner Station, the vaginal imagery associated with the river is heightened and further sexualized: "The reach was narrow, straight, with high sides like a
railway cutting. . . . When the sun rose there was a white fog, very warm
and clammy. . . . At eight or nine, perhaps, it lifted as a shutter lifts. We
had a glimpse of the towering multitude of trees, of the immense matted
jungle" (73). Within that immense matted jungle lurk the "savages" who
protect Kurtz and the Inner Station from these intruders. The only casu-
alty of the attack Kurtz orders is the black helmsman who dies so vividly
at (actually on) Marlow's feet (it is important to remember that the attack, since ordered by Kurtz, is not a manifestation of the evil of the
maternal heart of darkness but rather a manifestation of Kurtz's evil).

The helmsman's death is explicitly sacrificial, but the sacrifice brings
about no redemption: that dynamic is part of one overall configuration of
meaning in this text, the bleak or "nihilistic" vision so often associated
with modernist works.[25] The death of the helmsman, and the extent to
which Kurtz is associated with, rather than differentiated from, the heart
of darkness—he is its offspring as well as its invader and ravager—constitute the segment of the text that narrates the fear of the new that forms the
negative side of Conrad's male modernist ambivalence.

The relationships among Marlow, the helmsman, and Kurtz are remarkably complex. They form a triangulated cluster of doubles (Marlow,
the harlequin, and Kurtz form another such cluster). Marlow and Kurtz
are, of course, the primary pair of doubles, Kurtz representing for Marlow both the incarnation of the ultimate horror of his Company's (his
culture's) enterprise and also the potential of human achievement, specifically artistic achievement (Kurtz is a painter, writer, musician), a potential that has become a victim of that corrupt enterprise. Again, the object
of Marlow's truth-quest is "exclusively" Kurtz, the nightmare of his
choice, the locus of revelation for Marlow of the horror of what his culture has wrought.

The helmsman is killed by a spear in his side, reminiscent of Christ's
wound: again, he dies as a human sacrifice to Kurtz, or, in the regressed
text, to the heart of darkness, foreshadowing the heads on the stakes. He
falls on Marlow's feet, filling his shoes—identity symbol like the hat in
"The Secret Sharer"—with blood.[26] Marlow finds the blood in his shoes
intolerable and hastens to throw them, along with the dead helmsman
himself, overboard. The helmsman, and Marlow's connection to him,
have been sacrificed not to the maternal but to Kurtz, though Kurtz him-

self, in the obverse construction of this segment of the narrative, is also sacrificed to phallo-imperialism. The helmsman has been Marlow's "savage" guide into the wilderness, but it is the pilgrims' culture, with Kurtz its ultimate incarnation, not the wilderness, that claims his life. Kurtz (indirectly) orders his death; moreover, he dies as a result of his similarity to Kurtz, his lack of "restraint"—his contamination not by the heart of darkness but by imperialism: he dies shooting at his fellow Africans with Marlow's rifle, a weapon Marlow himself does not use.

As Marlow drags the helmsman to the railing, "his shoulders were pressed to my breast; I hugged him from behind desperately" (88). This explicit homosexual connection, paralleling the harlequin's devotion to Kurtz, provides, I would argue, in the form of a male homosexual bond, a mediation of the terrifying, fascinating sexual appeal of wilderness femininity. The helmsman, the harlequin, and Kurtz are all intimately connected to that femininity; through them Marlow establishes a safely displaced sexual connection himself.

Once he throws the dead helmsman and the bloody shoes overboard, Marlow is ready to consummate his connection to Kurtz and to the maternal heart of darkness. In doing so he reverts partly to the old-text vision of gender he expounds before he sets out for Africa. He thinks of the Intended and reiterates his Brussels vision of the feminine house of cards: "They—the women I mean—are out of it—should be out of it. We must help them to stay in that beautiful world of their own, lest ours gets worse" (84). He has thrown overboard, in a terrible sacrifice demanded by Kurtz and the horror he represents, the firm vision of the new text he saw as he opened the vaginal passage up the river. The bleak climax and denouement of the narrative do not abandon that vision, but they do severely qualify and reduce it.

At the Inner Station, Marlow's language continues to lose power, becoming pat, trite, banal, and melodramatic; at the same time it reverts to misogyny and racism: "I assure you that never, never before, did this land, this river, this jungle, the very arch of this blazing sky, appear to me so hopeless and so dark, so impenetrable to human thought, so pitiless to human weakness" (94). The rhythm of this writing is forced and conventional, as are its sentiments.

The language revives momentarily in the descriptions of Kurtz and his fabulous house with its heads on stakes, but sinks again, as in the following:

I tried to break the spell—the heavy, mute spell of the wilderness—that seemed to draw him to its pitiless breast by the awakening of forgotten and brutal instincts, by the memory of gratified and monstrous passions. This alone, I was convinced, had driven him out to the edge of the forest, to the bush, towards the gleam of fires, the throb of drums, the drone of weird incantations; this alone had beguiled his unlawful soul beyond the bounds of permitted aspirations. (107)

Banal conventionality speaks here, as the maternal is safely reinscribed in its shackled monstrosity, the pre-Oedipal concomitantly reverting, as lodged in African culture, to "forgotten and brutal instincts . . . gratified and monstrous passions." The "atavism" motif is, of course, part of the regressed text.

The obverse of the monstrosity of the shackled maternal is Kurtz's "savage and superb, wild-eyed and magnificent" (101) African lover. At an early stage in the development of my current reading, I saw her as a positive manifestation of the wilderness-as-feminine in this text, since she provides such conclusive evidence that the heart of darkness is the sexuate mother: "And in the hush that had fallen suddenly upon the whole sorrowful land, the immense wilderness, the colossal body of the fecund and mysterious life seemed to look at her, pensive, as though it had been looking at the image of its own tenebrous and passionate soul" (101). Subsequently, however, I have come to see her not as the culmination of the opening of the vaginal passage but rather as an element of the conventional adventure-romance into which the text temporarily degenerates.[27] Kurtz's jungle lover is part of, rather than different from, the forgotten and brutal instincts, the gratified and monstrous passions of the shackled maternal.

She is, in fact, visibly shackled. Her "barbarous ornaments" consist of "brass leggings to the knees, brass wire gauntlets to the elbow . . . innumerable necklaces of glass beads on her neck . . . she must have had the value of several elephant tusks upon her" (100–101). She also wears "bizarre things, charms, gifts of witch-men," but the "barbarous ornaments" that Marlow names specifically are the currency of the one-sided imperialist "trade" with the Africans. The bankrupt currency of imperialism *is* the shackle of the fecund mother/native, disguised as precious ornamentation (in some feminist arguments, all women's jewelry is seen as displaced shackle, and certainly as token of male ownership and of currency in the exchange of women). She is a walking objective correlative of imperialist plunder, with "the value of several elephant tusks upon her" (note the ambiguity of "upon," suggesting burden as well as ornament).

As the steamer pulls away from shore with Marlow and Kurtz aboard, it leaves behind not the empowered maternal origin it had been steaming toward, but the seductive body representing the re-shackled maternal monster, her brass-wire-gauntleted arms helplessly outstretched, the only figure left standing in place after Marlow literally blows the whistle on the whole scene. Although we are left to wonder whether she may be cut down by the pilgrims' belated gunfire, she is defined by our final view of her, unmoving—she "did not so much as flinch and stretched tragically her bare arms after us over the sombre and glittering river" (109). Simultaneously murdered and immortal, like the feminine itself in patriarchal culture (think of "Matter" as discussed by Plotinus), she recalls our initial glimpse of the African coast, with the French gunboat firing impotently at the untouched wilderness.

But the echo of that earlier scene should also fix in our minds how large a change has actually taken place, despite the regressive elements of the depiction of the Inner Station. Initially, Africa was entirely alien, horrific, death-dealing. The jungle woman the African wilderness has become is sympathetic, "tragic," "savage and superb, wild-eyed and magnificent," with a "tenebrous and passionate soul." The role of villain has been taken over by the pilgrims, the invading male Europeans, and Kurtz's own dark heart. The African feminine-maternal, though reduced and trivialized by insertion in the adventure-romance text, is victim rather than aggressor. The jungle woman does acquire stature in her final tableau, as she withstands unflinching the steam-whistle blasts of Western technology, with bare arms outstretched. She is neither evil like Kurtz nor ridiculous like the pilgrims. Even if Conrad could not find the fictional resources to accomplish it, his intention was to make her "magnificent."

Additionally, Marlow says "I had turned to the wilderness really, not to Mr. Kurtz" (103). Marlow learns from turning to the wilderness that while some men are celestial, wholly absorbed into the order of the father, never touched by the order of "earth" (the maternal), and some men are "fools," with insufficient imagination to participate in the (modernist) dream/nightmare of the maternal,

> most of us are neither one nor the other. The earth for us is a place to live in, where we must put up with sights, with sounds, with smells, too, by Jove!— breathe dead hippo, so to speak, and not be contaminated. And there, don't you see? your strength comes in, the faith in your ability for the digging of unostentatious holes to bury the stuff in—your power of devotion, not to yourself, but to an obscure, back-breaking business. (86)

This is the position opened up by Marlow's passage to modernism. The maternal is no longer simply horrific and deadly. It allows the masculine subject who seeks access to it room to maneuver, assaulting him with troubling sights and sounds and nauseating smells, but not overwhelming him, allowing him even a modicum of the repression necessary to survival ("unostentatious holes to bury the stuff in") since he has a source of "strength" in the reconstituted paternal, the superego that gives him a "power of devotion" not merely to himself but to worthy effort (read seamanship and writing for Conrad, in addition to the "back-breaking business" of digging the "unostentatious holes to bury the stuff in" suggested by the syntax of Conrad's sentence). This masculine subject is "neither one nor the other": not just neither "fool" nor "thunderingly exalted [Jovian] creature" but, more importantly, also, in Kristeva's phrase, "never the one without the other": occupying precisely the passage between.

As Marlow's steamer speeds back down the river, away from the magnificent woman the wilderness has become, the river is totally reinscribed within Victorian figuration, becoming the river of life coursing inevitably toward death:[28] "The brown current ran swiftly out of the heart of darkness, bearing us down towards the sea with twice the speed of our upward progress; and Kurtz's life was running swiftly, too, ebbing, ebbing out of his heart into the sea of inexorable time" (109). And though Marlow pays lip service to the jungle-as-heart-of-darkness here, it is Kurtz's heart that has assumed the text's burden of darkness. Kurtz is Marlow's "choice of nightmares forced upon me in the tenebrous land invaded by these mean and greedy phantoms" (110). Kurtz's voice "survived his strength to hide in the magnificent folds of eloquence the barren darkness of his heart" (110). "His was an impenetrable darkness" (111). Kurtz has Marlow close the shutter of the pilot house, where he, like the black helmsman, dies (though the helmsman's tragic error was to *open* the shutter to the wilderness); "'I can't bear to look at this . . . Oh, but I will wring your heart yet!' he cried at the invisible wilderness" (110).

I do not want to dwell on Kurtz's famous and endlessly discussed last words. Their status in the text is multifariously ambiguous, and they can be used in the service of any number of readings. For my purpose here, I read "the horror! the horror!" as part of Kurtz's burial in the earth— "next day the pilgrims buried something in a muddy hole" (112). As Marlow says several times, Kurtz was more or less already dead by the time he got on board the steamer. Kurtz is part of the "stuff" to be buried in "unostentatious holes": not dead hippo, or the sights, sounds, and smells of earth, but the bankrupt eloquence of the "voice" of the father, of the old text and the phallo-imperialism it represents. Conrad is burying premodernist fiction in that "muddy hole" opened in the maternal. "The horror! the horror!" is not the truth of the maternal heart of darkness, but rather the fate of "A voice! a voice!" (110) that has betrayed the maternal, that vows to "wring [its] heart yet," that "hide[s] in the magnificent folds of eloquence the barren darkness of his heart," discoursing on "My Intended, my station, my career, my ideas" (110), and recommending, as the means of an "enlightened" suppression of savage customs that is actually informed by the confounded fact of the profit motive, "exterminate all the brutes." "The horror! the horror!" is Kurtz's historically specific despair as the muddy hole closes over him, the despair of the imperialist ravagers, not of culture or humanity or the self or language or writing or any such dehistoricized, departicularized abstraction. Conrad makes that very clear when he has Marlow see on Kurtz's "*ivory* face the expression of sombre pride, of ruthless power, of craven terror" (111, italics added).

After Kurtz dies, the text retreats from this radical position. Marlow's near-death allies him too closely to Kurtz, making him forget that he had turned to the wilderness and not to Kurtz: "next day the pilgrims buried something in a muddy hole. And then they very nearly buried me" (112); "it is his extremity that I seem to have lived through" (113). The text now covers over the historical particulars of Kurtz's story with the "nihilistic" ideology that we have already seen at work in the useless sacrifice of the helmsman: "Droll thing life is—that mysterious arrangement of merciless logic for a futile purpose. The most you can hope from it is some knowledge of yourself—that comes too late—a crop of unextinguishable regrets" (112). Kurtz is posthumously recast as a "remarkable man" because "he had something to say" in the face of death, that "unexciting contest" that "takes place in an impalpable greyness . . . in a sickly atmosphere of tepid scepticism." Marlow did not have to face the ultimate moment that time but he feels "with humiliation that," unlike the remarkable Kurtz, "probably I would have nothing to say" (112).

Not only did Kurtz have something to say in his new heroic incarnation, he pronounced accurate judgment on "all the hearts that beat in the darkness. He had summed up—he had judged. 'The horror!' . . . it had the appalling face of a glimpsed truth" (113). Not only is the lying Kurtz's utterance "truth," which has now come full circle in *Heart of Darkness* to be relodged in the male representative of the old order, the old text, but "it was an affirmation, a moral victory, paid for by innumerable defeats, by abominable terrors, by abominable satisfactions. But it was a victory!" (113). Only by rewriting Kurtz as an existential hero of consciousness, unafraid of his death-vision of the abyss, achieving "moral victory" by enunciating a bottomless revulsion against life, can Conrad reenter Marlow into the "sepulchral city," reinserting him in the civilization that has produced the real "horror! horror!" Any other version of Kurtz—particularly the version established just before his death—would be unable to maintain its existence in the deadly, moribund universe of culture and representation Conrad designates the "sepulchral city."

Without a heroic version of Kurtz, this narrative would leave the old text too far behind. Ironically, the character (Kurtz) who enunciates the emptiness (or the "horror") of the center, the absence of meaning (or who generates meaning or "truth" by means of that enunciation), cannot himself be an empty center. At the turn of the century that would not yet be possible, and it would certainly be a different literary phenomenon from the modernist *sous-rature* Conrad was creating.

The "sepulchral city" is the home of Kurtz's "Intended," who has "a soul as translucently pure as a cliff of crystal" (113). The "cliff of crystal" is the obverse of the matted vegetation rising up on either side of the African vaginal passage. What Kurtz, the old text, "intended" was the plunder of the whore-mother to maintain the "purity" of this virgin, who dies a living death in her beautiful world of illusion, dedicated to preserving (embalming) not her own independent feminine delusion but specifically Kurtz's lie, the lie of imperialism that it serves ideals rather than profit. The Intended represents conventionally encultured gender relations with a vengeance.

The culture of bourgeois "safety" shocks and offends Marlow—he now knows upon what repression and violence its safety is constructed. The mortality earlier associated with the maternal heart of darkness comes to reside at the end in the place that constructs the suppression of the maternal: we feel the presence of institutionalized death much more forcibly in the Brussels sequence than we did in Marlow's very abstract description of his near-fatal illness, a presence seen particularly at the Intended's house, with its

> high and ponderous door . . . the tall houses of a street as still and decorous as a well-kept cemetery . . . The tall marble fireplace had a cold and monumental whiteness. A grand piano stood massively in a corner; with dark gleams on the flat surfaces like a sombre and polished sarcophagus. . . . She came forward, all in black, with a pale head, floating towards me in the dusk. She was in mourning. (116–17)

Once we are inside the Intended's house, confronted by Kurtz's hypocrisy made visible, Kurtz again becomes demonic. The reality of his life and death is the "horror" the utterance of which would "knock down" the Intended's carefully preserved illusion. Marlow believes he cannot utter it, just as he believes he would have nothing to say in the face of death. The truth about the lie Kurtz embodies becomes more and more vivid to Marlow's senses as he listens to the Intended's encomia. He suspects that Kurtz had not even given him the right bundle of papers—that the Intended's letters were not at all what Kurtz wanted to preserve, that he had instead meant to entrust Marlow with "another batch of his papers which, after his death, I saw the manager examining under the lamp" (119).

As the Intended asks Marlow about Kurtz's last words, "the horror! The horror!" beats in his ears "in a whisper that seemed to swell menacingly like the first whisper of a rising wind" (121). Then Marlow "pull[s] [him]self together" and utters his famous "lie," his statement to the Intended that Kurtz's last word was "your name." It is crucial that we do not know her name. The only named characters in the entire text are

Kurtz and Marlow. I would argue that at an important level of the text, in the configuration of meaning I have been developing throughout this reading, Marlow does not lie. The "name" of the Intended *is* "the horror! The horror!"[29] Marlow's "lie" is the climax of the text not because it preserves the possibility of hope or light or goodness in a world that would otherwise be "too dark—too dark altogether" (121), but because it reinscribes in bourgeois patriarchal imperialist culture the truth of the vaginal passage. Marlow explicitly links the Intended to the text's repudiation of Kurtz at his death: as a horrific representative of what Western culture has made of femininity, she is part of the horror of the Kurtzian phallo-imperialist occupation of the maternal. In her icy, sarcophagal, deluded asexuality, she is that horror just as much as are the heads on stakes or the sagas of monumental plunder.

Conrad makes a crucial distinction, however, between the Intended as female victim of the Kurtzian system and Kurtz as its male perpetrator, a distinction for which he provides a powerful figuration: "She put out her arms as if after a retreating figure, stretching them black and with clasped pale hands across the fading and narrow sheen of the window. . . . a tragic and familiar Shade, resembling in this gesture another one, tragic also, and bedecked with powerless charms, stretching bare brown arms over the glitter of the infernal stream, the stream of darkness" (120). Although in Brussels the vaginal stream must again be seen as "infernal . . . the stream of darkness," the female victims of Kurtz's horror are dissociated from the ominous knitters of black wool or bustling aunts enforcing the system of sentimental tommyrot of the first part of the text, where the female is represented as complicit in, and perhaps even responsible for, the corruption of the masculine ideal Marlow sees in the practice of Belgian imperialism. As Marlow learns that all European imperialism is a corruption of the masculine ideal, instituted by men as a ravaging and occupation of the maternal, the female becomes, by the end of the narrative, though still obligatorily "infernal," at the same time also "tragic" and "powerless." The maternal has been re-repressed, made powerless, or rather its powerlessness has been represented accurately as the text reenters Europe, but the passage to the maternal origin opened by Marlow and his text has demystified that origin, putting alongside the sinister, death-dealing maternal monster required by the old text both a fecund veracity and a pitiable but dignified victimhood.

For Marlow, the great snake uncoiled was a charm, a fascinating lure into the terrifying maternal heart of darkness. For Rachel Vinrace, the beauty of the jungle river and the perfection of the lives of the women in the "native camp" one reaches by journeying up that river—positive figural components in this section of the text of the maternal itself—are the fascinating lure, but danger lurks within that perfection in the form of a snake. As we have seen, Helen Ambrose, the maternal character, "promised" Rachel "a river," and Rachel stays with Helen because she has "visions of a great river, now blue, now yellow in the tropical sun and crossed by bright birds, now white in the moon, now deep in shade with moving trees and canoes sliding out from the tangled banks" (86). This vision is inspired by the tapestry Helen is embroidering. But, as we have also seen, Helen reads a black book of philosophy as she embroiders on board the *Euphrosyne*, and she subsequently presides over the romance plot of the fourth and fifth parts of the novel, a plot that coincides with Rachel's death. Unconsummated betrothal and death coincide, as in *Heart of Darkness*, with the passage of the novel into a formal mode that disrupts realist convention much more concertedly than did the first three sections, heightening and intensifying dreamlike, surreal image-sequences and destabilizing conventional linguistic signification.

Woolf's river passage seems consciously to evoke Conrad's:

> They seemed to be driving into the heart of the night, for the trees closed in front of them, and they could hear all round them the rustling of leaves. The great darkness had the usual effect of taking away all desire for communication by making their words sound thin and small. . . . He [Hewet] was drawn on and on away from all he knew, slipping over barriers and past landmarks into unknown waters as the boat glided over the smooth surface of the river. . . . By degrees the river narrowed, and the high sandbanks fell to level ground thickly grown with trees. (265–67)

Within this briefly sketched, quasi-Conradian setting of the river of narrow high banks, matted vegetation, and the silent but mysteriously noisy darkness of the unknown, Woolf places a set of characters very different from Conrad's: no rapacious European pilgrims or restrained cannibal crewmen, but rather the inhabitants of an upper-middle-class English drawing room, their clothes, behavior, and values untouched by the vaginal passage opening around them. Woolf makes the group both ludicrous and inevitable, with their strict adherence to the routines of a leisured English day, their elaborate impedimenta of books, paintboxes, and tea things, awnings, shawls and constricting clothes, their stilted conversation and prudery, their sense that no other way of life is conceivable.

During their two romantic upriver encounters, Terence and Rachel leave this group behind and also (however minimally) violate its rules. As they set out on their first excursion into the jungle, Hirst warns them "beware of snakes" (270). Hirst and Helen, not voyagers out for all their insouciance, refuse to go into the jungle, but wait for Rachel and Terence on the shore of the river, safely in sight of the boat and the rest of the group. Rachel and Terence begin conventionally enough, on "a wide pathway striking through the forest at right angles to the river" that "resembled a drive in an English forest" (270). However,

> As they passed into the depths of the forest the light grew dimmer, and the noises of the ordinary world were replaced by those creaking and sighing sounds which suggest to the traveller in a forest that he is walking at the bottom of the sea. The path narrowed and turned; it was hedged in by dense creepers which knotted tree to tree, and burst here and there into star-shaped crimson blossoms. . . . The atmosphere was close and the air came at them in languid puffs of scent. . . . Not only did the silence weigh upon them, but they were both unable to frame any thoughts. (270)

This jungle path reproduces the river as vaginal passage, with the silence, the dense vegetation, and the "close" atmosphere again evoking Conrad. For Woolf, however, this jungle with its star-shaped crimson blossoms and languid puffs of scent is more a place of magical sensual beauty than of ominous threat.

In this ambiguous setting, Rachel and Terence strangely declare themselves to one another in a love scene that opens a new channel for fiction. Terence asserts their love as a fact and Rachel merely echoes him: "We are happy together," he says, "Very happy," she replies; "We love each other," he says, "We love each other," she replies. The snake of which Rachel must beware is, I would argue, the inevitable supremacy of the male in the situation of overt courtship, a situation that no longer allows the meeting of the minds in programs for gender equality that characterized their love when it was undeclared, but instead involves a brute assertion of male possession. The modernist writing that represents this scene demystifies the language of love, revealing it as a language of domination. The language that breaks the silence of the maternal (a silence filled, like Conrad's, with powerful, mysterious, "inarticulate" noise, here of bird cries and monkey chuckles) is Terence's only (paralleling his desire to write a novel that would *speak* silences)—all Rachel can do is echo it.

They are late when they return from this expedition, thereby violating the rules. Rachel has detached herself from the ludicrous and moribund world of English bourgeois gentility, but the alternative passage to the maternal is as fraught with danger as is Conrad's, containing a snake in the form of domination by Terence and his defamiliarized but ineluctable language, and also bearing the seeds of death: when she returns from this betrothal scene, Rachel is exhausted and her cheeks are white.[30]

One standard reading of Rachel's death sees it as an expression of Woolf's fear of heterosexuality: Rachel's marriage with Terence cannot be consummated in Woolf's imagination—literally, she would rather (Rachel) be dead.[31] But I would argue that the really deadly snake is bourgeois marriage rather than heterosexuality per se. Although Terence and

Rachel leave the sphere of the hotel denizens, violate its rules, and enter the wild jungle to avow their love, that avowal will lead them right back to the heart of the drawing room. As we will see, Rachel does not fall ill until the utterly conventional, repressive nature of her future life with Terence becomes clear to her. Embracing and kissing in the jungle may be the source of the infection, but only because the embracing and kissing are constructed by the interpretive community (which includes Terence and Rachel themselves) as a proposal of marriage.

The maternal, in the form of Helen, is in collusion with this particular snake (remember Helen reading her black volume of philosophy). It is helpful and I think justifiable here to read *To the Lighthouse* back into *The Voyage Out*. Mrs. Ramsay, Woolf's ultimate ambiguous mother, is seen as culpable in that novel in the way she forces younger people into marriage—not into sex, but into marriage. It is Lily Briscoe's triumph to continue to love Mrs. Ramsay and yet to resist that pressure; Lily Briscoe's triumph is twenty years in the future for Woolf as she writes this novel.

Mr. Flushing, the organizer of the expedition, stops the boat just short of its final destination, the native village, so that whoever wants to can walk the rest of the way. Rachel and Terence take advantage of this opportunity to go off alone together again into the jungle. Rachel continues to experience a discrepancy between her inchoate feelings and the language and social conventions that are supposed to express and contain them: being in love, being happy, getting married. Woolf is struggling toward a new social/literary text in which Rachel's experiences and emotions would be allowed to be whatever they are, to determine their own forms of verbal and social expression. But here, in this initiatory work of modernism, the new text is still in equipoise with the old.

Going through the obligatory list of his "faults," Terence says "I ought never to have asked you to marry me, I expect" (280–81). Rachel replies, "Am I in love—is this being in love—are we to marry each other?" (281). Again, she cannot make her feelings correspond to the naming of these monolithic social institutions. Terence assures her, in an overly sanguine prediction that at once touches the heart of Rachel's dilemma and radically underestimates its intractability, "Oh, you're free, Rachel. To you, time will make no difference, or marriage" (281). As it turns out, death is Rachel's only road to freedom—her voyage out of cultural and textual constraint must also be a voyage out of life. Terence fantasizes his marriage to Rachel as an end to his loneliness; he sees them walking together through London streets. That is precisely what can never happen: married in London, Rachel would lose herself, to look ahead (or, chronologically, back) to Edna's formulation in *The Awakening*. Walking the London streets, Rachel and Terence would reproduce the opening scene of the novel, which established the unsatisfactory marriage of Helen and Ridley (as it turns out Helen spends most of her time in South America escaping from Ridley into her ambiguous friendship with St. John Hirst) and the alienation of bourgeois marriage in modern industrial culture—precisely the setting out of which the novel attempts to voyage.

Rachel and Terence have a triumphant moment of union honest to their actual emotion and experience before convention reabsorbs them. First they voice their alienation from the social construction of their experience:

> "What's happened?" he began. "Why did I ask you to marry me? How did it happen?"
>
> "Did you ask me to marry you?" she wondered. They faded far away from each other, and neither of them could remember what had been said. (281)

Then they return to a relatively unmediated and simple recollection of what actually happened between them, and that brings them to a harmonious happiness:

> "We sat upon the ground," he recollected.
>
> "We sat upon the ground," she confirmed him. The recollection of sitting upon the ground, such as it was, seemed to unite them again, and they walked on in silence. . . . Long silences came between their words, which were no longer silences of struggle and confusion but refreshing silences, in which trivial thoughts moved easily. They began to speak naturally of ordinary things. . . . Very gently and quietly, almost as if it were the blood singing in her veins, or the water of the stream running over stones, Rachel became conscious of a new feeling within her. She wondered for a moment what it was, and then said to herself, with a little surprise at recognising in her own person so famous a thing:
>
> "This is happiness, I suppose." And aloud to Terence she spoke, "This is happiness."
>
> On the heels of her words he answered, "This is happiness," upon which they guessed that the feeling had sprung in both of them the same time. (282–83)

This time Rachel speaks first, and Terence echoes her. Their feelings are in harmony with one another and with the words that express them. Silence is not a measure of linguistic inadequacy but a measure of peace and of synchrony with the fecund maternal silence around them, a "refreshing" silence out of which a new language might emerge to give voice to the "blood singing" in Rachel's veins.

This scene takes place within the very womblike destination of the river passage. Just before the boat landed, the "wall of trees" on either side of the river "came to an end," as the "light suddenly widened out":

Woolf's version of the Inner Station is much more explicitly and positively womblike than Conrad's. Into this momentary uterine utopia, the
ambiguous mother violently inserts herself: "A hand dropped abrupt as
iron on Rachel's shoulder; it might have been a bolt from heaven. . . .
Helen was upon her" (283). Helen's approach seems at first (and indeed
figurally it is) to be part of their uterine bliss, her voice part of its powerful
pre-Oedipal language. What they take to be the noises and internal movements of the womb ("the waters in which they were now sunk") are really
the sounds of Helen's approach:

> Voices crying behind them never reached through the waters in which they
> were now sunk. The repetition of Hewet's name in short, dissevered syllables
> was to them as the crack of a dry branch or the laughter of a bird. The grasses
> and breezes sounding and murmuring all round them, they never noticed that
> the swishing of the grasses grew louder and louder, and did not cease with the
> lapse of the breeze. A hand dropped . . . (283)

What follows, in a scene deploying for modernist form the powerful
overdetermination of the dream and of language, is a mysteriously violent
and sexual encounter between Helen, Terence, and Rachel, with Rachel
the passive victim, Helen the primary aggressor, and Terence at once
complicit and removed:

> She [Rachel] fell beneath it [Helen's hand on her shoulder], and the grass
> whipped across her eyes and filled her mouth and ears. Through the waving
> stems she saw a figure, large and shapeless against the sky. Helen was upon her.
> Rolled this way and that, now seeing only forests of green, and now the high
> blue heaven, she was speechless and almost without sense. At last she lay still,
> all the grasses shaken round her and before her by her panting. Over her
> loomed two great heads, the heads of a man and woman, of Terence and Helen.
>   Both were flushed, both laughing, and the lips were moving; they came to-
> gether and kissed in the air above her. Broken fragments of speech came down
> to her on the ground. She thought she heard them speak of love and then of
> marriage. Raising herself and sitting up, she too realised Helen's soft body, the
> strong and hospitable arms, and happiness swelling and breaking in one vast
> wave. When this fell away . . . she was the first to perceive a little row of human
> figures standing patiently in the distance. . . . Falling into line behind Mr.
> Flushing, they were careful to leave at least three yards' distance between the
> toe of his boot and the rim of her skirt. (283–84)

I read this strangely wonderful scene as the fall into the sexualized, Oedipal family, with its alienated language of "love and . . . marriage." Terence functions simultaneously as Rachel's and as Helen's mate, putting
Terence, appropriately for bourgeois marriage, also in the position of
Rachel's father.

Helen's sexuality is excruciatingly ambiguous for Rachel. Helen's sexual encounter with Terence, the kiss, is a betrayal and an ominous threat. The enormous figure of adult heterosexuality looms over the prostrate virgin, the mother figures as the daughter's sexual rival, and, most important, the mother abrogates her role as nurturer by inappropriately flaunting her sexuality. That is the meaning of Helen's violent embrace of Rachel. The painful, disorienting knocking about in the grass, which Terence may or may not join Helen in inflicting on Rachel, and then the "soft body, the strong and hospitable arms, and happiness swelling and breaking in one vast wave," in the context of the violent attack on Rachel and the kiss between Helen and Terence looming enormously over her head, are an abuse of maternal nurturance in the service of sexual exploitation. We are reminded of Helen's various sinister moments in relation to Rachel on board the *Euphrosyne*. Like the jungle womb itself, which betrays Rachel into betrothal and death precisely at the moment that it offers her perfect "happiness," Helen's vast wave of maternal/sexual jouissance is the lure that leads Rachel right back to the "little row of human figures" waiting to reabsorb her into the old text of bourgeois culture. Remember, Helen's purpose in approaching the two lovers is to reunite them with the "little group of figures" from which they have again too long strayed.

After this scene, the native village is an anticlimax. Mr. and Mrs. Flushing fulfill their purpose in this sequence by making "purchases" of native jewelry, which they fear is insufficiently authentic. And as they fear, the "native" culture available to them for purchase inevitably shows "signs here and there of European influence" (286). One wonders whether they paid for their "brooch" and "pair of ear-rings" with strands of brass wire.

Rachel makes no purchases. She feels alienated from and inadequate before the utterly natural native women who dominate the village, "squatting on the ground in triangular shapes, moving their hands, either plaiting straw or in kneading something in bowls" (284). A woman openly nurses her baby, and Rachel feels even worse. Woolf narrates her characters' response to this anticlimax in a passage that not only requires no explication, but is itself an explication:

> Seeking each other, Terence and Rachel drew together under a tree. Peaceful, and even beautiful at first, the sight of the women, who had given up looking at them, made them now feel very cold and melancholy.
>
> "Well," Terence sighed at length, "it makes us seem insignificant, doesn't it?"
>
> Rachel agreed. So it would go on for ever and ever, she said, those women sitting under the trees, the trees and the river. They turned away . . . They had not gone far before they began to assure each other once more that they were

in love, were happy, were content; but why was it so painful being in love, why was there so much pain in happiness? (285)

The empowered maternal to which this novel has opened a passage is both the only source of happiness, harmony, and authentic language—the new text—and also, at the same time, violent, exploitative, betraying, and hopelessly alienated. At the end of the chapter, the darkness that earlier offered Rachel refuge from London's blazing light has taken on the sinister tones of Conradian darkness: "darkness poured down profusely, and left them with scarcely any feeling of life, except that they were standing there together in the darkness" (289).

Rachel's relationship with Terence, or rather Terence's attitude toward Rachel, changes utterly after their return from this river passage, when they must reenter the social nexus as an engaged couple. Woolf pays narrative lip service to their ostensible perfect happiness, without which there would be no novel to write here, no old text to work against, just as Conrad must provide a heroic version of Kurtz. But in fact, Terence becomes assertive, highly critical of Rachel, and oppressively determined to observe the conventions. He insists that they go to tea at the hotel, mocking her self-consciousness (she can't bear the thought of all those eyes upon her) by informing her that she is "consumed with vanity," "a monster of conceit" (308) to think that anyone will be looking at her. He tells her that she is "'a person of no conceivable importance whatever—not beautiful, or well dressed, or conspicuous for elegance or intellect, or deportment. A more ordinary sight than you are,' he concluded, 'except for the tear across your dress has never been seen'" (308). The tear across the dress had been used before: by Jane Austen, in *Pride and Prejudice*, to figure Lydia's disastrous seduction by Wickham.

Earlier, Terence had interrupted Rachel as she tried to play a difficult late Beethoven sonata, insisting on telling her about his work as he belittled her music in terms reminiscent of Dr. Johnson on the subject of women preachers: the sonata is "merely like an unfortunate old dog going round on its hind legs in the rain" (292). Rachel is a fine pianist. Woolf has developed her piano playing throughout the novel as the locus of her modernist heroinism, her capacity for profound, difficult, unconventional, authentic behavior and expression. *The Voyage Out* is of course a *kunstlerroman*; where Kurtz is a universal artist, painter-writer-musician, Rachel has specialized. Music is a figure here of the attempt to create a new language uncontaminated by the old social/literary text. In her disgust with the false, artificial congratulatory "notes" to which Terence is forcing her to write stilted replies, she erupts, "They're sheer nonsense! . . . Think of words compared with sounds!" (292). "Sounds" are, of course, what she and Terence had heard on the river passage, in the jungle, and in the native village. Rachel wants to create her own "notes."

In a reversal of his earlier feminist position, Terence goes on to sneer at women, who are "optimists" because "they don't think" (291). He insists that Rachel stop playing the piano and write replies to the nonsensical notes of congratulation. While she grudgingly obeys, he looks at the politically engaged books lying about ("antiquated problem plays, harrowing descriptions of life in the east end," as he contemptuously describes them [292]) and tells her that she reads "trash" and then that she never will "care with every fibre of your being for the pursuit of truth! You've no respect for facts, Rachel; you're essentially feminine" (295). Under the guise of praising her charming idiosyncrasies, he tells her she is "not beautiful," her eyes "never see anything," her "mouth's too big," and her "cheeks would be better if they had more colour in them" (297). What he likes about her face is that it " 'makes one wonder what the devil you're thinking about—it makes me want to do that—' He clenched his fist and shook it so near her that she started back, 'because now you look as if you'd blow my brains out. There are moments,' he continued, 'when, if we stood on a rock together, you'd throw me into the sea' " (298). This is a neat reversal of his earlier, feminine-identified position, when women's oppression made his blood boil, and he imagined himself as a woman wanting to blow someone's brains out. He has become that "someone."

Rachel has a surprising but appropriate reaction to Terence's vision of the rock and the sea: "To be flung into the sea, to be washed hither and thither, and driven about the roots of the world—the idea was incoherently delightful. She sprang up, and began moving about the room, bending and thrusting aside the chairs and tables as if she were indeed striking through the waters" (298). Terence interprets her actions as "cleaving a passage for herself, and dealing triumphantly with the obstacles which would hinder their passage through life" (298). This makes him feel that their "marriage will be the most exciting thing that's ever been done!" (298). He catches her in his arms, and they struggle "for mastery . . . At last she was thrown to the floor, where she lay gasping, and crying for mercy" (298). Her escape from this situation will be precisely to the underwater womb-world she imagines as a refuge from her impasse with Terence on the rock: " 'I'm a mermaid! I can swim,' she cried, 'so the game's up.' " Her game is also up, however: "her dress was torn across."

Rachel obeys Terence—they go to the hotel to tea. In the hotel sequence, Woolf moves through various minor characters' points of view, as she has intermittently throughout the novel. Rachel's more overtly rebellious double, Evelyn M., who has refused a number of offers of marriage, thinks about the hotel social circle's two engaged couples (Susan is

Mrs. Paley's conventional niece, Arthur her equally conventional intended), offering a crude, simplified version of Woolf's critique of bourgeois marriage:

> They moved so slowly because they were not single but double, and Susan was attached to Arthur, and Rachel to Terence, and for the sake of this one man they had renounced all other men, and movement, and the real things of life. Love was all very well, and those snug domestic houses, with the kitchen below and the nursery above, which were so secluded and self-contained, like little islands in the torrents of the world; but the real things were surely the things that happened, the causes, the wars, the ideals, which happened in the great world outside, and went on independently of these women, turning so quietly and beautifully towards the men. She looked at them sharply. Of course they were happy and content, but there must be better things than that. Surely one could get nearer to life, one could get more out of life, one could enjoy more and feel more than they would ever do. (320)

Evelyn M. is not quite right, and her critique, still so often heard, comes a bit too easily. The key word in this passage is "double." "The causes, the wars, the ideals, which happened in the great world outside and went on independently of these women" are not any more "the real things" than are the "snug domestic houses." What Woolf reveals here is precisely the trap of the either/or, of phallogocentric dualism. Just before Rachel's death, Woolf is constructing for us in the sharpest possible terms the dualistic trap out of which she is trying to voyage by opening the passage between the masculine-paternal "great world outside" and the feminine-maternal "snug domestic house." The passage between has been opened, its opening and the passage itself are associated with water, and as we have seen over and over this underwater world is at once magically liberating and terrifyingly deadly. In it Rachel is about to drown.

The death sequence opens with Terence and Rachel sitting on the terrace of the Ambroses' villa on a desperately hot afternoon, with Terence reading aloud to Rachel from *Comus*. He has chosen Milton on this hot afternoon because "the words of Milton had substance and shape, so that it was not necessary to understand what he was saying; one could merely listen to his words; one could almost handle them" (326). Rachel, however, the feminine modernist protagonist, cannot receive Milton that way. Partly because these words function pre-Oedipally as well as symbolically—"one could almost handle them"—she knows they hold for her a crucially "different," subversive meaning: "The words, in spite of what Terence had said, seemed to be laden with meaning, and perhaps it was for this reason that it was painful to listen to them; they sounded strange; they meant different things from what they usually meant" (326).

In part, Milton here is the great patriarchal "bogey,"[32] and Terence's choice of Milton, along with his prerogative itself of choosing and enunciating language at all, particularly this prime patriarchal language, while Rachel passively, uncomprehendingly listens as she begins to die, is further evidence of Terence's new oppressive position in relation to Rachel as her future lord and master. I would argue that Woolf is also using Milton for more complex purposes. Here is the passage Woolf quotes from Terence's reading of *Comus*:

> There is a gentle nymph not far from hence,
> That with moist curb sways the smooth Severn stream.
> Sabrina is her name, a virgin pure;
> Whilom she was the daughter of Locrine,
> That had the sceptre from his father Brute.

As Catherine Belsey argues in *John Milton: Language, Gender, Power*,[33] Sabrina erupts in *Comus* as one of those instances of the subversive feminine that crop up throughout the not at all monolithically patriarchal Great Tradition. The new, different meaning Rachel is trying to grasp in this passage, I would argue, is her identification with Sabrina, the powerfully virginal underwater goddess, granddaughter of masculine "Brute" strength, who "sways the smooth Severn stream," governing the (vaginal) river that Rachel has been unable to harness for her own liberation from the old text.

The next passage Terence reads reinforces this interpretation:

> Sabrina fair,
>   Listen where thou art sitting
> Under the glassy, cool, translucent wave,
>   In twisted braids of lilies knitting
> The loose train of thy amber dropping hair,
> Listen for dear honour's sake,
>   Goddess of the silver lake,
>   Listen and save!

It is Sabrina who saves the chaste Lady from rape by Comus. In Milton's version of Sabrina's rather obscure story, she plunged into the Severn in flight from an evil "stepdame" (Belsey, 51). Sabrina represents the possibility of feminine power through sea-change, a power attained in spite of, or even in response to, the distortion of maternal succor for girls in patriarchy—a power derived from reclaiming the maternal origin for oneself (Sabrina's "stepdame" is "enraged" by some sort of sexual jealousy, making us think of that surreal scene in the jungle with Rachel, Terence, and Helen). Sabrina is like the triumphant "mermaid" Rachel imagines she will become when she imagines being flung from the rock into the sea.

I would argue that as allusion, the passage from *Comus* suggests the Kristevan impossible dialectic, the Irigarayan opening of the equalizing vaginal passage *between* the paternal and the maternal. The Severn is a boundary, simultaneously separating ("sever") and joining England and Wales, Woolf's oppressive dominant culture and a wilder (in popular mythology) culture it has oppressed. Sabrina herself, heroine-savior of her endangered sister, plunges into the vaginal river a persecuted daughter and emerges a powerful goddess. Woolf harnesses Milton, as allusion, to her own feminist-modernist project, without denying him his remarkable literary power—if anything, Milton's language is heightened, made even more magical, by the context in which Woolf embeds it—the incantatory repetitions that give it the power of charm or mantra. This vaginal river marks a genuine two-way traffic between Woolf and Milton, the maternal redeemed from the evil stepdame and the paternal redeemed from "Brute."

It is important to remember at this point that contrary to stepdame Helen's negative expectation of Rachel at the beginning of the ocean voyage (Helen thinks with irritation that Rachel will confide in her that she does not get on with her father), Rachel *likes* Willoughby, feeling a comfortable, easy identification with him. Willoughby Vinrace, though an imperialist, is not an oppressive imperialist ideologue or sexual exploiter like Richard Dalloway, Mrs. Paley's cohabitor of the blocked passage. In fact, he is the one who goes farthest up the river; he virtually disappears up the river after the boat lands.

Again, in this modernist text, as in *Heart of Darkness*, the momentary vision of the opened passage is inevitably unstable: Sabrina and the mermaid dissolve as Rachel dies. The modernist sea-change is entirely ambiguous, consisting of suffering and annihilation as well as triumph and escape ("death or some unexampled joy").

In her fevered delirium, Rachel sinks beneath the "glassy, cool, translucent wave," a phrase she fixes on obsessively. Helen nurses her, wanting a better doctor for her than the obviously incompetent village man Terence insists on retaining because he assures them that Rachel's illness is not serious. In this sense, Helen is a positive nurturing presence, and significant blame for Rachel's death can be assigned to Terence: perhaps, if they had called in the competent doctor sooner, as Helen wished, Rachel need not have died.[34]

Helen's presence, however, becomes sinister to Rachel. Just before Rachel's death, "Helen's form stooping to raise her in bed appeared of gigantic size, and came down upon her like the ceiling falling" (347), reminding us of the jungle encounter. Also, Helen is strangely calm and unmoved at the moment of Rachel's death. Woolf carefully preserves her maternal ambiguity.

Terence's reaction to Rachel's death is overtly touching and pathetic but at another level shocking and almost diabolical. He holds her hand as she dies and feels "happiness . . . perfect happiness":

> An immense feeling of peace came over Terence. . . . Once he held his breath and listened acutely; she was still breathing; he went on thinking for some time; they seemed to be thinking together; he seemed to be Rachel as well as himself; and then he listened again; no, she had ceased to breathe. So much the better—this was death. It was nothing; it was to cease to breathe. It was happiness, it was perfect happiness. They had now what they had always wanted to have, the union which had been impossible while they lived. (353)

Of course, Terence still lives. Rachel has died into the perfection of his union with her (not hers with him).

Rachel's own experience of her illness and death, the most difficult part of the novel for Woolf to write because it took her so close to her own experience of madness, finds representation in the novel's most important modernist figuration.[35] She returns to the dream-vision she had on the *Euphrosyne*, after Richard Dalloway's kiss, of the long tunnel with damp bricks ending in the claustrophobic vault inhabited by a deformed little man with long nails. But now the vault is inhabited by actual rather than transformed women: Helen and the nurse who is also taking care of Rachel—the overly hot (sexual) and the overly cold mother (Rachel sees Nurse McInnis playing cards and thinks "that a woman who sat playing cards in a cavern all night long would have very cold hands" [331]).

After seeing the nurse as the woman with cold hands playing cards in a cavern, Rachel shuts her eyes. When she opens them, the "woman was still playing cards, only she sat now in a tunnel under a river, and the light stood in a little archway in the wall above her" (331). Woolf is gradually reconstituting Rachel's earlier nightmare. Rachel shuts her eyes again, and

> [finds] herself walking through a tunnel under the Thames, where there were little deformed women sitting in archways playing cards, while the bricks of which the wall was made oozed with damp, which collected into drops and slid down the wall. But the little old women became Helen and Nurse McInnis after a time, standing in the window together whispering, whispering incessantly. (331)

The incomprehensible pre-Oedipal language so magical, authentic, and beautiful in the jungle has now become an ominous incessant whisper, as the womb itself again becomes a horrific death-vault. Under the glassy, cool, translucent wave *of the Thames*, the great river of the city to which Rachel must return, if she lives, as Mrs. Terence Hewet, is no Sabrina, but rather the maternal deformed by patriarchy. That is not a womb to which Rachel as modernist heroine can (re)turn.

Terence visits her, offering her, significantly, a bundle of letters from England. In her reply she speaks of "the old woman with the knife" and something that goes "rolling off the edge of the hill" (333). Terence is disconcerted, but Hirst comforts him. He pays another visit, this time kissing her. "She opened them [her eyes] completely when he kissed her. But she only saw an old woman slicing a man's head off with a knife" (339). The horrific old woman, associated with the women in the vault under the Thames, is Rachel's ally as well as her persecutor, expressing her rage at Terence just as Bertha expresses Jane Eyre's at Rochester.[36] But the vision of an old woman with a knife slicing off a man's head and of the head rolling down a hill is more terrifying than it is gratifying, and Rachel is figuring the impossibility of her situation, just as Jane did in her vision of the mad Bertha right before her escape from Thornfield.

Just before her death, Rachel does return to the womb. It is not the empowered womb at the end of the vaginal river passage, which was momentarily utopian in the jungle but has returned to its earlier encultured status as death-vault under the Thames. Rather, Rachel escapes to the ocean floor, becoming like the "monsters" of the ocean voyage. But those monsters no longer threaten violently to be born. They have given up:

> The heat was suffocating. At last the faces went further away; she fell into a deep pool of sticky water, which eventually closed over her head. She saw nothing and heard nothing but a faint booming sound, which was the sound of the sea rolling over her head. While all her tormentors thought that she was dead, she was not dead, but curled up at the bottom of the sea. There she lay, sometimes seeing darkness, sometimes light, while every now and then some one turned her over at the bottom of the sea. (341)

This is a far cry from the swimming mermaid, or Sabrina, or the perfect harmony and authenticity at the end of the river passage, before the snake struck. All Rachel's power is gone. She is entirely passive, her view of "darkness" or "light" dependent on "some one" who "turns her over."[37] Her fetal position is a figure of withdrawal and defeat, affording only the peace of escape and protection from "her tormentors." This is the womb-death feared by post-Freudian patriarchal culture—the "return to the womb" as entropic death-wish, as desire to regress, to shed adult responsibility and difficulty, to become again passive, helpless, and protected. It is the masculine fear of the empowered maternal displaced as fear of emasculation: Woolf has reinstated the patriarchal maternal just as Conrad did. The ending of The Voyage Out is just as bitter, just as is defeated by the old text, as is the ending of Heart of Darkness. The passage, however, was opened, and through it two modernist narratives were born.

Chapter 5

THE DESTRUCTIVE ELEMENT: *THE AWAKENING* AND *LORD JIM*

THE FULLY realized *sous-rature* we will see in *The Awakening*, 1899, and *Lord Jim*, 1899–1900, also characterizes later works of "high" modernism, in poetry as well as narrative (see Part III).[1] Gender, race, and class are no longer the erupting forces they were in the texts I have previously discussed, where they marked sites of initiatory formal innovation. As in subsequent works of modernism, male and female modernist ambivalence in *Lord Jim* and *The Awakening* concerning the "revolutionary horizon" of reconstitution of gender, race, and class relations is not represented overtly. These novels feature no ambitious governesses or (literally) imprisoned wives, no black men or women simultaneously dying and being born, no passages to a third world of the empowered maternal. Instead, as in high modernism, modernist ambivalence and the historical referents to which it is a response are suppressed and reinscribed primarily in form.[2] Detached from specific historical referents, history and the feminine become, in these two novels as in high modernism, abstractions that are organizing textual principles.

There is no controversy involved in claiming *Lord Jim* as an originary work of modernism. Formally, it is characterized by some of the most widely recognized features of modernist narrative: indeterminacy, nonlinear chronology, unreliable first-person narration. In coupling *The Awakening*—definitely not generally considered an originary work of modernism—with *Lord Jim*, I am again, as I did with "The Yellow Wallpaper," moving toward a reconsideration of the position of female-signed texts in the engendering of modernist narrative.[3] *The Awakening* is in many ways a less likely candidate than "The Yellow Wallpaper" to be considered a groundbreaking feminine modernist narrative, since it would appear, and has appeared to almost all its critics, to be comfortably ensconced within realist convention. Unlike "The Yellow Wallpaper," which (apart from recent feminist analysis) has received little critical attention, *The Awakening* has been carefully located by critics within various nineteenth-century or nonmodernist subgenres, particularly Romanticism, the French novel, impressionism, American realism, naturalism, regionalism or local color, and seen as defined by the influence of two important (male) nineteenth-century precursors: Flaubert and Whitman.[4] At the same time, *The Awak-*

ening, like "The Yellow Wallpaper," has become a crucial text in the emerging feminist (anti-)canon of fiction by women.[5] When it is judged by the standards of realistic convention, however, *The Awakening* appears problematically inconsistent or even badly written—out of narrative control. When *The Awakening* is viewed as a work of modernism, it becomes clear that this troublesome "inconsistency" is the radical disjunctiveness of modernist *sous-rature*.[6]

The novel's opening greets us with the voices of two caged birds. Thrust as they are before our attention, those birds are evidently a composite figure of Edna's caged marriage: she is only a bird in a gilded cage, as the lyric goes. But she is two birds, in two dialectically related cages. One is a parrot, whose only speech is repetition of what it hears others say; the other is a mockingbird, whose expression is also founded on imitation. Moreover, only the mockingbird understands the parrot's private language: "He [the parrot] could speak a little Spanish, and also a language which nobody understood, unless it was the mocking-bird that hung on the other side of the door" (3).

This doubled, caged bird is a consummate figure of a markedly feminine *sous-rature*: decorative, imprisoned, isolated from the world, it has a private language that is split between assertion and (using the connotations of "mockingbird") self-mockery. Neither part of this split voice has autonomy, whether it is the beautiful parrot, echoing the voices it hears, or the equally caged mockingbird, hung symetrically "on the other side of the door, whistling his fluty notes out upon the breeze with maddening persistence" (3). Like the parrot's speech, the mockingbird's song is associated in this passage with futile anger.

What the parrot says echoes and reinforces the figure of the double cage: "Allez vous-en! Allez vous-en! Sapristi! That's all right!" (3). The parrot's anger shields itself in the Creole French that defuses it, makes it comical and harmless, much as the extramarital sexual desire felt among the novel's Creole characters is trivialized and made safe by the mocking, bantering tone they use to express it. The parrot's outburst of anger is immediately neutralized, in "serious" English, by "that's all right!"

If we want subsidiary evidence of Chopin's modernist formal technique in *The Awakening*, we might look at her use of stylized, heightened, repeated language, particularly in the famous passage describing the sea, which appears at the beginning and the end of the novel:

> The voice of the sea is seductive; never ceasing, whispering, clamoring, murmuring, inviting the soul to wander for a spell in abysses of solitude; to lose itself in mazes of inward contemplation.
>
> The voice of the sea speaks to the soul. The touch of the sea is sensuous, enfolding the body in its soft, close embrace. (15, 113)

This is clearly "poetic" language, set apart in tone, diction, and cadence from Chopin's cool, detached, mildly ironic, firmly "prosaic" standard narrative prose, which we can see in sentences such as the one immediately following the first appearance of the sea passage: "Mrs. Pontellier was not a woman given to confidences, a characteristic hitherto contrary to her nature" (15). The repeated, highly abstract motif of the lovers and the woman in black has a similar function in the novel, interrupting the narrative and stylizing its prose surface.

The sea, particularly as Chopin evokes it in the passages repeated at the beginning and end of the novel, is itself the novel's most important figural locus of *sous-rature*, at once liberating and deadly, like "the light which, showing the way, forbids it" (14). The sea is very explicitly an empowering/deadly feminine-maternal site at once of autonomy and death, as it is in *The Voyage Out*. It is strongly connected with Edna's awakening, her growing determination to belong to no one but herself. It is the place where she literally learns adult mastery, by learning to swim. But in becoming the source of mastery, it becomes at the same time the source of danger:

> Edna had attempted all summer to learn to swim. . . . But that night she was like the little tottering, stumbling, clutching *child*, who of a sudden realizes it [*sic*] powers, and walks for the first time alone, boldly and with over-confidence. . . . A feeling of exultation overtook her, as if some power of significant import had been given her soul. She grew daring and reckless, overestimating her strength. She wanted to swim far out, where no woman had swum before. (28, italics added)

As we see in this passage, Chopin's irresolvable ambivalence toward empowering Edna is the source of the novel's *sous-rature*. The narrator begins by telling us that Edna has not been able to learn to swim because of her "ungovernable dread." There is no ambivalence in Chopin's rejection of Edna's passive, frightened condition. But in the moment of empowering Edna, Chopin herself becomes frightened and retreats in midsentence, making Edna a "little tottering, stumbling, clutching child, who of a sudden realizes it [*sic*] powers, and walks for the first time alone, boldly *and with over-confidence*" (italics added). Chopin cannot leave it at "boldly": for Edna, to be bold is to be overconfident. In the next paragraph, Chopin allows Edna to exult, to feel "as if some power of significant import had been given her soul." But she characterizes Edna's desire "to swim far out, where no woman had swum before" as "daring and reckless, overestimating her strength" (28). Chopin ends the novel by proving that Edna's desire is, as literally as can be, self-annihilating.

We see the same ambivalence toward Edna's awakening in the "voice of the sea" passage. That voice is "seductive," "speaks to the soul," and has a touch that is "sensuous, enfolding the body in its soft, close embrace" (15). But the voice also clamors, murmurs, and invites the soul to "wander for a spell in abysses of solitude; to lose itself in mazes of inward contemplation" (15). At the end of the novel, the sea invites Edna to stand gloriously "naked under the sky," feeling "like some new-born creature, opening its eyes in a familiar world that it had never known." Edna seems to achieve the rebirth that eludes Rachel Vinrace as monster/fetus returned to the ocean womb. But the sea's "foamy wavelets" also coil "like serpents about her ankles" (113), and on the next page the sea kills her. She dies swimming "boldly," exhausting her strength and saving herself (if not her life) from the chains of patriarchal domesticity. She does not sink down to the bottom of the sticky pool, as Rachel does, passively shoved about, waiting to die. But her ultimate fate and Rachel's are nonetheless the same.

The shifts from positive to negative imagery in the "voice of the sea" passage, and elsewhere, are seamless—there is no corresponding shift in tone, no indication in the prose of intentionality or even self-consciousness. Chopin's ambivalence is so deeply embedded that to narrate this story, to move through it from one moment to the next, is to oscillate between positive and negative emotions as if there were no oscillation, no shift, as in a moebius strip.[7]

The clearest instances of the doubleness of Chopin's relation to her material come throughout the novel in the narrative voice itself. One of the starkest examples of this double stance appears early in the novel when Edna, having been needlessly awakened (irony, *double entendre*) by her husband and forced to attend to a child he imagines ill, goes out on the porch to cry. The narrator begins her description of Edna's emotional state in a serious tone:

> An indescribable oppression, which seemed to generate in some unfamiliar part of her consciousness, filled her whole being with a vague anguish. It was like a shadow, like a mist passing across her soul's summer day. It was strange and unfamiliar. . .

Suddenly, in midsentence, the narrator's tone changes radically:

> . . . it was a mood. She did not sit there inwardly upbraiding her husband, lamenting at Fate. . . . She was just having a good cry all to herself. The mosquitoes made merry over her, biting her firm, round arms and nipping at her bare insteps. (8)

In the first half of the paragraph, the narrator presents Edna's feeling as the initiation of genuine rebellion, a first assertion of autonomy. The second half of the paragraph shifts abruptly into trivializing, antifemale irony: Edna is just a "moody" woman having a good cry, mocked, with sexually charged aggression ("firm, round arms ... bare insteps"), by mosquitoes who are, it would seem, the narrator's surrogate. Like the parrot, Chopin's narrator has said to the reader "Allez vous-en! Sapristi! That's all right!"

In the next chapter, the narrator describes Edna's relation to her children in unambiguously approving terms, a judgment that is considerably complicated by the end of the novel. Here in chapter 4, the narrator emphasizes in a positive way the boys' sturdiness and self-reliance, which differentiate them from the weaker "mother-tots." The narrator's description of the "mother-women," Edna's maternal antitheses, is highly sarcastic: "It was easy to know them, fluttering about with extended, protecting wings when any harm, real or imaginary, threatened their precious brood. They were women who idolized their children, worshiped their husbands, and esteemed it a holy privilege to efface themselves as individuals and grow wings as ministering angels"(10). Chopin retreats in fear at the strength and clarity of this statement. She has her narrator begin the next paragraph in a violently contradictory vein: "Many of them were delicious in the role; one of them was the embodiment of every womanly grace and charm. If her husband did not adore her, he was a brute, deserving of death by slow torture" (10). The artificial sarcasm here, so different from the authentically angry sarcasm of the preceding paragraph, seems to mask, or express in displaced form, the anger Chopin feels, I would argue, at capitulating to her fear. Her fantasy of M. Ratignolle's death by slow torture parallels, in its displacement of anger, the figure of the mosquitoes attacking Edna's firm arm and bare instep.

In describing Edna's marriage, the narrator reverses herself, again within two paragraphs. The first paragraph begins, as did the others, with feminist assertion: "Her marriage to Léonce Pontellier was purely an accident, in this respect resembling many other marriages which masquerade as the decrees of Fate" (19). The paragraph continues in the same vein: "She fancied there was a sympathy of thought and taste between them, in which fancy she was mistaken." The next paragraph retreats suddenly and completely from this strong position: "As the devoted wife of a man who worshiped her, she felt she would take her place with a certain dignity in the world of reality, closing the portals forever behind her upon the realm of romance and dreams." Despite the qualification "she felt," this sentence has the ring of authorial endorsement. Suddenly Edna's marriage is no longer "purely an accident," a mismatch of two people who have no "sympathy of thought and taste." Instead, it is a step for Edna from the childish "realm of romance and dreams" into the adult "world of reality."

In chapter 18, Edna spends an evening with the Ratignolles. This time the narrator begins with a categorically approving judgment of their

highly conventional marriage, which she erodes and then shatters in subsequent paragraphs. First we hear that "the Ratignolles understood each
other perfectly. If ever the fusion of two human beings into one has been
accomplished on this sphere it was surely in their union" (56). Two paragraphs later, we see Madame Ratignolle "keenly interested in everything
he said, laying down her fork the better to listen, chiming in, taking the
words out of his mouth." The narrator's ill-concealed disgust at this ostensibly positive detail erupts in the next paragraph: "Edna felt depressed
rather than soothed after leaving them. The little glimpse of domestic
harmony which had been offered her, gave her no regret, no longing. It
was not a condition of life which fitted her, and she could see in it but an
appalling and hopeless ennui."(56).

The narrator steps back to assess the state of Edna's spiritual progress
in the wake of her strong reaction against that evening with the Ratignolles. First we hear that Edna now considers breaking the vase and
stamping on her wedding ring "very foolish, very childish . . . She was
visited by no more outbursts, moving her to such futile expedients." Instead, as if it were different or better, "She began to do as she liked and
to feel as she liked . . . going and coming as it suited her fancy, and, so far
as she was able, lending herself to any passing caprice" (57). We wonder
in what way this aimless self-indulgence, this devotion to instantaneous
gratification with a concomitant refusal of analysis, decision, responsibility, or acknowledgment of underlying desire, is in any meaningful way
less childish than smashing the vase and stamping on the wedding ring.

Narrative stance in the novel is further complicated when, in defense of
Edna against M. Pontellier's notion that she is becoming "a little unbal-
anced mentally," the narrator tells us that Edna is not merely doing as she
pleases moment by moment but rather "that she was becoming herself
and daily casting aside that fictitious self which we assume like a garment
with which to appear before the world" (57). Clearly, Chopin has two
irreconcilably contradictory assessments of Edna, exactly as Conrad has
of his hero in *Lord Jim*; in each work these contradictory assessments are
embedded in the language of the text.[8] In response to Dr. Mandelet's
persuasive elaboration of a naturalist credo, seemingly endorsed by
Chopin[9]—"youth is given up to illusions. It seems to be a provision of
Nature; a decoy to secure mothers for the race" (109–10)—Edna replies
with all of Chopin's ambivalence: "Yes, . . . The years that are gone seem
like dreams—if one might go on sleeping and dreaming—but to wake up
and find—oh! well! perhaps it is better to wake up after all, even to suffer,
rather than to remain a dupe to illusions all one's life" (110).

Unlike Dr. Mandelet, Edna seems to think a woman can avoid becoming a victim of romantic illusion by choosing to discard it. While he sees
illusion as inevitable, attributing it to a reified Nature, she implies that it

is an alterable social construct. However, to discard the illusion, repressive as it is, is only to suffer. To awaken, rebel, become free, is "perhaps" better than to remain Léonce Pontellier's loveliest object, but it is no real escape. Edna is defeated by this insight and retreats to her habitual childish posture. She tells the doctor not to "blame [her] for anything" (110). Chopin has retreated with her.

Chopin could not have realized this material in fiction without fashioning modernist narration for herself. Bound by the constraint of the (at least nominally) consistent narrative stance demanded by realist convention, the novel could not have been written, since its stance is premised on two contradictory assertions: that Edna's awakening is good and that it is bad. On the one hand, Chopin believes Edna's awakening frees her, makes her whole and autonomous, puts her in touch with the things that matter, offers her salvation from her deadened, passive married life. On the other hand, Chopin believes that Edna's awakening is not only Pyrrhic, doomed, and megalomaniacal, but also itself superficial and passive, consisting of no more than a regression to a childish state of self-indulgence in which Edna follows every passing whim, shedding not so much false values as adult responsibilities, and ending in reckless, unconscious, but nonetheless wilful self-annihilation. Because this *sous-rature* involves a desire for freedom contradicted by a fear of punishment, it is historically particular to female-signed modernism.

Race and class are simultaneously suppressed and pervasive in this narrative. Edna's drama of awakening does not overtly engage those issues, but the world of the novel that constructs that drama is inconceivable without its class and race assumptions. By marrying Léonce, Edna becomes part of a rigidly hierarchical, European-style class society. The impedimenta of her female, wifely oppression are precisely the impedimenta of her upper-middle-class status. Her first open conflict with Léonce after their return from Grand Isle comes as a result of her failure to be "at home" for people he considers socially important. That failure is a direct result of her first act of female rebellion—her attempt to reclaim her time and movements for herself by abrogating the figurally apt feminine ritual of the "at home." The accoutrements within that home, like the home itself, mark simultaneously class and female boundaries. At the same time that she stamps (ineffectually) on her wedding ring, she breaks a vase. She is Léonce Pontellier's "loveliest object"—her status as oppressed woman, again, is inseparable from her status as upper-middle-class wife, reified as object just as Léonce's capitalist culture reifies the rest of the world. When she moves to the freer "pigeon house," she makes her famous comment about her decline on the material plane corresponding to a rise on the spiritual. Mlle. Reisz, her inspiration for that move, is simultaneously free and déclassée.

As part of Southern culture, New Orleans Creole society as represented by Chopin in this novel functions on the basis of the subservience, oppression, and near-invisibility of blacks. Here again, as with class, and in fact inextricable from class, race functions covertly as a coordinate of freedom and oppression. The drudgery of the maternal function is undertaken by a nameless "quadroon" nurse, without whom the oppressive upper-middle-class female life of uselessness and conspicuous consumption (as both consumer and consumed) personified by Adèle Ratignolle, and expected of Edna by Léonce, would be impossible. Given that it is her responsibility to her children ("think of the children," admonishes Adèle) that finally defeats Edna, at least in her own mind, the "quadroon" nurse is the novel's figure of patriarchal culture's enslavement of the mother. We always see her mutely following about after Raoul and Etienne (and it is of course important that they are male children) as if she were shackled to them. As "quadroon," she is both white enough and black enough to take care of white children—white enough not to contaminate them, black enough to be enslaved to them. She represents directly the position of race in this culture, and by metonymy the position of the mother: neither a full participant in the culture ("white") nor separate from it ("black").[10]

Brown skin and low class are also joined, and linked to a somewhat threateningly, disgustingly liberated female sexuality, in the person of Robert's "friend" Mariequita. We meet her on the crucial trip to the *Chênière Caminada*. Chopin's description of her is highly suggestive. She is

a young barefooted Spanish girl, with a red kerchief on her head and a basket on her arm, bringing up the rear. Robert knew the girl, and he talked to her a little in the boat. No one present understood what they said. . . . She had a round, sly, piquant face and pretty black eyes. Her hands were small, and she kept them folded over the handle of her basket. Her feet were broad and coarse. She did not strive to hide them. Edna looked at her feet, and noticed the sand and slime between her brown toes. (34)

Mariequita and Robert speak the oppressed-class language of sex, incomprehensible to Edna. Mariequita's class and race position ("bringing up the rear" suggests sexuality as well as class and race) signifies that female sexuality can be freely expressed only in that language, making it socially powerless, expurgated from the dominant race and class. That is perhaps the most important fact in Edna's suicide, as inspired by Adèle's admonition to "think of the children": Edna may have the right to exile herself from her race-class position, but she does not have the right to threaten the position of her sons.

Mariequita's "earthy" sexuality, fascinating, threatening, and disgusting to Edna, is connected to the notion of illicit extramarital sex. Mariequita immediately senses the attraction between Robert and Edna, jealously asking whether Edna is his "sweetheart" and belittling Robert's response that she is "a married lady, and has two children" because "Francisco ran away with Sylvano's wife, who had four children" (34). All this reinforces the notion that Edna and Robert must violate the laws of their class-race as well as the laws of patriarchy (which Robert, with his inadequate imagination, cannot do) in order to act upon their feeling for one another.

Mariequita returns at the end of the novel, immediately after Robert's failure to rise to Edna's challenge. She has become Victor's "friend" in Robert's absence. Her first appearance in the novel is recalled by the fact that she is now jealous of Victor's attraction to Edna, just as she had been of Robert's. But she sees quickly that this time the infatuation is all on Victor's side and lapses into admiration of "this woman who gave the most sumptuous dinners in America, and who had all the men in New Orleans at her feet" (112). This poignantly ironic admiration establishes a camaraderie of sorts between these two women, and Edna's last remark in the novel is addressed to Mariequita, as Edna takes from her some towels for her final swim: "I hope you have fish for dinner . . . but don't do anything extra if you haven't" (112). This remark establishes a friendliness, almost a complicity between Edna and Mariequita, where before Mariequita represented to her an inaccessible otherness of freed, earthy feminine sexuality linked to brown skin, low class, and the language in which they speak.

The "scene of torture" that interrupts Edna's near-consummation with Robert, that leads to Dr. Mandelet's profession of the naturalist sexual credo, and also inspires Edna's final despair is a scene of childbirth. While Edna reads Adèle's suffering in childbirth as a result of the ineluctable "ways of Nature," at the sight of which Edna feels "an inward agony . . . a flaming, outspoken revolt" (109), Chopin provides us with an alternative perspective. Edna thinks of her own "like experiences" as "far away, unreal, and only half remembered. She recalled faintly an ecstasy of pain, the heavy odor of chloroform, a stupor which had deadened sensation, and an awakening to find a little new life to which she had given being, added to the great unnumbered multitude of souls that come and go" (108–9). The experience of childbirth, to invoke a crude but apt banality, is relative, only partly a result of the inevitable "ways of Nature." Edna's "half remembered . . . stupor" that "deadened sensation" corresponds to the slumbering condition of her life the awakening from which is the subject of the novel. Similarly, Adèle's complaining, fussing, and melodramatic suffering are appropriate to her caricatured, conventional femininity. Childbirth, the function of the (repressed) maternal origin, is most alienated for Adèle, the novel's most conventional woman. For Dr. Mandelet it functions as lynchpin of his easy naturalist fatalism, a stance that cynically, ruefully, but resignedly supports the status quo.

Edna's remembered experience of childbirth encapsulates the ambivalence of her position in relation to feminine empowerment. "Ecstasy of pain" is a perfectly ambiguous (and eroticized) phrase, establishing the contradictory structure of this important sentence. Its crucial phrase is "an awakening to find a little new life to which she had given being." Taken by itself, particularly with the telling use of the keyword "awakening," a word whose allusion to the novel's title is emphasized by its being cast as a noun rather than a progressive verb, this phrase is a direct expression of a positive empowerment of the female origin: "*to which she had given being.*" Since this is a modernist work, however, that phrase and its implications are immediately put under erasure by the following phrase, "added to the great unnumbered multitude of souls that come and go." In its mournful, elongated vowel sounds and its almost Miltonic rhythm, as well as in its sense, that phrase expresses alienation, despair, helplessness—the opposite of the energized empowerment and autonomy expressed by the previous phrase.

Edna must "think of the children" and "that determination had driven into her soul like a death wound"—"I shouldn't want to trample upon the little lives" (110). Just as in patriarchy the power of female generativity becomes a weapon turned against women to deny that power and keep the mother in her subordinate place, so the "little new life" to which Edna "had given being" reverses its significance for her to become the source of her "death wound," her shackle to "the little lives" who become Léonce's allies in thinking they can "possess her, body and soul" (114). They are the force to which she must either "sacrifice herself" (113) or die: "The children appeared before her like antagonists who had overcome her; who had overpowered and sought to drag her into the soul's slavery for the rest of her days. But she knew a way to elude them" (113). Although Chopin's image of the "new-born creature, opening its eyes in a familiar world that it had never known" produces an ending less alienated and hopeless than that of *The Voyage Out*, Edna's method of eluding her children is no more a victory than Rachel Vinrace's method of eluding marriage-in-England to Terence Hewet.

The ending of *Lord Jim* parallels that of *The Awakening*: Jim dies a sacrifice to his "exalted egoism," going "away from a living woman to celebrate his pitiless wedding with a shadowy ideal of conduct" (253). He chooses at the end the sterility of the bankrupt Western code of masculine honor that makes him "one of us." He is defeated by outmoded patriarchal conventions for masculinity just as Edna is defeated by outmoded patriarchal conventions for femininity. In *Lord Jim*, just as in *The Awakening*, the empowered feminine ("a living woman") is the locus of poten-

tial for both liberation from those conventions and also for the protagonist's annihilation. As in *The Awakening*, the empowered feminine is
connected to otherness of race and class, and figurally to water: Stein's
famous injunction "in the destructive element immerse" is the best formulation I have seen of modernist *sous-rature*. Accordingly, as in *The Awakening*, narrative stance toward the protagonist is perfectly ambivalent: as
Albert Guerard says in *Conrad the Novelist*, concerning reader response
to Jim, "We must remember that in every chapter and on every page the
double appeal to sympathy and judgment is made" (see n. 8).

From the beginning, Conrad calls attention to an overdone insistence
on Jim's masculinity. The opening of this novel is just as packed with
significant information as is the opening of *The Awakening*, and as in *The
Awakening* a great deal of it is conveyed figurally. "He was an inch, perhaps two," hits us with the force of its strangeness as an introduction to
a male protagonist, and the normalizing phrase that follows, "under six
feet," does not entirely dispel that strangeness, with its suggestion of extreme tininess, one reading of which is the primal tininess of the infant in
relation to the mother. (At the same time, the emphasis on Jim's failure to
achieve the full six feet of towering manhood suggests a deficiency of
masculinity.) That tininess will reappear in Marlow's description of his
last sight of Jim, which I would argue is a womb image: "He was white
from head to foot, and remained persistently visible with the stronghold
of the night at his back, the sea at his feet . . . that white figure in the
stillness of coast and sea seemed to stand at the heart of a vast enigma. . . .
he himself appeared no bigger than a child—then only a speck, a tiny
white speck, that seemed to catch all the light left in a darkened
world" (204).

Marlow focuses on the whiteness "from head to foot" of that fetal
"tiny white speck." That whiteness is also emphasized in the novel's
opening paragraph: "He was spotlessly neat, apparelled in immaculate
white from shoes to hat" (3). As in *Heart of Darkness*, the maternal feminine is allied with the dark of night and of skin color, while Jim is the
dazzling white of an exaggerated version of his racial identity. As Jim's
whiteness is overdone, and therefore questionable, so is his masculinity:
"His voice was deep, loud, and his manner displayed a kind of dogged
self-assertion which had nothing aggressive in it. It seemed a necessity,
and it was directed apparently as much at himself as at anybody else" (3).
Conrad's description of a water-clerk's job also deliberately calls into
question Jim's masculinity: "To the captain he is faithful like a friend and
attentive like a son, with the patience of Job, the unselfish devotion of a
woman, and the jollity of a boon companion" (3). Much more immediately and clearly than in *Heart of Darkness*, Conrad is presenting for
critique the hegemonic alliance of whiteness and maleness embodied (ex-

aggerated and therefore undermined) in Jim. (Critique, of course, is in equipoise with sympathy, as Guerard says—Jim is, after all, "one of us.")

In the first pages of the book, we also learn that Jim is "Jim—nothing more. He had, of course, another name, but he was anxious that it should not be pronounced" (4). He has literally forfeited the name-of-the-Father, renouncing (or being stripped of) his patriarchal birthright. This forfeiture is emphasized later in the novel, again in a sequence depicting Jim's life as a water-clerk in an Eastern port. First Marlow berates him for having left the surrogate father who would have made his fortune: " 'Oh! you—you—' I began, and had to cast about for a suitable word, but before I became aware that there was no name that would just do, he was gone" (116). Jim's boss then duplicates Marlow's inability to name Jim properly: "D'ye hear, Mister What's-your-name?" (116).

Accordingly, or appropriately, Jim as water-clerk is drifting steadily East, away from his Western (white, imperialist, patriarchal) patrimony, toward (I would argue) the feminine. Thomas Moser has shown that the East was associated with death for Conrad;[11] I see it as also associated with the feminine. The evidence of that association in *Lord Jim* will emerge in the course of this reading. At this point I would like to cite what I see as the clearest evidence in Conrad's oeuvre of the femininity of the East—the passage in "Youth" where Marlow arrives at his first Eastern port (by now, after my reading of *Heart of Darkness*, I would hope the sexuate feminine-maternal imagery of this passage does not require explication):

> "And this is how I see the East. . . . I see a bay, a wide bay, smooth as glass and polished like ice, shimmering in the dark. A red light burns far off upon the gloom of the land, and the night is soft and warm. We drag at the oars with aching arms, and suddenly a puff of wind, a puff faint and tepid and laden with strange odours of blossoms, of aromatic wood, comes out of the still night— the first sigh of the East on my face. That I can never forget. It was impalpable and enslaving, like a charm, like a whispered promise of mysterious delight. . . . The scented obscurity of the shore was grouped into vast masses, a density of colossal clumps of vegetation probably—mute and fantastic shapes. And at their foot the semicircle of a beach gleamed faintly, like an illusion. There was not a light, not a stir, not a sound. The mysterious East faced me, perfumed like a flower, silent like death, dark like a grave.
>
> "And I sat weary beyond expression, exulting like a conqueror, sleepless and entranced as if before a profound, a fateful enigma."[12]

The East is a locus of death indeed, just like the heart of darkness, the fearful maternal origin of life and therefore death, the womb-tomb ("perfumed like a flower, silent like death, dark like a grave"). It is the "mère de glace" of the Irigarayan patriarchal maternal, its fecundity frozen over to provide a reflecting surface for the endless self-representations of masculine subjectivity.

Jim is driven farther and farther East by his "keen perception of the Intolerable"—Conrad is, in keeping with his impressionist method, tantalizing us with the intolerable "fact" (the *Patna* story) that Jim's "incognito" is designed to "hide," a fact we are not to learn for quite a while. What we do learn at the outset is that Jim's father, possessor and bequeather of that unspeakable surname, is the seemingly timeless type of the English parson, who "possessed such certain knowledge of the Unknowable as made for the righteousness of people in cottages without disturbing the ease of mind of those whom an unerring Providence enables to live in mansions" (4). In fact the parson-father is the opposite of timeless—he is eminently historical. What he represents seems about to be overthrown, for better and worse, by the twentieth century.

Conrad goes to significant lengths to establish the politics of Jim's situation: the patrimony that he has renounced/from which he is exiled (both are true) is not only almost ludicrously bankrupt ("such certain knowledge of the Unknowable") but, even more important, it is designed to maintain the status quo of class in a manner reminiscent of Marx's analysis of the function of religion in class society. Orthography and parallel structure link Jim's "Intolerable" with his father's "Unknowable." It is more than a truism to say that the most important intention in Conrad's fiction is to show that the Unknowable is not susceptible to any "certain knowledge." Perhaps it is precisely the Father's false and oppressive certainty that makes Western masculinity, with its concomitant race and class dominance, the Intolerable for Jim.

We move quickly from the parsonage of Jim's childhood to the training ship of his early manhood, where he is sent (with portentous irony) when "after a course of light holiday literature his vocation for the sea had declared itself" (4). There we see him in his characteristic posture:

> His station was in the fore-top, and often from there he looked down, with the contempt of a man destined to shine in the midst of dangers, at the peaceful multitude of roofs cut in two by the brown tide of the stream, while scattered on the outskirts of the surrounding plain the factory chimneys rose perpendicular against a grimy sky, each slender like a pencil, and belching out smoke like a volcano. He could see the big ships departing, the broad-beamed ferries constantly on the move, the little boats floating far below his feet, with the hazy splendour of the sea in the distance, and the hope of a stirring life in the world of adventure. (4–5)

This passage is irresistible to critics with political interests. Jameson uses it to attack modernism's conversion of the grimy "realities" of history to shining impressions, a conversion the impulse toward which he finds in the very rhythm of Conrad's sentences.[13] I have used this passage to begin to define precisely how modernist *sous-rature* works, emphasizing narrative distance from, and irony concerning, Jim's "station . . . in the foretop," which Conrad associates with the "stirring life in the world of adventure" offered by Jim's "course of light holiday literature" (see chapter 1). It is only from that lofty, self-deluded perch that grimy realities are converted to impressions, and the novel launches at this point precisely a critique of the world of masculine adventure fantasy.

Moreover, the imagery of the description of the factories undercuts this passage's distancing from industrial reality, invoking the explosive, leveling potential of industrial capitalism in the figure of the chimney "belching out smoke like a volcano." At the same time, "slender like a pencil" evokes self-reflexively—the impressionist's admonition to himself—the instability of a superficial, butterfly sort of impressionism that would attempt to fly above all darker, beetle knowledge (one thinks of a preternaturally sundrenched Monet or Renoir).[14] The writing pencil that would convert a smokestack into a pencil is slender indeed. Out of it a volcanic truth will inevitably erupt.

What holds me now in this passage is the "peaceful multitude of roofs cut in two by the brown tide of the stream," a stream that flows toward "the hazy splendour of the sea in the distance." Of course this brown stream severing peaceful roofs prefigures the geography of Jim's Patusanian village, and specifically foreshadows his confrontation with Gentleman Brown straddling that *brown* Eastern stream. "Cut in two" is a figure of some violence, particularly in conjunction with "peaceful multitude." Conrad could have used "divided" or could even have formulated the scene with the river simply running through the town. The violence of "cut in two" prefigures the violence of Gentleman Brown and of the novel's ending.

I would also argue that the overall tableau, including this violence, has an emblematic quality. It is an emblem of modernist *sous-rature*. The brown stream, the vaginal passage running to the hazy splendour of the oceanic maternal womb, cuts violently through the social-literary status quo, which has all along used this stream to construct itself as homogeneous on the basis of a concealed dualism or bipolarity. The town was built as one town "in two" parts on either side of this stream. But Conrad makes the stream the aggressor, cutting the town in two, and therefore revealing or making visible—putting under erasure—this bipolar structure's construction of its fallacious peace and sense of unity on the suppression of the vaginal passage. As in *Heart of Darkness*, Conrad reinscribes the passage into knowledge and representation. The violence of this reinscribed passage ("cut in two") parallels, and is linked to, the violence of the erupting industrial volcanoes—again, the historical forces associated with the construction of modernism are the forces engendering feminism and socialism.

Jim is linked for us subliminally in this passage both to the unstable status quo, associated with the fake world of masculine adventure fantasy, and at the same time to its undoing by means of the modernist making-visible of the violent brown stream. Jim simultaneously embodies the masculine code of honor—what Marlow calls "the sovereign power enthroned in a fixed standard of conduct" (31), his adherence to which makes Jim "one of us"—and also the bankruptcy and spuriousness of that code: he raises for Marlow "*the doubt of* the sovereign power enthroned in a fixed standard of conduct" (italics added). He carries an exaggerated defense of this masculine standard with him as he drifts farther and farther toward the feminine East.

He takes the questionable berth on the *Patna* in the first place as a result of a sequence of events highly significant for this reading. Having failed the training ship test of valor as a direct result of his fantasizing on his perch in the fore-top, he finds the sea devoid of the adventure he seeks. In a horrendous gale, he experiences the "earnestness of the anger of the sea" and is "disabled by a falling spar" (7), a figure suggestive of a simultaneously toppling and punitive masculinity, a double castration (a *falling* spar *disables* Jim). As a result of his importantly unnamed injury, he "spent many days stretched on his back, dazed, battered, hopeless, and tormented as if at the bottom of an abyss of unrest" (7–8). Helplessness, passivity, and despair are found "at the bottom of an abyss": deprived of (a questionable) conventional masculinity, Jim falls into the abyss of the alienated maternal.

Recovering from this injury in "the white men's ward" (8) of a hospital in an Eastern port, Jim is snared by the lure of the Eastern sexual feminine: "The hospital stood on a hill, and a gentle breeze entering through the windows, always flung wide open, brought into the bare room the softness of the sky, the languor of the earth, the bewitching breath of the Eastern waters. There were perfumes in it, suggestions of infinite repose, the gift of endless dreams"(8). The sexual feminine of the East is just as alienated for this wounded but untested white male as is the abyss of the maternal.

The stage is set for the pivotal drama of the *Patna* episode. The language Conrad uses in introducing the *Patna* is loaded with implications for my concerns here. The eight hundred nonwhite, non-Western pilgrims are clearly linked with feminine water imagery: the pilgrims and the feminine are the colonized, disenfranchised volcanic force that will destroy that spurious white male Western code of honor. They are the destructive element in which Jim at first fails to immerse. The skipper of the *Patna* is pure beetle, unredeemed by any element of butterfly; to him the pilgrims

are "cattle" to be "driven on board." The narrator dissociates himself
from this dehumanizing view of the pilgrims. He admires their response
to "the call of an idea," their "exacting belief" (10). At the same time, he
clearly describes their boarding the ship as a flood of the same sort of
rising water that figurally drowned Alvan Hervey in "The Return":

> They streamed aboard over three gangways, they streamed in urged by faith
> and the hope of paradise, they streamed in with a continuous tramp and shuffle
> of bare feet, without a word, a murmur, or a look back; and when clear of
> confining rails spread on all sides over the deck, flowed forward and aft, over-
> flowed down the yawning hatchways, filled the inner recesses of the ship—like
> water filling a cistern, like water flowing into crevices and crannies, like water
> rising silently even with the rim. (9–10)

The repetitions of "streamed," of "flowed" and "overflowed," and of
"like water" make the liquidity of the pilgrims ominous. This pilgrim-
water has the same silence of potent otherness as the maternal feminine
heart of darkness, like that of the maternal origin a silence filled with
compelling nonsymbolic (to these Western ears) language.

The Eastern sea in which the *Patna* floats enacts figurally the drama of
gender in patriarchy. During the day, "under a sky scorching and un-
clouded, enveloped in a fulgor of sunshine that killed all thought, oppressed the heart, withered all impulses of strength and energy"—an ex-
aggeration of overbearing paternal logos comparable to Jim's overdone
masculinity—the sea is very clearly an alienated maternal feminine:
"under the sinister splendour of that sky the sea, blue and profound, remained still, without a stir, without a ripple, without a wrinkle—viscous,
stagnant, dead . . . a lifeless sea . . . an abyss forever open in the wake of
the ship" (10–11). But at night, the benign maternal emerges and gains
ascendancy (one is reminded of the day/night gendered dualism of "The
Yellow Wallpaper"):

> The nights descended on her like a benediction. . . . A marvellous stillness per-
> vaded the world, and the stars, together with the serenity of their rays, seemed
> to shed upon the earth the assurance of everlasting security. . . . The propeller
> turned without a check, as though its beat had been part of the scheme of a safe
> universe; and on each side of the *Patna two deep folds of water* . . . enclosed
> within their straight and diverging ridges a few white swirls of foam . . . a few
> undulations that . . . calmed down at last into the circular stillness of water and
> sky. . . . Jim on the bridge was penetrated by the great certitude of unbounded
> safety and peace that could be read on the silent aspect of nature *like the certi-
> tude of fostering love upon the placid tenderness of a mother's face.* (11–12,
> italics added)

Conrad could not invoke the benign and sexuate ("two deep folds of
water") maternal more explicitly here.

This de-repressed, resplendent and nurturing nighttime sea (and night-time is also, of course, the "time" of the ascendant unconscious as well as of the empowered maternal feminine), not the "viscous, stagnant, dead" sea of patriarchal repression (evocative of the "sticky pool" in which Rachel Vinrace drowns), is the enabling "destructive element" of modernism (by metonymy, the empowered rising water of the nighttime sea also includes the nonwhite, non-Western pilgrims, who survive unharmed the nighttime sea's devastating attack on Jim and his fellow officers). In the simultaneity of its enabling and its destroying, Conrad's "in the destructive element immerse" is a succinct formulation of modernist *sous-rature*.

In the *Patna* episode, the maternal "element" proves its "destructive"ness by throwing in the path of the ship the mysterious and deadly obstruction that changes the course of Jim's life, an obstruction that Marlow will call "the suspended menace discovered in the midst of the most perfect security" (59):

> they looked upwards at the stars. What had happened? . . . suddenly the calm sea, the sky without a cloud, appeared formidably insecure in their immobility, as if poised on the brow of yawning destruction. . . . A faint noise as of thunder, of thunder infinitely remote, less than a sound, hardly more than a vibration, passed slowly, and the ship quivered in response, as if the thunder had growled deep down in the water. (17)

As always, the imposing silence of the empowered maternal actually proves the locus of a compelling, disturbing, presymbolic noise, rife with unreadable signification (note the remarkable similarity of this "thunder" to the Irigarayan echo).

Jim's first jump, his jump off the *Patna*, is an initial, failed attempt to come down off his perch "aloft" in the bankrupt, juvenile literary/social text of masculine adventure fantasy. Jim is a butterfly, a nightmare-suppressing dreamer of wish-fulfillment, denying the earthbound beetle existence that is the other half of the truth of life. He jumps down toward the destructive element of the repressed maternal, toward the lower (class) and the darker (race) of the cave of the maternal origin. However, he lands not in the destructive element itself but in a lifeboat designed to save him from it, manned by his co-conspirators in maintaining the social status quo. As Stein will instruct him (via Marlow), he can only "follow the dream" authentically if he renounces protection from the destructive element, if he in fact "immerses" in it.

Jim jumps in response to the officers' repeated calls to George, who unbeknownst to them lies dead on the deck. Our attention is focused primarily on Jim's paralysis and on the diabolical ironies, as Marlow repeatedly characterizes them, of the situation, ironies so thoroughly treated by critics of this novel that I will not rehearse them here.[15] I would only emphasize the rupture in Jim's identity signaled by his responding to a name other than his own—a name that begins with the "G" of Gentleman Brown—and by the symbolism of his cap flying off his head as he jumps.[16]

The gendered language Marlow uses to describe the jump confirms Jim's. Marlow quotes Jim and then echoes him:

> "She seemed higher than a wall; she loomed like a cliff over the boat. . . . I wish I could die," he cried. "There was no going back. It was as if I had jumped into a well—into an everlasting deep hole." . . . Nothing could be more true: he had indeed jumped into an everlasting deep hole. . . . He told me it was like being swept by a flood through a cavern. . . . for two or three minutes the end of the world had come through a deluge in a pitchy blackness. (68–69)[17]

Jim has jumped into the deep well-hole of the maternal, a hole deathly, inescapable, and overwhelming for him at this stage of the novel. Jim's first encounter with the maternal "abyss" had been entirely involuntary—it came as a result of his being "disabled by a falling spar," his first experience of deprivation of patriarchal masculine power. Its outcome was a passive alienation. In this second encounter he jumps voluntarily, though the motivation for the jump is entirely unconscious—he literally does not know what he is doing—and the destructive element he is jumping into is still fully alienated for him, both in his description of it and in the fact that he jumps into the lifeboat that simultaneously saves him from it and binds him to the worst version of the gender-race-class system that represses it.

The hideousness of the beetle-skipper with whom Jim has willy-nilly allied himself by jumping into the lifeboat forces the reader to acknowledge the real implications of Jim's betrayal of the pilgrims—his complicity in the attitude toward them ("Look at dese cattle" [10]) that allows the officers *including Jim* to abandon ship (Marlow deliberately uses the word "deserted" [68]). When Marlow watches Jim as he is on the point of finding out that the *Patna* did not in fact sink, he expects to see him "overwhelmed, confounded, pierced through and through, squirming like an impaled beetle" (26). At the same time, in the lifeboat sequence the beetle-skipper is associated with the tyranny of the phallus and of its oppressive ownership of language (he *becomes* a relentlessly talking erect phallus):

> The skipper started swearing, as hoarse as a crow. He wasn't going to talk at the top of his voice for *my* accommodation. "Are you afraid they will hear you on shore?" I asked. He glared as if he would have liked to claw me to pieces. The chief engineer advised him to humour me. He said I wasn't right in my head yet. The other rose *astern*, like a thick pillar of flesh—and talked—talked. (76, italics added)

Marlow's meditation on Jim's experience in the lifeboat reinforces the maternal imagery surrounding the jump and at the same time begins to explicate the significance of that imagery. Jim says, "We were like men walled up quick in a roomy grave" (74)—the familiar image of the womb-tomb. Marlow connects that "roomy grave" filled with life to "madness," to a dangerous freedom born of disconnection from the accustomed social milieu, to the "Irrational," and to the still alienated "Dark Powers":

> There is something peculiar in a small boat upon the wide sea. Over the lives borne from under the shadow of death there seems to fall the shadow of madness. When your ship fails you, your whole world seems to fail you; the world that made you, restrained you, took care of you. It is as if the souls of men floating on an abyss and in touch with immensity had been set free for any excess of heroism, absurdity, or abomination. . . . Trust a boat on the high seas to bring out the Irrational that lurks at the bottom of every thought, sentiment, sensation, emotion. . . . It was part of the burlesque meanness pervading that particular disaster at sea that they did not come to blows. It was all threats, all a terribly effective feint, a sham from beginning to end, planned by the tremendous disdain of the Dark Powers whose real terrors, always on the verge of triumph, are perpetually foiled by the steadfastness of men. (74)

Although the modernist vision of a salvation inseparable from immersion in the destructive element dominates this text, the traditionalist-conservative view of evil feminine "Dark Powers," associated with the "madness" of the repressed unconscious and held at bay only by "the steadfastness of *men*," inevitably crops up. It is particularly appropriate that it crop up here, before Jim or the reader has met Stein.

That meeting marks the turning point of the novel. Marlow signals to the reader to pay special attention to Stein's advice by calling him "one of the most trustworthy men I had ever known" (122), and also by making him a genuine (as opposed to fantasy) hero who "when a youth of twenty-two had taken an active part in the revolutionary movement of 1848" (124).[18] His collection of butterflies and beetles marks him as the site of modernist *sous-rature*. He unites within his "study" the two terms of the Irigarayan gendered dualism of phallogocentric patriarchy: the butterflies of light and transcendence and the beetles of dark, earthbound immanence. The two remain separate—he doesn't attempt a synthesis of them or a denial of their difference, yet neither one is privileged over the other: "Stein never failed to annex on his own account every butterfly or beetle he could lay hands on" (125). The syntax of that sentence maintains the distinction between butterflies and beetles, while at the same time establishing an equivalency between them, refusing to accord butterflies greater intrinsic value than beetles.

In his study, as in Conrad's study (*Lord Jim*), Stein enacts the Kristevan impossible dialectic of gender, never the one without the other. The description of the arrangement of butterfly and beetle exhibits establishes their separateness at the same time that it links them together:

> Narrow shelves filled with dark boxes of uniform shape and colour ran round the walls, not from floor to ceiling, but in a sombre belt about four feet broad—catacombs of beetles. Wooden tablets were hung above at irregular intervals. The light reached one of them, and the word *Coleoptera* written in gold letters glittered mysteriously upon a vast dimness. The glass cases containing the collection of butterflies were ranged in three long rows upon slender-legged little tables. (124)

The *Coleoptera* (beetle) label is presented in an image wonderfully suggestive of a butterfly: it "hung above" the beetle cases, "written in gold letters" that "glittered mysteriously upon a vast dimness." We move directly from that butterfly-like beetle label to the butterflies themselves, housed in earthbound "slender-legged little tables" suggesting beetles: again, the two are simultaneously separate and joined. Hierarchy is also undercut in "not from floor to ceiling."

The space (the "study") the butterflies and beetles cohabit is also figured as a cohabitation of the masculine and the feminine: "Only one corner of the vast room, the corner in which stood his writing-desk, was strongly lighted by a shaded reading-lamp, and the rest of the spacious apartment melted into shapeless gloom like a cavern" (124). The masculine power of writing and reading in the strong (but shaded) light is placed *within*, not above, the "spacious," "shapeless gloom like a cavern" of the maternal. Similarly, Stein attained his preeminent trading position in the Celebes by inheriting the fruits of a productive union between a Scotsman "with a patriarchal white beard" and "the chief ruler of Wajo States, who was a woman . . . very free in her speech" (125): a mutually beneficial, nonexploitative union of a white Western man and a dark Eastern woman, equally powerful each in his and her own way. (Stein also married an Eastern woman, "'my dear wife the princess,' he used to say" [125]—a union that of course prefigures Jim's with Jewel, as does that of the Scotsman with the Wajo chief.)

Stein's fabulous, rare specimens are, of course, pinned and no longer even wriggling—they are dead. The novel's simplest positive version of Stein—the wise, heroic, supremely trustworthy old sage who speaks the unmediated truth—is put under erasure throughout this sequence by his association with death, reification, eeriness, and the macabre. This association is given at least equal weight with Stein's wisdom and trustworthiness and in fact is presented as a concomitant of it, since his fame as collector would be impossible without this association with death (specimens are by definition dead). This conjunction gives him something of the stature of a shaman, wise through, rather than in spite of, his contact with the "Dark Powers." Only such a shaman, at home in the Platonic cave, could pronounce the crucial dictum "in the destructive element immerse."

To arrive at Stein's study, Marlow must "travers[e] an imposing but empty dining-room very dimly lit" (123). Stein's "elderly, grim" servant "vanished in a mysterious way as though he had been a ghost" (123). We have already seen the catacombs housing his beetle collection in the vast, dim, shapeless, cavern-like gloom of his study. Just before he delivers his crucial pronouncement on the destructive element, he is described by Marlow as a "shadow prowling amongst the graves of butterflies" (130). Stein's story of the capture of the rare butterfly specimen he is examining when Marlow finds him is a parable of the impossible dialectic of death and life, immanence and transcendence, feminine and masculine, that is summarized by "in the destructive element immerse." The story begins with an image of Stein's " 'princess,' his wife" that prefigures Jewel's heroism: Stein goes off on a dangerous journey, leaving his wife "in command" of their fortified house. She walks him to the gate; "she had on a white jacket, gold pins in her hair, and a brown leather belt over her left shoulder with a revolver in it" (127): a powerful *and* sexually appealing woman. "I liked to see her so brave and young and strong," says Stein (127).

Stein rides "four or five miles . . . there had been rain in the night, but the mists had gone up, up—and the face of the earth was clean; it lay smiling to me, so fresh and innocent— like a little child" (127). Stein and his princess have a daughter, Emma, a brown girl with a European name. The clean, "innocent" "face of the earth," suggestive of Stein's child (who, with the princess her mother, is shortly to die), immediately becomes the site of treachery and slaughter: an ambush by Stein's enemies. The innocence and freshness are not, however, a delusion or a snare— they *coexist with* treachery and death. Immediately following the phrase "like a little child" comes, "Suddenly somebody fires a volley—twenty shots at least it seemed to me." Stein feigns death, falling forward on his horse's neck, using death to preserve his life. Stein shoots his attackers as they approach him—they believe his ruse—and "then I sit alone on my horse with the clean earth smiling at me, and there are the bodies of three men lying on the ground" (127). Conrad could not make clearer the coexistence, the cohabitation of the "clean earth smiling" and the death that he carefully makes hideous: "one was curled up like a dog, another on his back had an arm over his eyes as if to keep off the sun, and the third man he draws up his leg very slowly and makes it with one kick straight again" (127).

Now comes the miraculous moment (I feel compelled to report here that it gives me chills every time):

> And as I looked at his face for some sign of life [the man who had horribly kicked his leg] I observed something like a faint shadow pass over his forehead. It was the shadow of this butterfly. Look at the form of the wing. This species fly high with a strong flight. I raised my eyes and I saw him fluttering away. I think—Can it be possible? And then I lost him. . . . At last I saw him sitting on a small heap of dirt ten feet away. . . . I got him! . . . I had greatly desired to possess myself of a specimen of that species when collecting for the professor. I took long journeys and underwent great privations; I had dreamed of him in my sleep, and here suddenly I had him. . . . On that day I had nothing to desire . . . even what I had once dreamed in my sleep had come into my hand, too!
> (128)

Just as he advises Marlow, Stein follows his dream (*the* dream—the unconscious) by immersing in the destructive element. The shadow of the butterfly appears on the forehead of the man Stein has killed. But Stein doesn't actually catch the butterfly—the thing itself rather than its shadow—until it lands "on a small heap of dirt," so suggestive of the maternal feminine as well as of death (the grave). Jim will not be able to follow his dream until he acknowledges his connectedness to the earth, dirt, the feminine: "This magnificent butterfly finds a little heap of dirt and sits still on it; but man he will never on his heap of mud keep still" (129).

Stein, inscribing the modernist moment of social-textual transformation, then rewrites the parable of Plato's cave. I will follow this crucial modernist parable sentence by sentence. "A man that is born falls into a dream like a man who falls into the sea" (130). This dream is the opposite of Jim's fore-top life of adventure fantasy, of escapist wish-fulfillment; this is precisely the falling-down that Jim initiated but avoided when he jumped from the *Patna* not into the destructive element but into the lifeboat. This dream has to do with being born and with the sea: it is the dream again as representation of the realm of the repressed maternal-unconscious, a representation in the image of which modernist form evolved.

"If he tries to climb out into the air as inexperienced people endeavour to do, he drowns—*nicht war*?" (130). Climbing out into the air from a sea-dream into which one falls at birth would seem to figure a positive, appropriate emergence from infancy, the presymbolic, the attachment to the mother's body, into the air, the only element that supports human life. "Climb out" suggests worthy endeavor, and the movement upward from sea to air recapitulates the Platonic trajectory from cave to sunlight. But this attempt to climb out into the air is one that only "inexperienced people" make, and when they do, they drown. As I read this, the time is past, historically, when the sea-dream, the destructive element, the lower-down and darker otherness of gender, race, and class can simply be left behind, remaining suppressed, invisible, and silent. The attempt to maintain that suppression will result in that deadly rising of the water that (figurally) drowned Conrad's unreconstructed representative of upper-class Western white male hegemony, Alvan Hervey, in "The Return." This suppression must be undone, and an alliance must be forged with the ineluctably powerful destructive element.

"No! I tell you! The way is to the destructive element submit yourself, and with the exertions of your hands and feet in the water make the deep, deep sea keep you up" (130). The verbs in this sentence constitute a fabulous conjuncture of passivity and activity, opposition and alliance, submission and manipulation, hostility and awe. The conceit of the entire parable is swimming as opposed to drowning—the "inexperienced" person in the water flails about, desperately attempting to get out, and therefore drowns; the good swimmer attempts to become one with the water, making the movements of "hands and feet" that will keep him afloat. This, however, is only the surface story. The crucial pair of verbs in this sentence is "submit" and "make": only by genuinely jumping into the destructive element, a jump that Stein reformulates on the next page as an immersion—a renunciation of will, mastery, control, dominance—can "you" then harness the power of the destructive element by appropriate "exertions of your hands and feet" and "*make*" it "keep you up." Will can only be exerted effectively in the destructive element *after* submission to it; submission and will conjoined form a productive alliance.

"Deep, deep" emphasizes simultaneously the power, the threat, the importance, the suppression, and the femininity of the destructive element, and at the same time allies it again with the unconscious. "Hands and feet" is a strange locution. I would surmise that Conrad uses it here rather than "arms and legs" in the service of a nonidiomatic strangeness we are to take as the German inflection he gives us elsewhere by means of syntax (the verb at the end of the sentence) and actual German interjections. But beyond that, it functions as an instance of impressionist method, bringing the image into sudden vivid focus by means of the unexpected detail derived from a stark sort of metonymy that follows the eroticized logic of dream displacement, reminding us that modernist narrative form in this text constitutes precisely the immersion in the dream that Stein here propounds. To "follow the dream" *is* "in the destructive element [to] immerse" (131). Having enunciated this modernist credo, Stein provides Jim the opportunity to enact it in Patusan, whose name simultaneously recalls and rewrites *Patna*, adding to it "us."

In Patusan, Jim immerses in the destructive element and for a time follows his dream. Again, the destructive element is constituted by dark-skinned race as well as the sexuate maternal feminine. Marlow introduces us to the geography of Patusan by means of an important symbolic tableau:

> Patusan is a remote district of a native-ruled state, and the chief settlement bears the same name. At a point on the river about forty miles from the sea, where the first houses come into view, there can be seen rising above the level of the forest the summits of two steep hills very close together, and separated by what looks like a deep fissure, the cleavage of some mighty stroke. As a matter of fact, the valley between is nothing but a narrow ravine; the appearance from the settlement is of one irregularly conical hill split in two, and with the two halves leaning slightly apart. On the third day after the full, the moon, as seen from the open space in front of Jim's house (he had a very fine house in the native style when I visited him), rose exactly behind these hills, its diffused light at first throwing the two masses into intensely black relief, and then the nearly perfect disc, glowing ruddily, appeared, gliding upwards between the sides of the chasm, till it floated away above the summits, as if escaping from a yawning grave in gentle triumph. (134–35)

The feminine sexual imagery is so obvious here that I hope I do not need lengthy argument to establish it. I will merely point to the empowerment of the feminine implied by the imposing stature of the vaginal figure of the two steep hills divided by a deep fissure (or the irregularly conical hill split in two, with the two halves leaning slightly apart) and to the repetition of Stein's butterfly parable (the rarest specimen found literally on the face of death) in the transcendent feminine moon rising between the hills "as if escaping from a yawning grave in gentle triumph." Here the butterfly parable becomes located entirely within the feminine, with the transcendent feminine moon taking the position of the butterfly, and death located in the yawning vaginal grave. I would also point, in this passage, to Jim's "fine house in the native style"—his affiliation with the feminine is linked to his integration into a nonwhite, non-Western culture (both embodied in Jewel). It is from the "open space in front of Jim's house" that this tableau of moon and hills is visible: in modernist narrative, vantage point is all (what you see from where you stand is what—as far as human mind can know—there is, and vice versa).

Finally, I think it is important that the moon, when it first rises, is "glowing ruddily." In the passage in "Youth" describing Marlow's first Eastern port, and in the sequence narrating Jim's jump from the *Patna*, the vaginal imagery incorporates a glowing red light (see n. 17). Marlow makes the significance of this suggestive red light clear in a passage a few chapters later, when, describing again the tableau of moon and hills as seen from Jim's house, he adds, in a description of the village, "Here and there a red gleam twinkled within the bamboo walls, warm, like a living spark, significant of human affections, of shelter, of repose" (151). It is the red light of the benign sexuate ("living spark") maternal.

The rest of that second description of the moon-and-hills tableau could not be more different from the first description, which was written to arouse awe and wonder rather than the eerie chill aroused by the second one (remember the alternation of admiration and fear aroused by the description of Stein, his house, and his collection, or, for that matter, the alternation of judgment and sympathy, as Guerard describes it, in our response to Jim in the *Patna* episode). We must remember that it is the *destructive* element in which Jim has immersed:

> There is something haunting in the light of the moon; it has all the dispassion-ateness of a disembodied soul, and something of its inconceivable mystery. It is to our sunshine, which—say what you like—is all we have to live by, what the echo is to the sound: misleading and confusing whether the note be mocking or sad. It robs all forms of matter—which, after all, is our domain—of their sub-stance, and gives a sinister reality to shadows alone. And the shadows were very real around us, but Jim by my side looked very stalwart, as though noth-ing—not even the occult power of moonlight—could rob him of his reality in my eyes. Perhaps, indeed, nothing could touch him since he had survived the assault of the dark powers. All was silent, all was still; even on the river the moonbeams slept as on a pool. It was the moment of high water, a moment of immobility that accentuated the utter isolation of this lost corner of the earth. The houses crowding along the wide, shining sweep without ripple or glitter, stepping into the water in a line of jostling, vague, grey, silvery forms mingled with black masses of shadow, were like a spectral herd of shapeless creatures pressing forward to drink in a spectral and lifeless stream. Here and there a red gleam twinkled. (150–51)

I quote this passage in full not only because I think all of it is highly significant for my argument, but also because I am impressed by the am-plitude of the passage itself, particularly the wonderful string of ghostly adjectives in the description of the village and the Poesque repetition in "spectral herd of shapeless creatures" and "spectral and lifeless stream."

The first part of the passage, evidently, establishes the schema of Iriga-ray's Plato. Marlow "sets up" the passage I have quoted by describing the moonlight, "after we had watched the moon float away above the chasm between the hills like an ascending spirit out of a grave," as possessing a "sheen" that "descended, cold and pale, like the ghost of dead sunlight." The feminine moon is only the reflection in the mirror of death of the living masculine sun of logos. Marlow's description of "echo" could have been taken directly from Irigaray's analysis of echo's significance in

Plato's cave. The presymbolic noise of the cave, displaced as "echo" of logocentric "sound" just as the feminine is ghostly shadow of the masculine, is "misleading and confusing." As such, however, this "echo" is an agent of modernist *sous-rature*, because it makes meaning undecidable, and the undecidable meaning itself, eminently modernist, is at once "mocking" and "sad" (think of Chopin's parrot/mockingbird).

"Our sunshine" is "all we have to live by"; moonlight "robs all forms of matter—which, after all, is our domain—of their substance, and gives a sinister reality to shadows alone." Again Marlow enunciates the conservative position, the hegemonic gender ideology, as he did in the earlier passage about the Dark Powers always on the verge of victory, held at bay only by the steadfastness of men. But Conrad has Marlow put his own enunciation under erasure. "Gives a sinister reality to shadows alone" is immediately followed by: "And the shadows were very real around us, but Jim by my side looked very stalwart, as though nothing—not even the occult power of moonlight—could rob him of his reality in my eyes. Perhaps, indeed, nothing could touch him since he had survived the assault of the dark powers." Jim is exempted from destruction at the hands of the "dark powers," here significantly lowercase, because in their element he has immersed. He is also exempted from shadowiness and unreality to Marlow for the same reason: Jim rewrites the hegemonic dialectic of gender by allying himself with the dark, occult power of moonlight. Marlow collapses his own distinction between shadow and reality in "the shadows were very real around us," preparing the way for the merging of Jim's "stalwart" masculine reality with the reality of those feminine shadows. The rest of the passage moves back and forth again between the eerie deathliness of the moonlit world, associated with "the moment of high water" that recalls the ominous rising water of the pilgrims boarding the ship and of the flood drowning Alvan Hervey in "The Return," and the "red gleam" of the benign feminine always in impossible dialectic with the deathly moon—the "red gleam" that "twinkled within the bamboo walls, warm, like a living spark, significant of human affections, of shelter, of repose."

Marlow distrusts Jim's Patusan triumph. He assumes in this section of the novel a softened, open-minded version of the famous Conradian conservatism, a conservatism enunciated at its extreme point in the beliefs Marlow attributes to the recipient of his letter narrating Jim's end:

> I remember well you would not admit he had mastered his fate. You prophesied for him the disaster of weariness and of disgust with acquired honour, with the self-appointed task, with the love sprung from pity and youth. You had said you knew so well "that kind of thing," its illusory satisfaction, its unavoidable deception. You said also—I call to mind—that "giving your life up to them" (*them* meaning all of mankind with skins brown, yellow, or black in colour)

"was like selling your soul to a brute." You contended that "that kind of thing" was only endurable and enduring when based on a firm conviction in the truth of ideas racially our own, in whose name are established the order, the morality of an ethical progress. (206)

Marlow's tone in reporting this familiar ideology is just ironic enough to distance, but not to detach him from it: "I affirm nothing" (206).

Marlow's own racism (and sexism) are decidedly more tempered than the letter recipient's, but they frame his view of Jim's experience in Patusan. Marlow dislikes Patusan. He describes his first view of it in highly sexual and markedly negative imagery:

The coast of Patusan (I saw it nearly two years afterwards) is straight and sombre, and faces a misty ocean. Red trails are seen like cataracts of rust streaming under the dark green foliage of brushes and creepers clothing the low cliffs. Swampy plains open out at the mouth of rivers, with a view of jagged blue peaks beyond the vast forests. In the offing a chain of islands, dark, crumbling shapes, stand out in the everlasting sunlit haze like the remnants of a wall breached by the sea. (148)

The "red trails . . . like cataracts of rust streaming under the dark green foliage" is as explicit a menstrual image as one is likely to find in Conrad.

Marlow attributes to Jim the gloomy view of Patusanian geography evident in this passage as "pathetic" projection of a cosmic depression:

At the first bend he [Jim] lost sight of the sea with its labouring waves for ever rising, sinking, and vanishing to rise again—the very image of struggling mankind—and faced the immovable forests rooted deep in the soil, soaring towards the sunshine, everlasting in the shadowy might of their tradition, like life itself. And his opportunity sat veiled by his side like an Eastern bride waiting to be uncovered by the hand of the master. (149)

But Jim's "opportunity" proves to be nothing like a veiled Eastern bride, and Jewel herself takes Jim's fate in her hands. The image of the veiled Eastern bride, like the tedious abstraction in the above passage ("the very image of struggling mankind"), bespeaks an uneasiness with the radical implications of Jim's actual experience in Patusan, comparable to the belated elevation of Kurtz to the status of existential hero in *Heart of Darkness*.

Marlow closes his narrative of his visit to Jim with an eruption of anti-maternal disgust and fear. Patusan becomes entirely the claustrophobic, deathly, *dark*, maternal, in which Jim is permanently exiled, reduced to the status of fetal "tiny speck." As Jim escorts Marlow down the river to the ship that will carry Marlow, but not Jim, back to Europe,

The boat fairly flew; we sweltered side by side in the stagnant, superheated air; the smell of mud, of marsh, the primeval smell of fecund earth, seemed to sting our faces; till suddenly at a bend it was as if a great hand far away had lifted a heavy curtain, had flung open an immense portal. The light itself seemed to stir, the sky above our heads widened, a far-off murmur reached our ears, a freshness enveloped us, filled our lungs, quickened our thoughts. . . . I breathed deeply, I revelled in the vastness of the opened horizon, in the different atmosphere that seemed to vibrate with a toil of life, with the energy of an impeccable world. This sky and this sea were open to me. (201)

Marlow will be delivered out of the fetid, sweltering, stagnant, fecund maternal into the wide-open, impeccable, sunlit horizon of paternal logos; Jim must remain behind, a white speck in a vast uterine darkness filled with dark-skinned people:

Their dark-skinned bodies vanished on the dark background long before I had lost sight of their protector. He was white from head to foot, and remained persistently visible with the stronghold of the night at his back . . . at the heart of a vast enigma. . . . he himself appeared no bigger than a child—then only a speck, a tiny white speck, that seemed to catch all the light left in a darkened world. (204)

Marlow articulates the race and gender ideology underlying this imagery in his descriptions of Dain Waris and Jewel. Again, Marlow mitigates the extremity of the racist beliefs Conrad ascribes to the letter recipient, but the very mitigation of this ideology, allowing one dark-skinned man and woman to stand above their peers, serves to normalize the radical implications of Jim's Patusan story by making Dain Waris and Jewel exceptions to the general rule of race and gender. If Jim triumphs and follows his dream by merging with brown people, one of them a woman, embodiments of the destructive element, then the representative of that race and that individual woman must be designated exceptional.

Marlow calls Dain Waris the "distinguished youth" who was the "first to believe in" Jim:

theirs was one of those strange, profound, rare friendships between brown and white, in which the very difference of race seems to draw two human beings closer by some mystic element of sympathy. Of Dain Waris, his own people said with pride that he knew how to fight like a white man. This was true; he had that sort of courage—the courage in the open, I may say—but he had also a European mind. You meet them sometimes like that, and are surprised to discover unexpectedly a familiar turn of thought, an unobscured vision, a tenacity of purpose, a touch of altruism. (160)

Marlow goes on to gild the lily, calling attention to the strain behind this racist elevation of Dain Waris above the rest of his race that makes "unobscured vision, tenacity of purpose and altruism" European, their absence "native": "Dain Waris had a proud carriage, a polished, easy bearing, a temperament like a clear flame. His dusky face, with big black eyes, was in action expressive, and in repose thoughtful. He was of a silent disposition; a firm glance, an ironic smile, a courteous deliberation of manner seemed to hint at great reserves of intelligence and power" (160). In light of the fact that Dain Waris barely exists in the text apart from this description and from his crucial role in the denouement, it seems likely that he functions as an ideological counterbalance, bolstering Marlovian conservatism, to the radical significance of Jim's immersion in the destructive element.

Marlow's introduction of Jewel inspires a similar and even more bizarre paean to this exceptional woman and her exceptional mother.[19] He calls women "the beings that come nearest to rising above the trammels of earthly caution," then expands on that obscure formulation:

> it is only women who manage to put at times into their love an element just palpable enough to give one a fright—an extraterrestrial touch. I ask myself with wonder—how the world can look to them—whether it has the shape and substance *we* know, the air *we* breathe! Sometimes I fancy it must be a region of unreasonable sublimities seething with the excitement of their adventurous souls, lighted by the glory of all possible risks and renunciations. However, I suspect there are very few women in the world, though of course I am aware of the multitudes of mankind and of the equality of sexes—in point of numbers, that is. But I am sure that the mother was as much of a woman as the daughter seemed to be. (169)

If Jim's saving destructive element is a woman, then she must be made as exceptional to her gender as Dain Waris is to his race. The over-the-top quality of this passage, even more embarrassing than the description of Dain Waris, lies less in the extravagance and fuzzy abstraction of the praise of women, which comes close to designating the female gender a separate species, than in the explanatory revelation that "there are very few women in the world," punch number one, followed by the knock-out punch, "equality of the sexes—in point of numbers that is." Lest anyone think Marlow a believer in "equality of the sexes," or lest anyone think that Conrad, given the story he is writing, is moved by feminism, the orthodox disclaimer is clearly made.

The imagery in which Jim's Patusanian rebirth is embedded reveals the text's positive valuation of the maternal origin that Marlow's antifemale ideology functions to counteract and obscure. This time, when Jim jumps, he actually lands in the destructive element rather than in a "lifeboat," and he takes refuge with nonwhite, non-Western people of both genders rather than with the degraded, corrupt representatives of his own ruling class, race, and gender. After flying over Tunku Allang's stockade like a butterfly, Jim leaps again. "He took off from the last dry spot, felt himself flying through the air, felt himself, without any shock, planted upright in an extremely soft and sticky mudbank" (155). Jim finally lands on (in) the mud, the mound of earth, as Stein's butterfly does.

In this maternal mudbank he flounders for what seems like an eternity. The description of this floundering is very like a description of a difficult birth: "He made efforts, tremendous sobbing, gasping efforts, efforts that seemed to burst his eyeballs in their sockets and make him blind, and culminating into one mighty supreme effort in the darkness to crack the earth asunder, to throw it off his limbs—and he felt himself creeping feebly up the bank"(155). He has immersed in the destructive element and emerged to follow his shining dream, heroically liberating the village from its oppression by Sherif Ali, with the help of the worthy Bugis of Doramin, *using* the vaginal geography of Patusan's two hills for his daring defeat of that brigand and then becoming Patusan's just and beloved Tuan Jim, with Jewel always at his side. It is significant that the character Conrad emphasizes in Doramin's compound, when Jim first reaches it after his rebirth, is Doramin's "old wife," who is kind to Jim. We have heard nothing of Jim's actual mother, only his parson-father of the unmentionable surname. In his Patusanian rebirth, Jim has acquired a good mother.[20]

The stunning, redeeming, heroic defeat of Sherif Ali could not have occurred without Jewel. Her agency is a crucial goad to the passivity Jim lapses into when he leaves Doramin to take over Stein's company compound after his escape from Rajah Allang's stockade. With the help of her initiative, Jim overcomes Cornelius's corruption of Stein's enterprise. It is she who takes the lead in the first defeat of Sherif Ali's men, keeping vigil, waking Jim in the night and virtually forcing him to defend himself, thrusting the red torch—the glowing red light of the benign sexuate maternal—through the window of the storehouse in which Sherif Ali's men lie in wait to kill Jim. As the men surrender, one of them calls Jim "Tuan."

In narrating the storehouse episode (reminiscent, of course, of Stein's ambush parable) and in his treatment of Jewel in general, Marlow emphasizes her union with Jim and its redeeming quality: "Their soft murmurs reached me, penetrating, tender . . . like a self-communion of one being carried on in two tones" (173). Further: "he realised that for him there was no refuge from that loneliness which centupled all his dangers except—in her. 'I thought,' he said to me, 'that if I went away from her it would be the end of everything somehow.' . . . He let her follow him without thinking of any protest, as if they had been indissolubly united" (182). Jim's union with Jewel, a brown woman, is, quite simply, his salvation. When he abandons her to "celebrate his pitiless wedding with a shadowy ideal of conduct," a shadowy ideal that makes him "one of us" and that is elsewhere described as a "firm conviction in the truth of ideas racially our own, in whose name are established the order, the morality of an ethical progress," it *is* "the end of everything."

The narration of Jim's Patusanian triumph unfolds toward Jewel. We get the story of Jim's war against Sherif Ali before "the story of his love" that precedes that war chronologically. This narrative positioning heightens the effect of the storehouse episode, making it, rather than the rout of Sherif Ali, the dramatic culmination of Jim's success. Further, Marlow has much more trouble telling "the story of his love," because it is a different kind of story altogether from the familiar masculine saga of the successful military venture.[21] If it were the kind of love story it seems to the letter recipient to be, Marlow would not have such trouble telling it; it would be just as familiar as the tale of military exploit. Even Conrad's embarrassment and inadequacy in the narration of sexual material would not produce precisely this disclaimer, which I cite in full because of its importance to my argument:

> I suppose you think it [the story of his love] is a story that you can imagine for yourselves. We have heard so many such stories, and the majority of us don't believe them to be stories of love at all. For the most part we look upon them as stories of opportunities: episodes of passion at best, or perhaps only of youth and temptation, doomed to forgetfulness in the end, even if they pass through the reality of tenderness and regret. This view mostly is right, and perhaps in this case, too. . . . [*sic*] Yet I don't know. To tell this story is by no means so easy as it should be—*were the ordinary standpoint adequate*. Apparently it is a story very much like the others: for me, however, there is visible in its background the melancholy figure of a woman, the shadow of a cruel wisdom buried in a lonely grave, looking on wistfully, helplessly, with sealed lips. The grave itself, as I came upon it during an early morning stroll, was a rather shapeless brown mound, with an inlaid neat border of white lumps of coral at the base, and enclosed within a circular fence made of split saplings, with the bark left on. A garland of leaves and flowers was woven about the heads of the slender posts—and the flowers were fresh. (168, italics added)

"The ordinary standpoint" is not "adequate" to this modernist treatment of the feminine. The conventional love story, which, because it involves a white European man and a brown non-Western woman, does not even qualify to "the majority of us" as a *love* story at all, cannot accommodate this material, *because* there is visible in its background the melancholy figure of a buried, silenced, horribly oppressed woman, whose position in this text is that of the mother.

As always with Conrad, the details of this passage invite explication. The stories that are not love stories at all appear to "the majority of us" as "stories of opportunities"—remember that Jim's "opportunity" was

supposed to have been always at his side "like a veiled Eastern bride."
However, the story of Jim and Jewel is *not* a story of the kind of "opportunity" Marlow imagines his audience to construct—it is a story of immersion in the destructive element. "The veiled Eastern bride" is just as
spurious as the "ordinary standpoint" of "the majority of us." Marlow
clearly dissociates himself here from the point of view of "the majority of
us" that he is carefully deferring to; that is the entire point of the necessity
for Conrad of inventing a new narrative form that problematizes "the
ordinary standpoint." The "us" Jim is "one of," the "we" to whom
women appear a separate species, "the majority of us" who are so cynical
about Jim and Jewel, are precisely the dominant race, gender, and class
whose "shadowy ideal of conduct," the "idea racially our own," constitutes the "ordinary standpoint" that this modernist narrative puts under
erasure.

The origin of that erasure is figured as the mother's grave, *not* the
mother-as-grave. The first emphasis is on the mother herself, "melancholy," "buried in a lonely grave, looking on wistfully, helplessly, with
sealed lips." Jewel's mother, the woman's mother rather than the man's,
is a figure of pathos rather than terror, whose maternal silence, here at
least, is no longer ominous or imposing but rather signals, as in truth it
does, suppression.

The description of the mother's grave, the familiar maternal feminine
figure of the "shapeless brown mound," reminds us of the crucial mound
of earth on which the butterfly alights ("small" or "little heap of dirt,"
"heap of mud" [128–29]). This brown mound, however, is distinguished
by "an inlaid neat border of white lumps of coral at the base." The dread
vaginal teeth, seemingly an inevitable component of sexuate maternal figuration for Conrad, have become here harmless, orderly, small, totally
nonthreatening, even poignantly decorative. Moreover, they are made of
coral: "of his bones are coral made." Without insisting on this point or
pushing it too far, I would suggest that this harmless, pathetic grave, gar-
landed about with fresh leaves and flowers suggesting rebirth, incorporates the sea-change of the paternal as an element of the modernist impossible dialectic.

We need not rely for this reading of the significance of Jewel's mother
on the above passage alone. Jewel tells Marlow that she does not want to
die weeping, as her mother did: " 'My mother had wept bitterly before she
died,' she explained" (190). This simple statement produces in Marlow a
remarkable reaction: "An inconceivable calmness seemed to have risen
from the ground around us, imperceptibly, like the still rise of a flood in
the night, obliterating the familiar landmarks of emotions. There came
upon me, as though I had felt myself losing my footing in the midst of
waters, a sudden dread, the dread of the unknown depths"(190). In the

clearest possible figuration in light of my argument here, Conrad shows us Marlow feeling the force of the destructive element as a direct result of understanding the oppression of women.

Jewel explains that Cornelius tried to enter her mother's death chamber, but Jewel, at her mother's order, succeeded in keeping him out. As Jewel keeps her shoulder on the door, with Cornelius shoving on the other side and yelling "Let me in! Let me in! Let me in!"

> "The tears fell from her eyes, and then she died," concluded the girl in an imperturbable monotone, which more than anything else, more than the white statuesque immobility of her person, more than mere words could do, troubled my mind profoundly with the passive, irremediable horror of the scene. It had the power to drive me out of my conception of existence, out of that shelter each of us makes for himself to creep under in moments of danger, as a tortoise withdraws within its shell. For a moment I had a view of a world that seemed to wear a vast and dismal aspect of disorder, while, in truth, thanks to our unwearied efforts, it is as sunny an arrangement of small conveniences as the mind of man can conceive. But still—it was only a moment: I went back into my shell directly. One *must*—don't you know?—though I seemed to have lost all my words in the chaos of dark thoughts I had contemplated for a second or two beyond the pale. These came back, too, very soon, for words also belong to the sheltering conception of light and order which is our refuge. (190)

Again, Marlow is intermediary in this novel between convention and the radical rewriting of the social and literary text proposed by modernity, positioned precisely in the space this novel's modernist *sous-rature* defines. He is sufficiently a conventional soul, "one of us," with whom the white male Western reader can identify, by whom he would not feel threatened. Yet he has wider imagination and a larger moral sensibility than "one of us" generally has. He knows at some level that the "truth" of the "sunny arrangement of small conveniences" (a phrase suggesting both logos and technology) is in fact a tortoise shell under which "one *must*" take refuge to protect oneself from that other truth of a vast and dismal disorder, a silent chaos of dark thoughts, associated here, again, not with the mother herself, as in patriarchal ideology, but with the oppression/suppression of the mother (in the person of Cornelius, and, significantly, of the antifemale social convention that forced Jewel's mother to marry him).

Jewel herself is figured as the destructive element. Her eyes are just the same sort of deep well that Jim lands in when he jumps off the *Patna*, and her teeth are not harmless:

> It was dark under the projecting roof, and all I could see were the flowing lines of her gown, the pale, small oval of her face, with the white flash of her teeth,

and, turned towards me, the big, sombre orbits of her eyes, where there seemed to be a faint stir, such as you may fancy you can detect when you plunge your gaze to the bottom of an immensely deep well. What is it that moves there? you ask yourself. Is it a blind monster or only a lost gleam from the universe? (186–87)

The destructiveness of the feminine element is a crucial part of the modernist *sous-rature* of this novel. Again, the other truth of which Marlow gets fitful glimpses is horrific to him, terrifying as well as redeeming, as it was to Conrad and to the male modernist writers who followed him. Even the harmless, pathetic grave of the mother can, in a certain cracked moonlight, reacquire its sinister, fearful, death-dealing patriarchal lineaments. Note in the following not only the remarkable chaplet of bleached skulls but also the *coal-black* double summit, the *black* crack across the face of the moon (again, the chained feminine monster is linked to blackness), the cavern, the heavily reiterated shadows, the deathliness, the warm, heavy incense, and the stumps of felled trees—a litany of Conradian alienation from the maternal feminine:

> The big hill, rearing its double summit coal-black in the clear, yellow glow of the rising moon, seemed to cast its shadow upon the ground . . . raising my eyes, I saw part of the moon glittering through the bushes at the bottom of the chasm. . . . it disengaged itself from the tangle of twigs; the bare, contorted limb of some tree, growing on the slope, made a black crack right across its face. It threw its level rays afar as if from a cavern, and in this mournful eclipse-like light the stumps of felled trees uprose very dark, the heavy shadows fell at my feet on all sides, my own moving shadow, and across my path the shadow of the solitary grave perpetually garlanded with flowers. In the darkened moonlight the interlaced blossoms took on shapes foreign to one's memory and colours indefinable to the eye, as though they had been special flowers gathered by no man, grown not in this world, and destined for the use of the dead alone. Their powerful scent hung in the warm air, making it thick and heavy like the fumes of incense. The lumps of white coral shone round the dark mound like a chaplet of bleached skulls. (196)

The feeling inspired in Marlow by this scene is precisely the "feeling which has incited me to tell you the story, to try to hand over to you, as it were, its very existence, its reality—the truth disclosed in a moment of illusion" (196). "The truth disclosed in a moment of illusion": Conradian impressionism, modernist *sous-rature*.

In the end, Conrad decides that Jim is, after all, too white, too much one of us, to sustain the remarkable fusion with the brown and the female that he temporarily achieves in Patusan. In the final sequence—the written narrative Marlow mails to the novel's ultimate representative of one-of-us-ness—Jim's whiteness, de-emphasized in the previous section (except for the tiny white speck at the end), suddenly becomes the most important thing about him, defining his foil relationship to "Brown": "Brown saw in a knot of coloured figures motionless between the advanced houses a man in European clothes, in a helmet, all white" (230). "And there was something in the very neatness of Jim's clothes, from the white helmet to the canvas leggings and the pipe-clayed shoes, which in Brown's sombre irritated eyes seemed to belong to things he had in the very shaping of his life contemned and flouted" (231). "I told him that sort of game was good enough for these native friends of his, but I would have thought him too white to serve even a rat so" (232). "You have been white once, for all your tall talk of this being your own people and you being one with them. And are you? And what the devil do you get for it; what is it you've found here that is so d——d precious?" (232). "Precious," of course, suggests Jewel, particularly in light of the wonderful rumor Marlow discovers at a trading outpost that Jim is in possession of a fabulously rare and precious emerald.

Jim is ineluctably white, European, a ruler: "Patusan was recovering its belief in the stability of earthly institutions since the return of the white lord" (236). He is also, for all his immersion in the river mud, still (or again) a butterfly susceptible to defeat by the return of his own repressed beetlehood as embodied in Gentleman Brown, in cahoots with the ultimate beetle Cornelius. In fact, Brown and Jim meet "not very far from the place, perhaps on the very spot, where Jim took the second desperate leap of his life—the leap that landed him into the life of Patusan, into the trust, the love, the confidence of the people" (231). Presumably, Conrad's locating Jim's defeat by Brown on that spot is designed to negate the rebirth, the immersion in the destructive element, that occurred there. I would argue that the negation is not retroactive; that, to put it colloquially, the rebirth was real while it lasted. It is (not surprisingly) put under erasure rather than proven false. (The doubles relationship between Jim and Gentleman Brown, down to the complementarity of their half-names, is too well documented to require rehearsal here.)[22]

The hegemonic status quo is inadequately reimposed at the end of this novel, just as it is at the end of *Heart of Darkness*. Marlow describes Gentleman Brown as "a blind accomplice of the Dark Powers" (215): Dark Powers have again become capitalized, returned to their consummate evil and inaccessible otherness. The difference, I would argue, is that the status quo is clearly reimposed here in the character of a dire and discredited inevitability, even to the point of Conrad's inviting us to judge Jim negatively for his adherence to it, his "pitiless wedding with a shadowy ideal of conduct." I see the relentless emphasis on Jim's whiteness as a measure of Conrad's disengagement from all that whiteness signifies, a disengagement revealed by his finding it ridiculous even as he invites us to admire it.

I would like to consider in some detail Conrad's treatment of the letter recipient.[23] He is "the privileged man" (205), privileged because he is the only one "of all these listeners ever to hear the last word of the story" (205), but the phrase itself ("privileged man") has other (rather obvious in relation to my preoccupations here) suggestions. He is important, of course, because the reader assumes his position at this point in the text. Until now, the reader was positioned as part of an undefined, anonymous group of listeners, a situation that more or less reproduces the condition of actual readership. Now that position changes markedly, and the reader must deal with the text's pressure simultaneously to identify and resist identification with a carefully located and specified single character, a character who, as we have seen, is credited with an extreme version of hegemonic racism and sexism.

Conrad's description of this man distances us radically from, and fundamentally discredits, the position we must assume as his co-recipients of the letter: in other words, our complicity in his "standpoint." Before he reads the contents of his packet, this man looks out of his window:

> His rooms were in the highest flat of a lofty building, and his glance could travel afar beyond the clear panes of glass, as though he were looking out of the lantern of a lighthouse. The slopes of the roofs glistened, the dark, broken ridges succeeded each other without end like sombre, uncrested waves, and from the depths of the town under his feet ascended a confused and unceasing mutter. The spires of churches, numerous, scattered haphazard, uprose like beacons on a maze of shoals without a channel; the driving rain mingled with the falling dusk of a winter's evening; and the booming of a big clock on a tower, striking the hour, rolled past in voluminous, austere bursts of sound, with a shrill, vibrating cry at the core. He drew the heavy curtains. (205)

This passage recalls Jim's fore-top view of the town and sea at the beginning of the novel. We have returned to a state of alienation, a vantage point too high up and too detached: too "privileged." Evidently, the tone of this passage is entirely different from that early, light, hopeful (if quietly ominous) fore-top vision. It is bleak and almost despairing, deathly, the end of the story, overwhelmed by the Dark Powers as figured, tellingly, in ocean imagery. This man stays high and dry only by drawing his curtains and *with*drawing from the world into his privilege, a privilege synonymous with isolation and moribundity. His windows may be clear, but he can't see through them. "The light of his shaded reading lamp slept like a sheltered pool ... his wandering days were over" (205). Stein's wandering days were over too, but his reading lamp lit up a corner of his otherwise dark museum of immersion in the destructive element. No heavy curtains shut out the darkness for him.

In the packet this man receives, in addition to the cover letter and long narrative written by Marlow and the fragment written by Jim, is a yellowed old letter from his father that Jim has evidently treasured, "found carefully preserved in his writing-case" (207). Jim has remained faithful, in the end, to the law of the Father. But what to Jim was a profoundly important document, we see, with Marlow's help, as "easy morality and family news . . . The old chap goes on equably trusting Providence and the established order of the universe. . . . One can almost see him, grey-haired and serene in the inviolable shelter of his book-lined, faded, and comfortable study, where for forty years he had conscientiously gone over and over again the round of his little thoughts about faith and virtue"(207). For this shadowy ideal of conduct, these little thoughts about faith and virtue, ideas racially our own, Jim, in his "exalted egoism," "goes away from a living woman." Appropriately, Jim's choice is aligned with the "standpoint" of the "privileged reader," stand-in for the father, and the Father, who "screwed up his lamp, and solitary above the billowy roofs of the town, like a lighthouse-keeper above the sea," ultimate figure of hegemonic, hierarchical masculinity, "turned to the pages of the story" (214).

Jim dies *following* a bankrupt Western masculine code of honor, enforced by the brown ("Brown") man who saved him after his Patusanian rebirth; a brown man who kills Jim as a father avenging the death of his own son. Edna dies *escaping* a bankrupt feminine code of maternal submission, dying in the very (destructive) element that awakened her to her first sense of mastery and power. In both novels, the central question concerns the efficacy or success of the protagonist's response to the modern challenge to rewrite the social text. Does Jim follow the dream *"usque ad finem"* by immersing successfully in the destructive element, or was his Patusanian triumph of fusion with the other always a delusion, Gentleman Brown always waiting in the wings of his own psyche? Does Edna fulfill her awakening by giving up for her children her life but not herself, or is her suicide the inevitable, defeated end of her regressive refusal to face adult responsibility? In both novels, the question is unanswered, or the answer is "both": the irresolvable ambivalence of modernist *sous-rature*. In both novels, the twentieth-century challenge to rewrite the social text produced the modernist literary text.

PART III

IN THE WAKE OF EARLY MODERNIST NARRATIVE

Chapter 6

(ANTI-)CANONICAL MODERNISM

T HE *sous-rature* or impossible dialectic whose progress I have been following through the development of early modernist narrative characterizes the generality of works in the ill-defined and massive corpus of modernism. In other words, the ambivalence toward the twentieth-century revolutionary horizon that characterized the modernist historical moment achieved the defining literary form(s) of modernism in the *sous-rature* developed in early modernist narrative. It would be impossible of course to "prove" such a claim, but I hope to illustrate it by looking at a range of works drawn from both the traditional "high modernist" canon and also the anticanonical modernism retrieved and engendered by feminist and African-American scholarship.[1]

In "To Let Go or to Hold On—?" from his 1929 book of poems, *Pansies*, D. H. Lawrence uncannily summarizes central theses of this study.[2] It is a speculative poem on the familiar Lawrentian/Nietzschean theme of the destruction or disappearance of "man" and contemporary civilization and their reemergence in a "higher" form. "Letting go" involves renouncing will or human agency, consigning the task of arriving at that "higher" form to "the creative future" that "is fecund with a new Day of new creatures" who are "different from us." "Holding on," the other path to super-humanity the poem offers, involves deploying will and agency "to get down and clear away the debris / of a swamped civilisation, and start a new world for man / that will blossom forth the whole of human nature." The poem ends "Must we hold on? / Or can we now let go? / Or is it even possible we must do both?"

Lawrence's Nietzschean preoccupations concern me here only insofar as they mark his modernist anxiety about the revolutionary horizon of the twentieth century. That anxiety generates in this poem a complex *sous-rature* (most obviously, though not exclusively, in its last line) in relation to cataclysmic historical change. Using water imagery to deploy the contradictory dynamic of the destructive element, Lawrence converts an anguished, immobilizing dichotomy of gendered modes of action into a relatively enabling simultaneity.[3]

"Letting go" is aligned in the first stanza (and throughout the poem) with the feminine, figured as immersion in the oceanic-maternal destructive element:

Shall we let go,
and allow the soul to find its level
downwards, ebbing downwards, ebbing downwards to the flood?
till the head floats tilted like a bottle forward tilted
on the sea, with no message in it; and the body is submerged
heavy and swaying like a whale recovering
from wounds, below the deep black wave?
like a whale recovering its velocity and strength
under the cold black wave.

Immersion, just as in the Conrad texts, is deathly, a renunciation of the mastery of language ("with no message in it"), associated with the blackness and "downwardness" of the Platonic-maternal cave. The rhythms of the stanza plunge "downwards, ebbing downwards, ebbing downwards": the language floods out cathartically. Moreover, just as in Conrad, "letting go" into the feminine is saving in its deathliness: the "heavy, swaying" whale, which here almost suggests pregnancy, though the focus will shift to the whale's sperm in the third stanza, is "*recovering* / from wounds,*" "recovering its velocity and strength." The maternal-feminine may castrate, but it also provides the medium for restoring the castrated phallus, just as in Stein's formulation of the destructive element in *Lord Jim*.

   "Holding on" is aligned in the second stanza and throughout the poem with the masculine:

Or else, or else
shall a man brace himself up
and lift his face and set his breast
and go forth to change the world?
gather his will and his energy together
and fling himself in effort after effort
upon the world, to bring a change to pass?

Although the overt tone of this stanza is stalwart, resolute, and hopeful, where the tone of the first stanza was gloomy to the point of despair, the subtext of this stanza is significantly more defeated and fatalistic than that of the first stanza, where the "whale" is "recovering its velocity and strength." In the second stanza, we feel the terrible cost to the "man" of that repeated "bracing up," requiring a resolve signaled by "Or else, or else," a forcing of his "will and energy" into erection again and again to "fling himself in effort after effort" upon the massively resistant "world." (One thinks of Walter Morel flinging himself in futile effort after effort at the unyielding rock face in the mine of *Sons and Lovers*.)[4] The costs of the feminine "letting go" are obvious but the less obvious benefits are great; the benefits of the masculine "holding on" are obvious but the less obvious costs are great. This poem is informed well before the concluding line by the double logic of modernist *sous-rature*.

After the first two stanzas, the poem devotes a great deal more space to the feminine than to the masculine, seeming to become fascinated by it, and allowing it to take on aspects of both genders while remaining primarily feminine. The third stanza opens with a vision of total "annihilation" in the "dark flood" of letting go, an annihilation that "leaves no peak emerging": an almost self-parodically clear articulation of castration fear. But that vision of annihilation is immediately reformulated in a much more positive light:

Shall we be lost, all of us
and gone like weed, like weed, like eggs of fishes,
like sperm of whales, like germs of the great dead past
into which the creative future shall blow strange, unknown forms?

"Eggs of fishes," "sperm of whales," together constituting "germs of the great dead past" to be wrought into new life by "the creative future," evoke the kind of powerful, mystic-cosmic vision of world-historically transforming gender fusion for which Lawrence is famous.[5] It is important to note that this vision is evoked within feminine letting go. The conjunction of "sperm" and "whales" emphasizes the masculinity of the wounded, recovering whale of the first stanza.

The language of the second part of the third stanza becomes as loose and vague as the cataclysmic vision it articulates:

Are we nothing, already, but the lapsing of a great dead past?
Is the best that we are but sperm, loose sperm, like the sperm of fishes
that drifts upon time and chaos, till some unknown future takes it up
and is fecund with a new Day of new creatures? different from us.

I would point here to the "loose sperm" that becomes "sperm of fishes," joining or even collapsing together the earlier female "eggs of fishes" with the male "sperm of whales." I would also note that the adjective "fecund" makes the creative power of the "unknown future" explicitly feminine. ("Time and chaos" also evokes a biblical-Miltonic, or Platonic-Plotinian universe of unformed feminine matter.)

The speaker then considers again, briefly, the masculine possibility, making explicit the poem's mythic and Biblical allusions:

Or is our shattered Argosy, our leaking ark
at this moment scraping tardy Ararat?
Have we got to get down and clear away the debris
of a swamped civilisation, and start a new world for man
that will blossom forth the whole of human nature?

The language and figuration here are terse, tight, and controlled, while in the previous stanza they were loose and vague.[6] Again, we feel the defeat to the point of hopelessness ("shattered Argosy," "leaking ark") and the terrible effort ("get down and clear away the debris / of a swamped civilisation," "start a new world") of the masculine task. The onerousness of this task and the speaker's reluctance to undertake it are clearest in "have we got to." Additionally, the potential rewards of success are less than those of feminine letting go: while holding on and starting "a new world for man" "will blossom forth the whole of *human* nature," letting go will generate a form of life superior to any human nature can produce. It is also interesting that the masculine task involves "clear[ing] away the debris / of a *swamped* civilisation": the great deep flood of the empowered feminine becomes, in the vision of the masculine, a mere swamp, a fetid obstacle to progress.

If the speaker's emerging preference for feminine letting go has not been made clear by the reluctant tone of this stanza, it is revealed decisively in the next two stanzas:

> Must we hold on, hold on
> and go ahead with what is human nature
> and make a new job of the human world?
>
> Or can we let it go?
> O, can we let it go
> and leave it to some nature that is more than human
> to use the sperm of what's worth while in us
> and thus eliminate us?
>
> Is the time come for humans
> now to begin to disappear,
> leaving it to the vast revolutions of creative chaos
> to bring forth creatures that are an improvement on humans,
> as the horse was an improvement on the ichthyosaurus?

We feel poignantly here the speaker's urge to "let it go . . . let it go," expressed most explicitly, again, in the formulations "*must* we hold on" as opposed to "*can* we let it go? / O, can we let it go." That "O" is a cry of pained desire. Concomitantly, the speaker invokes Darwinian evolution and the authority of a somewhat arcane scientific nomenclature ("ichthyosaurus") to make the vast power of feminine "creative chaos / to bring forth creatures that are an *improvement* on humans," appear inevitable as well as desirable. The frightening, deep-dark-deathly feminine proves the provider of the broadest, most liberating, most desirable vision, *while retaining its fearsomeness*, whereas the invigorating, will-and-mastery-preserving self-mobilization of conventional masculinity, *while retaining its appealing clarity and firmness,* proves an onerous, futile, and narrow task, reducing cataclysmic social change to "a new job."

In other words, since it is deeply structured by modernist *sous-rature,* the poem insists on preserving the undecidability of the two gendered modes of (symbolically) enabling the utter change threatened/promised by the twentieth century. What makes this poem a prime instance of high modernist writing is its self-conscious articulation of that irreducible undecidability:

> Must we hold on?
> Or can we now let go?
>
> Or is it even possible we must do both?

"We must do both": Kristeva's impossible dialectic, Irigaray's two-way passage, set appropriately at the historical juncture of all that had gone before and the possibility of its utopian/dystopian transformation.

Just before "To Let Go or to Hold On—?" in *Pansies* is a brief poem called "After Dark," which, in terms of my preoccupations in this study, is a fitting supplement to the longer poem:

> Can you, after dark, become a darkie?
> Could one, at night, run up against the standing flesh of you
> with a shock, as against the blackness of a negro,
> and catch flesh like the night in one's arms.

Where the "we" and the addressee of "To Let Go or to Hold On—?" were rhetorical positions, the "one" and the "you" of "After Dark" are particularized as the self—presumably the speaker—and an eroticized other. The body of this sexual other becomes impressively massive ("run up against the standing flesh of you") and electrifying ("with a shock") when transformed by night into "a negro" who is "like the night." The speaker clearly desires this transformation: "Can you." The figural "black wave" of "To Let Go" is here embodied as a black person. Again, as in the narratives of Part II, the desirable/dangerous sexual other is at once of the night (the dream, the subconscious, the dark underside of life, birth-site of modernist form) and racially black. Race (black) is concatenated with the night-change ("*become* a darkie") the poetic speaker desires. The contemptuous "darkie" is a feeble assertion of the white speaker's control over that desire for, and concomitant fear of, this powerfully embodied other.

Forster's *Howards End* of 1910 is an even more schematic enactment (many find it too schematic a novel altogether) of the theses of this study than were the Lawrence poems.[7] It emphasizes the issue of class in relation to gender in formulating its version of the impossible dialectic, though race, as imperialism, is an important component of the novel's thematic structure. Quite straightforwardly, the Schlegels represent Culture, which, as Margaret says, is "irrevocably feminine" (44); the Wilcoxes represent patriarchal capitalist imperialism (Forster carefully makes Henry Wilcox not just a capitalist but an imperialist, and Paul must "make his way in Nigeria")—the world of telegrams and anger, which Margaret calls "irrevocably masculine, and all its inmates can do is to see that it isn't brutal" (44). Telegrams and anger are no good, but society requires for mere survival the vitality and commonsense of the masculine. Howards End itself, fallen on evil modern days, would have gone out of the family if Ruth Howard had not married Henry Wilcox. Forster's social-cultural-aesthetic project is "only" to "connect" the two, weeding out the extremes on both sides: the effete Tibby Schlegel, who passes from childhood straight to middle age, and Charles and Paul Wilcox (Charles's "brutality" is eventually punished by the state, whose law, the narrator says, is made in his image). This connection is consummated only partly in the marriage of Margaret and Henry. Henry, blind adherent to the sexual double standard, cannot connect his affair with Jackie to Helen's with Leonard Bast. Class is admirably inextricable from gender in this equation, *pace* the inadequacies of Forster's ability to represent the working class—"We are not concerned with the very poor. They are unthinkable . . ." (45).

The grand connection Forster offers at the end is represented by the baby boy, culturally illegitimate child (literally, outside the laws of the deadly, nonconnecting culture) of feminine high-culture Schlegel and working-class Bast, "down in the field," otherwise "the sacred center of the field," with his nursemaid Tom the peasant boy, who introduces himself by saying "Please, I am the milk" (299).[8] That baby's symbolic provenance embraces, in addition to breaking and remaking the laws of both class and patriarchal marriage, the victims of Wilcoxian imperialism: when Henry, announcing the terms of his will to his family, refers to the baby as Margaret's "nephew, down in the field," Paul says "Down in the field? Oh, come! I think we might have had the whole establishment, piccaninnies included" (341). Helen Schlegel's and Leonard Bast's baby, Margaret's (if not Henry's) nephew, is inheritor of Howards End, the great authentic heritage of precapitalist, preimperialist, pastoral England. Tom, *a boy*, is "the milk" of the great mother Ruth—he "connects" the novel's rigid gender division. Ruth was betrayed, neglected, silenced at the beginning of the novel, murdered by patriarchy; she is triumphantly arisen at the end. Her milk will flow from the past to nourish the future. The Wilcoxes of course, except for tamed, moribund Henry, sneeze themselves right out of the picture. Margaret inherits Howards End as the earth mother Ruth Wilcox intended her to—Henry's betrayal in burning her deathbed bequest is righted. The earth mother presides over the final scene. As Margaret says, "she is everything. She is the house, and the tree that leans over it" (313). Margaret believes that, in spite of the encroachment of London, Howards End "is the future as well as the past" (339). But it is precisely that encroachment of London that makes the "only connect" of this novel modernist *sous-rature* rather than sentimental pastoral wish-fulfillment.

The Schlegels as well as the Wilcoxes, like Bloomsburyite Forster himself, are, with irreducible modernist doubleness, *of* London. "Creeping London," visible on the horizon not only from Howards End but also from "Surrey and Hampshire" and, in its more general incarnation as urban modernity, from "Oniton, the Purbeck Downs, the Oderberge," is described as "a red rust" (339). If benign peasant boy Tom is the derepressed great mother's revivifying milk, creeping London is her terrifying, threatening uterine blood. Again, the male modernist fears destruction at the hands (in the engulfing womb) of the empowered maternal he himself has entered into representation.

Irigaray's Platonic paradigm emerges into overt symbolism in Forster's *A Passage to India*, 1924.[9] But Forster despairs here of the possibility that modern fiction can enact the impossible dialectic or realize the potential Jameson formulates in *The Political Unconscious*, where using the Lévi-Straussian model of art, in its derivation from ritual, as the place where social contradictions are symbolically resolved, he says that "modernism . . . is a symbolic act which involves a whole Utopian compensation for increasing dehumanization on the level of daily life" (42). Mrs. Moore enters the Platonic-maternal (Marabar) cave, which is also the locus of ineluctable otherness of race and culture, is horrified by her physical contact with what turns out to be an Indian baby, hears the leveling Irigarayan echo ("ou-boum"), and finds that it is the existential abyss: "The crush and the smells she could forget, but the echo began in some indescribable way to undermine her hold on life. . . . it had managed to murmur, 'Pathos, piety, courage—they exist, but are identical, and so is filth. Everything exists, nothing has value.' If one had spoken vileness in that place, or quoted lofty poetry, the comment would have been the same—'ou-boum.'" (143–44). After the Great War, the cultural leveling associated with the entry into representation of the empowered maternal—the Marabar Caves that dominate the novel and determine its events—has come to be, for Forster, unredeemed destruction (contrast Woolf's treatment of the new postwar order in Part 3 of *To the Lighthouse*, where Lily can both finish her painting and refuse to marry). Mrs. Moore's subsequent deification as the Hindu goddess Esmiss Esmoor stands in hopelessly ironic relation, I would argue, to the cruel, blank meaninglessness of her death: not a symbol of redemption or transformation but, again, of cultural incommensurability. Ruth Wilcox is a genuinely empowered great mother; the name Esmiss Esmoor, with its linguistic dislocation (like "god si love"), is (mostly) a joke.

Despite Adela's climactic recantation at the trial, and despite Ralph and Stella's sympathy for Professor Godbole's all-encompassing religion—a religion that Forster represents as at once hopeful, in its embrace of absolutely everything and its understanding that "absence implies presence," and also absurd in its "primitive" idolatry—the rifts opened by the maternal cave, embedded in "India" as site of otherness, cannot be knit together in the novel by any representations of connection available to Forster, as his ending makes clear:

> "Why can't we be friends now?" said the other [Fielding], holding him [Aziz] affectionately. "It's what I want. It's what you want."
>
> But the horses didn't want it—they swerved apart; the earth didn't want it, sending up rocks through which riders must pass single file; the temples, the tank, the jail, the palace, the birds, the carrion, the Guest House, that came into view as they issued from the gap and saw Mau beneath: they didn't want it, they said in their hundred voices, "No, not yet," and the sky said, "No, not there." (316)

The vaginal "Passage" to the racial-sexual-cultural otherness of "India," Forster has come to believe, cannot be traversed until all forms of hierarchical self-other dualism end at the political-social level. He has renounced his Bloomsbury faith in the transcendent power of personal relations, and with it all his hope and optimism. As Aziz says to Fielding, just before the above closing sequence: " 'If I don't make you go, Ahmed will, Karim will, if it's fifty-five hundred years we shall get rid of you, yes, we shall drive every blasted Englishman into the sea, and then'—he rode against him furiously—'and then,' he concluded, half kissing him, 'you and I shall be friends' " (316).

In Picasso's "Les demoiselles d'Avignon" of 1907, which has acquired an iconic status in our culture as a work of modernist origination and as a general emblem of modernism in the arts, I see another quintessential figuration of the theses of this study.[10] "Les demoiselles" is a painting of nude female bathers, linking (to state the obvious) the feminine and water. Since these bathers are prostitutes, their nudity is explicitly sexualized and that sexuality is marked simultaneously by degradation and by accessibility to the male viewer/voyeur/customer. It is, for 1907, a radically stylized painting, not only in the harsh discord of its treatment of the women (a harshness that still now strikes the viewer powerfully), but in its introduction of the vocabulary of cubism: the overall composition organized by, and the contours of the figures broken into, angular geometric shapes, the three-dimensionality or depth-illusion of traditional pictorial representation flattened, the figures radically stylized and distorted so as to seem splayed against the surface of the canvas, and the overtly nonrealistic conventions influenced by African tribal masks in the drawing of three of the five faces.[11]

"Les demoiselles" fuses the invention of these modernist formal practices with representation of an empowered sexual feminine. The female bathers are degraded within dominant convention (nude prostitutes, by definition lower class), but are transformed here *by modernist form*, including alliance with racial blackness (through both allusion to African art and literal dark paint on the three Africanized faces), into a powerful force, which, like the modernist texts I discussed earlier and will discuss in this chapter, retains its great strength now. It was in the process of painting (repainting and repainting) these women that Picasso invented (his version of) modernist art. By means of that modernist art, these women become awesome, frightening, magnificent, powerful figures. They are figures of modernist art as the release into new form of the sexual feminine; of the new form as release into representation of the power and terror of the sexual feminine; of the irresolvable ambiguity, the *sousrature* (the figures are just as hideous and distorted as they are powerful and riveting) of that feminine.[12] I would argue, further, that the conventionalized cluster of fruit at the bottom of the canvas suggests the vagina and the "fruit of the womb," linking the sexual feminine, again in characteristic modernist fashion, with the empowered maternal.

. . . . .

If modernism was invented by turn-of-the-century fiction, it was established as a movement by early twentieth-century poetry. Although fiction evidently continued to be just as important to modernist writing as poetry, a significant segment of that fiction (Stein, Proust, Joyce, Woolf, H.D., Toomer, Faulkner, Barnes) moved toward, or incorporated modes of, poetic writing in its prose. "So as everybody has to be a poet, what was there to do," said Gertrude Stein in 1913,[13] looking back at her own shift from narrative to poetry around 1911. It is as a set of theories of poetics that Anglo-American modernism's self-articulations have mainly persisted, and it is primarily as a poetics that modernism was canonized by the New Critics.

Poetry is the medium in which formal heightening or stylization is both most apparent to the reader and most readily accessible to the writer. It is the genre that almost inherently foregrounds the question of form. Narrative has a compelling, perhaps inevitable engagement with representation and referentiality, while poetry can shape itself in a more unmediated way as a *"language art,"* as Marjorie Perloff calls it.[14] Early modernist narrative represented the promise/threat of social renewal/destruction offered by the revolutionary horizon of the twentieth century in the modernist formal practices it invented. While the writers of early modernist narrative represented in their fiction their irresolvable ambivalence toward that revolutionary horizon, the self-conscious, self-defining Anglo-American modernists of the early twentieth century, with the exemplary exception of Woolf, repudiated revolutionary social change altogether, expressing an attraction to the reactionary right if expressing any political affinity at all, largely because reaction was compatible with their program for cultural renewal based on a revivification of the supposedly integrated or culturally authentic artistic modes of the distant past. The revolutionary impulse of modernism came to reside entirely in the realm of form. It is in poetry, or poetic prose, that form by itself can most readily bear the weight of so much cultural and political responsibility. The issues which, for early modernist narrative, were raised by actual political movements, socialism and feminism, and by the deformations of patriarchy-capitalism-imperialism to which those movements were a response, came to be assigned in high modernism to history itself, the feminine itself.

If Imagism is to modernist poetry as cubism is to modernist painting, then Pound's "In a Station of the Metro" is comparable to "Les demoiselles d'Avignon" as a founding work and cultural icon. Pound's emphasis in his parable of the composition of that poem is on compression:

> I wrote a thirty-line poem, and destroyed it because it was what we call work "of second intensity." Six months later I made a poem half that length; a year later I made the following *hokku*-like sentence:
>
> The apparition of these faces in the crowd;
>   Petals on a wet, black bough.[15]

We admire, as we are meant to, the unrelentingly high standard of the poet who will "use absolutely no word that does not contribute to the presentation." But we might also notice that what has taken place over the year and a half of the gestation of this poem is a powerful compression and containment of an erotic response. What he calls his "metro emotion" begins as a sudden vision of "a beautiful face, and then another and another, and then a beautiful child's face, and then another beautiful woman" (148). The poem that finally emerges abstracts these incarnated women's and children's faces first to apparition, then to flora. The eroticism of what Pound describes as his initial response is sublated in the transcendent Image, controlled through separation and abstraction. As Hugh Kenner tellingly formulates it, "Satisfaction lay not in preserving the vision, but in devising with mental effort an abstract equivalent for it, reduced, intensified."[16] The wetness and blackness of female, racial otherness are reassigned to the bough, a figure of rugged masculine potency, over which the light-colored, feminine petals now presumably droop. We can take those petals as synecdoche of moribund flowers, the classic poetic emblem of a mortality linked to the feminine.

Hugh Kenner considers the title a crucial part of the poem—he calls it "a poem which needs every one of its 20 words, including the six words of its title" (184)—and Pound's epithet for his inspiration, "my metro emotion," does more than locate neutrally the site of the poem's inception. The metro station operates in a complex way in the poem, and Kenner admirably unpacks the variegated resonances of Pound's title:

> We need the title so that we can savor that vegetal contrast with the world of machines: this is not any crowd, moreover, but a crowd seen underground, as Odysseus and Orpheus and Koré saw crowds in Hades. . . . Flowers, underground; flowers, out of the sun; flowers seen as if against a natural gleam, the bough's wetness gleaming on its darkness; in this place where wheels turn and nothing grows. So this tiny poem, drawing on . . . the Metro of Mallarmé's capital and a phrase that names a station of the Metro as it might a station of the Cross. (184–85)

The dark, underground "place where wheels turn and nothing grows" is the Platonic-maternal cave transmogrified into the hell of degraded modern mass democratic culture, locus of "the crowd," foreshadow of that ultimate modernist cliché, the urban "waste land." The vision of beautiful faces, the apparition of petals, is taken by Kenner exclusively as a contrast: the "vegetal contrast with the world of machines." It is that, of course. The mythic past is invoked against the banal present, as in Eliot and Joyce; the luminosity and fertile pathos of nature's cycles against the empty, mechanical reiterations of the turning wheel. But the female face-petals underground are at the same time, as figuration of modernist *sous-rature*, a product or appropriate denizen of the metro, an eruption into displaced representation of the fecundity of that maternal cave. They are *of* the underground cave just as much as they are its antithesis.

Moreover, the station of the metro is compared nonironically as well as ironically to the stations of the cross. The metro station becomes a place of suffering and negation that nonetheless, *and* therefore, generates redemptive vision. The erotic response to the sexuate woman is embedded in this degraded, mechanistic, mass urban setting, enabled as well as compromised by it. Without the "crowd" there would be no "apparition of these faces *in* the crowd"; without the dynamism, the dangerous energy of the modern underground, the modern machine, and the modern city, there would be no "metro emotion," no vision that is just as much inspired by the metro experience as it is compensation for it.[17]

As title, "In a Station of the Metro" is relegated to a position outside the poem and also elevated to a metatextual plane. It is a necessary part of the poem, as Kenner argues, but it also operates differently from the equation of apparition and petals, functioning outside the Imagist dynamic of radical metaphoric substitution and inside a more traditional referentiality: naming, locating, specifying, simultaneously generalizing (*"a* Station") and particularizing (*"the* Metro"). As an evocation of urban technology and mass democratic social leveling (as a TV ad for the *New York Newsday* subway column says, "nobody rides first class down here"), its referentiality points to the history of the modern.

Since it is a quintessential modernist text, "In a Station of the Metro" enacts *sous-rature* preeminently in relation to history and the feminine. The poem pointedly and literally locates itself "in" contemporary history and also repudiates that history; it is birthed (inspired) by and yet annihilates the women's faces, sublating them in the Image, the "petals" that simultaneously embody and disembody nature. The fate, the position, of history and of woman are the same: simultaneously enabling, necessary, defining, and also negated, rejected, countered by an extremely equivocal masculine ahistorical poetic transcendence—literally, *sous-rature*.

New Critical arguments that discover the entire poem in one line, the play in one speech, the novel in one scene, are out of date and perhaps suspect. But they do bear an affinity to the New Historical practice of discovering an entire moment of culture in one (preferably obscure or unlikely, inevitably nonliterary) document. This general methodology will allow me both to use "In a Station of the Metro" as a key to understanding the position of history and the feminine in modernist writing by men and also to allow Eliot and Joyce to stand, as they so often do, for white male high modernism (or, as they used to and probably often still do, for Anglo-American modernism in toto).[18]

Until the final section of Eliot's "Prufrock," women notoriously "come and go / Talking of Michelangelo" or they have arms "braceleted and white bare / [But in the lamplight downed with light brown hair!]"[19] They are either the banal degraders of high culture, dispensers of quotidian "teas and cakes and ices," or the disappointing and even disgusting, yet unattainable, objects of Prufrockian desire, the cause of his inability to say just what he means. Yet the poem's greatness lies in its precise articulation, through the modernist poetic practice of image juxtaposition, of the inability to say just what one means (because one means mutually contradictory things) as a representation of the modernist predicament, a predicament ascribed, here, to the troubling lure of woman.

When Prufrock takes his final "walk upon the beach," he has arrived there by traversing with the reader ("you and I") the streets of the modern city, streets that are just as much Hadean as is Pound's metro station. At the end of those streets, at the end of the poem, he finds that "we" have all along been "linger[ing] in the chambers of the sea," a figure that, like the one in Rachel Vinrace's nightmare, is clearly uterine. That figure retroactively makes the streets, with their "tedious argument / Of insidious intent" and their final "overwhelming question," at least partly a representation of the vaginal passage. The repressed maternal womb of patriarchy, erupting in modernism, is, then, the "overwhelming question." Again, as in "Metro," the nightmarish but/and enabling city of modernity is in the realm of the womb, and the alluring but unattainable women, mermaids or "sea-girls," are at once compensation for and products of that city: products to the extent that the entire poem has been written "in the chambers of the sea."

Prufrock claims that the mermaids will not sing to him, but at the same time he has heard them "singing, each to each," and that song echoes through the poem's beauty. He has had his vision of mermaids "riding seaward on the waves"; though they ride "seaward," away from Prufrock standing on the beach with "the bottoms of [his] trousers rolled," the magnificent language of the last two stanzas offers the vision to us. That vision is part of the night-sleep, the realm of the dream, the unconscious, the mother, that gave birth to modernism. At the same time, as in "Metro," it is part of a male modernist aesthetic (heretofore considered *the* modernist aesthetic) that, having de-repressed the mother, attempted re-repression by means of escape into a masculinist poetic transcendence above both history and woman. "Human voices wake us" from that sleep; "we drown" out of the life of the poem, destroyed by the destructive element of the feminine and the modern, but we have also realized their promise in this poem.

The themes of death and transformation through sea-change—immersion in the destructive element—are so apparent and so thoroughly explicated in Eliot's *The Waste Land* that I need do little more than point to them and remind the reader that sea-change occurs in the realm of the maternal feminine.[20] In "The Burial of the Dead," following the logic of "in the destructive element immerse," "the cruellest month" brings rebirth, water that stirs the life asleep within the maternal earth. This immersion in the destructive element is immediately located in the history of the modern, as the impersonal voice of the first four lines is suddenly embodied in a named feminine voice ("Marie") of pre–Great War upperclass European anxiety: Marie's freedom, exactly like that of the modernists, is the same as her fear. Similarly, where "the dry stone" brings "no sound of water," we see the poem's vision of "fear in a handful of dust," but death by water is, of course, equally the referent of the poem's fear: the ludicrous but compelling Madame Sosostris utters the command

"Fear death by water," but also links the "drowned Phoenician Sailor" to the locus classicus of positive sea-change, "those are pearls that were his eyes." The hyacinth girl establishes in the poem an actual space of *sous-rature*—the undecidable space between life and death—by linking the visionary "heart of light" to the maternal sea (*"Öd' und leer das Meer"*). This space is revealed at the end of "The Burial of the Dead" as the "Unreal City" of historical modernity. As in "Metro" and "Prufrock," urban modernity is the site and enabler of this irresolvably ambivalent encounter with the empowered (maternal) feminine, whose empowerment is precisely a function of that modernity.

Ariel's song, marking the salvation of culture offered by immersion in the maternal destructive element and woven through the poem in equal parts with the "fear death by water" motif, appears first in the context of the terminally degraded modern femininity of "A Game of Chess," the section of the poem whose vicious representations of women have been allowed to define Eliot's relationship to the feminine. (It should be noted here that this poem of homage to the great ancient masculine myth of Percival and the Fisher King is chock-full of women.) At the geographic center of the poem, lower class is linked to crass and disastrous female fecundity and sexuality—the working-class pub denizens are connected both ironically and nonironically to Ophelia's suicide just as the station of the metro is ambiguously linked to the stations of the cross. Lower class is linked as well to the actual cataclysm of the Great War and to the modernist sense of an impending, even greater cataclysmic change: "HURRY UP PLEASE IT'S TIME." On the other side of class valorization, the comic vitality of the working class women's voices, the vitality of Eliot's beloved music hall, is contrasted to the infuriating effeteness of the "so elegant / So intelligent" contemporary upper-middle-class neurasthenic Cleopatra of the first part of this section.

"The Fire Sermon" is written in and about a wide range of women's voices with just as much empathy as contempt. The feminine and its attendant water imagery are the locus here of the undecidable modernist simultaneity of destruction and renewal through two contradictory, thoroughly co-entangled themes—the theme of rebirth through a traversal of modern urban degradation and, at the same time, the theme of decline and perhaps destruction of culture from the beautiful and meaningful past to the degraded present:

> Weialala leia
> Wallala leialala

"Trams and dusty trees.
Highbury bore me. Richmond and Kew
Undid me. By Richmond I raised my knees
Supine on the floor of a narrow canoe."

Tiresias, as hermaphrodite and "most important personage in the poem" (if not "uniting all the rest"),[21] just as depressing and disgusting as he is visionary and oracular, is a prime figure of modernist *sous-rature*.

Part IV, "Death by Water," is the most self-evident exemplum of the themes of this study: Phlebas the Phoenician is just as much magically reborn à la Ariel—Madame Sosostris's drowned Phoenician sailor—as he is horribly destroyed by maternal feminine sea-change. "A current under sea / Picked his bones in whispers" is another deprivation, or muting, of language enacted by the maternal feminine upon the "he" who "was once" potently masculine—"handsome and tall as you." Finally, the speaking thunder (perhaps) bringing a destroying/reviving rain, conjoined with the "Murmur of maternal lamentation" and the "whisper music" fiddled on the woman's "long black hair," is the summarily ambiguous sound of the poem itself.

A Portrait of the Artist as a Young Man opens not with Eliot's anguished birth/death liminality but with the very good pre-Oedipal time and language of the benign, all-fulfilling maternal "moocow." On the other side of the old Western dualism, the other side to which Stephen inevitably crosses in his tormented adolescence, the maternal moocow becomes the locus of bodily shame and disgust. Stephen's heart is sickened by the "filthy cowyard at Stradbrook with its foul green puddles and clots of liquid dung and steaming brantroughs . . . The cattle which had seemed so beautiful in the country on sunny days revolted him and he could not even look at the milk they yielded."[22] The first trial of his early childhood at Clongowes is his Oedipal rebirth into patriarchy's degradation of the maternal, when he is shouldered into the square ditch full of cold, slimy water, where "a fellow had once seen a big rat jump into the scum" (11). The moocow maternal feminine becomes a filthy ditch in patriarchal culture, particularly in the extremist version of it Stephen/Joyce experiences in his Jesuit Irish Catholic upbringing. Thinking of the scummy ditch immediately makes Stephen think of his mother, in association as well as compensation: "How cold and slimy the water had been! A fellow had once seen a big rat jump into the scum. Mother was sitting at the fire with Dante waiting for Brigid to bring in the tea. She had her feet on the fender and her jewelly slippers were so hot and they had such a lovely warm smell!" (11).

But Stephen is also Dedalus, the modernist *Artist*; for him the filthy ditch of the maternal feminine is allowed rebirth as "a day of dappled seaborne clouds." That day and its magically transforming cloud language carry him through the "gray warm air" to the sea: "The clouds were drifting above him silently and silently the seatangle was drifting below him; and the grey warm air was still: and a new wild life was singing in his veins" (170). Paternal skyclouds and maternal seatangle contribute equally to Stephen's exultation. At the sea he is granted the epiphany of the fully sexual but simultaneously transcendent bird-girl—no more oscillation between Mother Mary and the filthy ditch—whose wreathing seaweed, unlike that of Prufrock's mermaids, is a green sign of both life-acceptance and Irish self-acceptance: "Stephen's Green." (Prufrock's red and brown, the threatening colors of female sexuality and of excrement, mark his hopeless division from the "sea-girls.")

On the way to that sea epiphany, as his friends call to him using variations on his Father-name, Stephen has the patriarchal vision of the fabulous artificer, rife like Plotinus with Irigaray's language and themes, a vision that is usually taken straight as Joyce's modernist view of himself as *The Artist*:

> Now, at the name of the fabulous artificer, he seemed to hear the noise of dim waves and to see a winged form flying above the waves and slowly climbing the air. What did it mean? Was it a quaint device opening a page of some medieval book of prophecies and symbols, a hawklike man flying sunward above the sea, a prophecy of the end he had been born to serve and had been following through the mists of childhood and boyhood, a symbol of the artist forging anew in his workshop out of the sluggish matter of the earth a new soaring impalpable imperishable being? (168–69)

But it is impossible to take this straight. The hawklike being who flies too close to the Father's sun is the opposite of imperishable—his Icarian-Oedipal wings are about to melt; he is about to plunge down into the sea.[23] His mistake, in fact, is to try to leave that maternal sea too far behind, to rise entirely into paternal logos. Repressed, the sea becomes his death. Further, "soaring impalpable imperishable" is too excessive to be anything other than ironic, and "sluggish matter of the earth" must make us suspicious after the novel's clear condemnation of the Jesuit hatred of the body and matter, the realm of the feminine maternal. Joyce is depicting ironically in this passage Stephen's masculine megalomania, the sterile megalomania Stephen has just perceived and rejected in the Jesuit priesthood, but that he cannot escape, as we see again in his arrogant aesthetic theorizing in chapter 5. He (Stephen) is about to fall into the same trap in his vision of the fabulous artificer, but Joyce saves him from it (for the moment) by means of the visionary but real seaborne bird-girl who stays on earth, the impossible dialectic of masculine clouds and feminine sea.

In *Ulysses* (among the innumerable other things that happen) these themes are embedded in history. Deferring the riches of Leopold and Molly, and of "Circe,"[24] in relation to my concerns here, I would like to point for brevity's and continuity's sake to the very clear enactment of this study's themes in "Telemachus."[25] Almost schematically, the sea is, as Mulligan asserts, the "grey sweet mother," also the "snotgreen sea.

The scrotumtightening sea. *Epi oinopa ponton . . . Thalatta! Thalatta!* She is our great sweet mother. . . . Our mighty mother" (5). Joyce might have gotten "snotgreen" from that modernist precursor Rimbaud's "morves d'azur" in "Le bateau ivre,"[26] but it comes more immediately from Stephen's dirty handkerchief, that Mulligan insists on pulling from his pocket: "the bard's noserag. A new art colour for our Irish poets: snotgreen" (5).

From Homer to Swinburne, with the possible exception of Rimbaud, what white male Western bard would call the great sea mother snotgreen? It had been for the poet to idealize her (an idealization that freed him to express unlimited contempt if he chose for actual women, living and literary), for the philosopher to belittle her. Joyce as modernist bard finds representation for the simultaneity of his cultural moment's homage to the power of the mother and disgust at her embodiedness, her link to repulsive body products. Both Molly and Leopold are part of this irreducibly ambiguous, low and disgusting, savingly life-affirming eruption of body parts and products, culturally feminine, into representation. The feminine body is *at once* for Joyce the great sweet mother and the snotgreen sea, "the ring of bay and skyline" holding "a dull green mass of liquid"—remember, as Joyce no doubt means us to, Stephen's scummy ditch at Clongowes—that becomes for Stephen the bowl by his mother's "deathbed holding the green sluggish bile which she had torn up from her rotting liver by fits of loud groaning vomiting" (5). This horrific maternal vomiting, the irrepressible eruption (literally an eruption into representation) of the "murdered" (repressed) mother who refuses to die out of her artist-son's consciousness ("agenbite of inwit") is in impossible dialectic with the masculine mythmaking and father-searching that, as in *The Waste Land*, has come, as a result of academic New Criticism, to define this text almost exclusively. Again, to the extent that white male high modernism has been appropriated by New Criticism in the academy as a reactionary cultural formation, its actual subversiveness in relation to gender and history has been elided. This impossible dialectic of empowered/deathly maternal and reinvigorated/castrated paternal is, as we have seen again and again, characteristic of modernist writing.

In two great works of the Harlem Renaissance, Langston Hughes's 1926 poem "The Negro Speaks of Rivers" and Jean Toomer's *Cane* of 1923, the empowered/deathly maternal is a figure of suffering, racial suffering, and racial redemption, with which the speaker identifies, and not, as it is to so many white male modernists, a figure (partly) of horror.[27] The ambivalence toward the maternal feminine in these two works seems to be a function of resenting that suffering. Despite the identification, and perhaps partly because of the resentment, the works assume a dominant, superior, in some ways condescending paternal position in relation to the redemptive maternal feminine, using its power in order to transcend it. The ambivalence toward that paternal superiority is expressed either as what Arnold Rampersad calls "liquidation" of the father or as guilt.[28] The history within and out of which these works were written, of course, is the history of the African-American struggle against racial oppression.

"The Negro Speaks of Rivers" allies both the suffering and the great historical stature of the African-American heritage with the maternal feminine as river: the Congo "lulled" the speaker "to sleep"; the speaker has "seen" the Mississippi's "muddy bosom." The speaker's soul, like the soul of his race, encompasses the history of the human race, from its birth by the Euphrates, through its early manhood by the Congo and its (enslaved) great achievement of pyramids upon the Nile—the poem emphasizes, obviously, the importance of these last two African rivers to the history of the human race—to its liberation by Abe Lincoln on the sunset Mississippi. While the poem's emphasis falls on the depth and ancientness of these rivers and therefore of "The Negro"'s soul that "has grown deep like the rivers," the feminine rivers themselves are distanced and objectified by the speaker to the status of instrumentality in his active development: "*I bathed in* the Euphrates," "*I built* my hut *near* the Congo," "*I looked upon* the Nile," "*I heard* the singing of the Mississippi." These verbs simultaneously connect the speaker to the rivers and separate him from them, establishing a contrast between his self-producing activity and their monumental, eternal passivity. The male speaker, therefore, while asserting his identification with the maternal feminine rivers, at the same time establishes his poetic voice as an active masculinity working upon that feminine to transcend it: again, the male modernist ambivalence toward the maternal feminine as history.

In *I Too Sing America*, Arnold Rampersad uses the terminology of irresolvable contradiction to discuss this poem:

> With its allusions to deep dusky rivers, the setting sun, sleep, and the soul, "The Negro Speaks of Rivers" is suffused with the image of death and, simultaneously, the idea of deathlessness. . . . From the depths of grief the poet sweeps back to life by clinging to his greatest faith, which is in his people and his sense of kinship with them. His frail, intimidated self, as well as the image of his father, are liquidated. A man-child is born, soft-spoken, almost casual, yet noble and proud, and black as Africa. The muddy river is his race, the primal source out of which he is born anew; on that "muddy bosom" of the race as black mother, or grandmother, he rests secure forever. (40)

Rampersad refers to Hughes's actual oppressive father and enabling grandmother, but, as his analysis makes clear, those actual progenitors achieve cultural-symbolic status in the poem.

Jean Toomer's *Cane* is full of strong women tormented by the exploitation of their sexuality, women with whom the male speaker empathizes and identifies. As in "The Negro Speaks of Rivers," women and female procreativity are identified with African-American suffering and strength. At the same time, the speaker clearly establishes his masculine distance from, and superiority to, these women, as well as his guilt at that superiority and at his (sometimes resentful) helplessness before the spectacle of their suffering.

"Fern" is particularly interesting to me because of its use of water imagery. Fern is sexually "easy," but she somehow mysteriously inspires guilt and respect in the men who "were everlastingly bringing her their bodies" (14). They all want to do something for her, but cannot think what. She lounges silently on her front porch with her head resting on a nail—a crucifixion image. The narrator says, "at first sight of her I felt as if I heard a Jewish cantor sing" (15), and her name, as we find out at the very end, is Fernie May Rosen. She embodies the contradiction/fusion of suffering and the possibility of redemption; of commingled (white) Jews and blacks; of the exploited sexuate feminine and an ideal of self-sacrificing altruism, enforced by guilt, in relation to an ironized feminine purity ("she became a virgin").

In the beginning of "Fern" clearly eroticized water imagery displaces the vagina oddly and powerfully upward to the eyes: "Face flowed into her eyes. Flowed in soft cream foam and plaintive ripples . . . you will know my feeling when I follow the curves of her profile, like mobile rivers, to their common delta" (14). Later, when the narrator has a disastrous quasi-sexual, quasi-religious encounter with Fern on the bank of a "branch . . . where reddish leaves had dammed the creek a little" (17), "face" becomes "God": "Her eyes, unusually weird and open, held me. Held God. He *flowed in* as I've seen the countryside flow in" (17, italics added). In response to this vision, the narrator "must have done something—what, I don't know, in the confusion of my emotion" (17). Fern responds with anguish: "her body was tortured with something it could not let out. Like boiling sap it flooded arms and fingers till she shook them as if they burned her" (17). He has impregnated her with, projected onto her, his own suffering, a suffering that has no place to go:

> I too had my dreams: something I would do for her. I have knocked about from town to town too much not to know the futility of mere change of place. Besides, picture if you can, this cream-colored solitary girl sitting at a tenement window looking down on the indifferent throngs of Harlem. Better that she listen to folk-songs at dusk in Georgia . . . love is not a thing like prejudice which can be bettered by changes of town. Could men in Washington, Chicago, or New York, more than the men of Georgia, bring her something left vacant by the bestowal of their bodies? (15–16)

The narrator has identified himself as "from the North," as Toomer of course actually was. Just before his encounter with Fern on the red-leaf-dammed creek, with its characteristic repressed-maternal attributes of redness and blockage, he tells us that he "felt strange, as I always do in Georgia, particularly at dusk. I felt that things unseen to men were tangibly immediate. It would not have surprised me had I had vision. People have them in Georgia more often than you would suppose. A black woman once saw the mother of Christ and drew her in charcoal on the courthouse wall" (17). In this extremely complex piece written in a deceptively casual narrative voice, the black woman is the irreducibly ambiguous carrier of suffering and redemption, despair and vision, earth-power and earth-contamination, guilt-inducing and spurious, but also altruism-inducing and genuine, transcendence. On her body are written irresolvable American contradictions of region (North and South), race (black and white), religion (Christian and Jew). The subordinate-transcendent masculine narrating voice Toomer constructs finds itself simultaneously saved and damned by what he projects onto the black woman, baffled by the irreconcilability of his superiority and inferiority to her, within the cultural contradictions he uses her to represent.

. . . . .

Because Gertrude Stein wrote as a woman, her ambivalence involved not alienation from the flood of the historical-maternal "new" she helped release, as was the case with the male modernists, but a fear of punishment for the unequivocal assertiveness of her program for that release of the twentieth-century revolution of the word. That fear emerges in diction of violence and anxiety. I would like to use a piece entitled "Sugar" from the "Food" section of her great assemblage of prose-poetry *Tender Buttons* in the same paradigmatic way for the female modernists that I used "In a Station of the Metro" for the male modernists.[29]

In a startlingly erotic passage from "Poetry and Grammar," 1934, Stein's fear of the poetic project she initiated in *Tender Buttons* erupts in a series of predominantly anxious and violent verbs: "Poetry is concerned with using with abusing, with losing with wanting, with denying with avoiding with adoring with replacing the noun. . . . Poetry is doing nothing but using losing refusing and pleasing and betraying and caressing nouns."[30] Similarly, Stein associates the process of making poetry with a painful intensification of erotic feeling: "you can love a name and if you love a name then saying that name any number of times only makes you love it more, more violently more persistently more tormentedly" (232).

In "Transatlantic Interview" of 1946, Stein assesses "Sugar" very favorably (she finds "unsuccessful" several other quotations from *Tender Buttons* the interviewer presents to her for comment).[31] "Sugar" begins

> A violent luck and a whole sample and even then quiet. Water is squeezing, water is almost squeezing on lard. Water, water is a mountain and it is selected and it is so practical that there is no use in money. A mind under is exact and so it is necessary to have a mouth and eye glasses.
>
> A question of sudden rises and more time than awfulness is so easy and shady. There is precisely that noise. (485)

Stein particularly liked those opening paragraphs. Their overall tone expresses an excitement tinged with violence, not simply in the opening "violent luck" but in the repetition of "squeezing," counterbalanced by an unexpected "quiet," which reinforces by opposition that violent excitement. I also hear excitement in the slightly disgusting erotic suggestiveness of water squeezing on lard, and violence in the suggestion of drowning in "a mind under." Again, the energy required for what Stein called breaking and remaking the rigid form of the noun is a threateningly violent force; the erotic charge of that breaking is tinged with disgust.[32]

Unlike the longer sections at the beginning of "Food," "Sugar" goes on for just another page but is still too long to quote in its entirety. The following excerpts, which continue the tone of the opening lines, taken together represent approximately half of the poem:

> A question of sudden rises and more time than awfulness is so easy and shady. . . . Put it in the stew, put it to shame. . . . A puzzle a monster puzzle, a heavy choking, a neglected Tuesday. . . . Wet crossing and a likeness, any likeness, a likeness has blisters, it has that and teeth, it has the staggering blindly. . . . Cut a gas jet uglier and then pierce pierce in between the next and negligence. . . . A collection of all around, a signal poison, a lack of languor and more hurts at ease. (486)

It does not take a detailed reading to make apparent the violence and anxiety of Stein's sounds as they hit the ear and of the troubling connotations and resonances that match and support those sounds as they take shape in the reader's mind. "Sugar" ends on a relaxed, affirmative note, "A nice old chain is widening, it is absent, it is laid by," which does not, however, wholly assuage the anxiety about that nice old chain articulated in the body of the piece.

Stein says in "Transatlantic Interview" that she had in mind "a great body of water" as she wrote "Sugar" (29). Water is an important recurring motif throughout *Tender Buttons*, particularly in conjunction with containment and vision.[33] Several titles within the "Objects" section

("Rooms" has no subdivisions) concern water either explicitly or obliquely, especially in relation to containment or protection, such as "Mildred's Umbrella," "A Seltzer Bottle," "A Mounted Umbrella," and "A Little Bit of a Tumbler." The opening section of "Objects," and therefore of *Tender Buttons*, condenses (as it were) the motifs of water, containment, and vision: "A Carafe, That Is a Blind Glass" (the second poem of "Objects" is entitled "Glazed Glitter," continuing the "blindness," or opacity, of the opening glass carafe).

"Sugar," as Stein seems to acknowledge in "Transatlantic Interview," constitutes a culminating moment for the major preoccupations of *Tender Buttons*. "Sugar" associates water not only with anxious sexuality and violence, as we have already seen, but also with the crucial modernist issues of democratic leveling and apocalyptic historical change. The "great body" of mother/water, the maternal feminine, the enabler of the new writing, can also drown, obliterate, prevent vision: "A mind under is exact and so it is necessary to have a mouth and eye glasses." In some of its polysemous associations, this sentence connects a drowned mind, the exactness of the symbolic, its exigency ("necessary"), the pre-Oedipal mouth that utters the presymbolic and attaches to the body of the mother, and the "eye glasses" that protect symbolic vision from presymbolic annihilation and that also suggest the "glasses" that contain water.

Water is also "a mountain" and involves "a question of sudden rises." Later, "crestfallen" is associated with "open," "mounting" with "chaining," and a "wet crossing" with "a likeness, any likeness, a likeness has blisters, it has that and teeth." At an obvious level, "a great body of water" has waves: mountains, sudden rises, that can become *crest*fallen. Waves rise in contradiction to the leveling force of water ("water seeks its own level"), a leveling force that suggests, for modernist writing, as we have seen, the representation of the eruption of the maternal feminine as twentieth-century egalitarianism.

Stein's position in relation to twentieth-century democratic, egalitarian leveling, like the positions of the other modernists, was as equivocal as her position in relation to female self-assertion. She hated Roosevelt and the New Deal, distrusted "big government," and allied herself politically, if at all, with an anarchic but generally right-wing American "rugged individualism." She was a close friend in the thirties and forties of the collaborationist Bernard Faÿ, whose interventions on her behalf with the Vichy government enabled Stein and Toklas, two Jews, to remain miraculously unmolested in occupied France. But, on the other side, "The Winner Loses, A Picture of Occupied France" is a tribute to the *maquisard* Resistance near her home in Belley, she excoriates Hitler as "Angel Harper" in *Mrs. Reynolds*, and, most importantly, she links to the egalitarian-democratic principle of "one man, one vote" her notion of the "twentieth-century composition" as having no dominant center, in fact no center at all: each of its elements is as important as every other element and as important as the whole.[34]

"Crestfallen and open," "mounting and chaining": these water-related conjunctions are perfect representations of Stein's ambivalence. "Crestfallen" has negative connotations of defeat, but/and denotes leveling and is linked to "open," which has positive political and literary connotations. "Mounting" has predominantly positive connotations but also denotes hierarchy as well as hierarchical, animalistic sex, and is linked to "chaining," which has negative connotations, invoking the constraints of the old order, again both political and literary (chains suggest linearity). Similarly, "wet crossing and a likeness" links representation ("a likeness") with water and transgression, or at least stepping over (boundaries), going from one side to another. Concomitantly, "any likeness, a likeness has blisters, it has that and teeth, it has the staggering blindly": sucking mouths develop teeth, as do threatening vaginas, which enable them to speak as well as to bite; blisters come from (subversive) friction; staggering blindly, again, is the terrifying punishment for the wet crossing. All these are developed as properties of "any likeness": any representation at all and especially any representation that deploys the nineteenth-century aesthetic of illusionist verisimilitude that Stein rejects.

The polysemy of Stein's experimental work makes it at once repository of modernism's richest possibilities and also repository of such near-limitless suggestiveness that its specific relevance to the modernist issues I am developing in this study could be questioned. Nonetheless, I think Stein's importance to the predominant concerns of female modernist aesthetic practice has been so amply demonstrated that I can assume it here without denying her concomitant relevance to various other strands of aesthetic and cultural history or of interpretive orientation.[35]

The same, of course, can be said of any of the other writers and works I discuss, and is particularly relevant to H.D.'s "Sea Rose" of 1916, a poem usually discussed in relation to Poundian Imagism. It is in fact a powerful and radical work of feminist modernism.[36] The title itself is jarring in its linkage of the small, perfected, fragile accultured beauty of the rose, prime Western symbol of patriarchal appropriation of female sexuality, with the vast power of the sea. "Rose" in the title can also be read as a verb—literally, the sea rose: paradigm of modernist sea-change (this reading gets some support from "Oread" of 1914, which begins "Whirl up, sea—").

The poem opens with an even more jarring invocation:

Rose, harsh rose,
marred and with stint of petals,
meagre flower, thin,
sparse of leaf

"Harsh" releases the rose of female sexuality from its imprisonment in a gentle, perfected beauty, allowing it its raw power, as does the title's conjunction of "rose" with "sea." "Marred" insists on the vitality of the rose's *im*perfection, in a cultural tradition that links its perfection to its reification. "Marred" also insists on the poem's rejection of the deadly conventions of female beauty within patriarchy. "Stint," "meagre," "thin," "sparse" all contradict the opulence, the concupiscent lushness, of conventional images of the rose. At the same time, radically subversive though they are, these adjectives do not cancel their own negative connotations. To fly (literally) in the face of that long tradition of oppression is to breast punishment, ostracism, "harsh" judgment: to be scorned as a marred, stinted, meagre, thin, sparse "spinster" or "old maid," one whose sexuality has been withdrawn from the economic sphere of male traffic in women. (One thinks of Woolf's "puckered-up" Lily Briscoe, whose name enacts a similar association of a flower with the "brisk"—very close to "crisp"—that is her nickname.)

The second stanza makes the speaker's polemic position clear:

more precious
than a wet rose,
single on a stem—
you are caught in the drift.

This harsh, marred, meagre sea rose is *"more precious /* than a wet rose, / single on a stem"—not only the conventional rose, but the sexually available (wet) rose linked to (impaled on?) the phallic stem. The sea rose, unlike the single possession of the single stem, is "caught in the drift." I take that as a simultaneous evocation of the maternal feminine sea, the crowd of urban modernity, and the radical transformations of sea-change itself. Again, while it is better to be caught in the drift than to be single on a stem, the negative connotations of "caught in the drift" are allowed to stand, in this poem of modernist *sous-rature*.

The two terms of the impossible dialectic of that *sous-rature* are elaborated in the third stanza:

Stunted, with small leaf,
you are flung on the sand,
you are lifted
in the crisp sand
that drives in the wind.

The first line recapitulates the first stanza. The second line reiterates "caught in the drift," emphasizing the helplessness of that "stunted," "small" sea rose within the great (historical) forces that create and propel it. The speaker's tone changes drastically in the third through fifth lines.

"Crisp," of course, is the key adjective—it is not just the compensation for all this stunted meagreness, but it is, I would argue, what the speaker *really* thinks of the sea rose that hegemonic culture perceives as stunted, meagre, marred, but that she perceives (as we will see in the final stanza) as vigorously, powerfully "crisp." (One thinks immediately of modernist aesthetics here, particularly the Imagism whose practice H.D. was in fact adapting to her feminist concerns.) The verbs of these three lines ("lifted" and "drives") are equally positive, literally uplifting and energizing. The sea rose clearly benefits here by the unleashed power of the realm of the sea, but at the same time we are not allowed to forget the rose's helplessness within that power.

In the final stanza, the sexuality of the sea rose itself is redeemed and made superior to that of the wet rose single on a stem:

> Can the spice-rose
> drip such acrid fragrance
> hardened in a leaf?

The "spice-rose" may or may not be equivalent to that wet rose single on a stem, but it is certainly suggestive of the rose's sexuality, here seemingly released ("drip") by its association with the sea rose. But the sea rose itself is superior to the "spice-rose" in the dripping (manifest) acridness of its fragrance: a wonderfully ambiguous choice of adjectives for the sea rose's sexuality, clearly presented as desirable by the syntax of the sentence but nonetheless carrying negative connotations. The "hardened" "leaf" reminds us again of the sea-rose's powerful difference from the soft rose petals of feminine subservience.

Two decades later and in another country, Zora Neale Hurston's *Their Eyes Were Watching God*, 1937, while affirming the autonomy and strength of black culture in general, of black women in particular, and of the feminine narrative voice, in the face of murderously repressive racism and sexism, refuses to choose black conclusively over white, or female over male.[37] In the courtroom scene that is the climax of the novel, Janey is surrounded by a sympathetic group of white women, protected from the black men who, in an eruption of male bonding, despise her for shooting her lover Tea Cake in self-defense, insisting on believing her guilty of murder: "And the white women cried and stood around her like a protecting wall and the Negroes, with heads hung down, shuffled out and away" (279–80).

The painful implications of that scene (particularly evident in the bowed heads and the shuffling) are quickly undercut. The narrator, Janey's surrogate, provides Janey with a rationalization of the behavior of Tea Cake's friends—"she knew it was because they loved Tea Cake and didn't understand" (281)—and in fact it turns out they do understand. It is Janey who makes the first gesture of reconciliation, but the men relent easily and apologize to her, drawing her back within the warm circle of black community at Tea Cake's funeral.

That circle is not always a reliable defense against racism, however, any more than either Tea Cake's relatively egalitarian love for Janey or her nurturing friendships with other women are a reliable defense against sexism. Earlier in the novel, Tea Cake beats Janey in a fit of jealousy of Mrs. Turner's brother. Janey is innocent. Mrs. Turner is a racist light-skinned black woman who identifies with whites and hates Tea Cake for his dark skin. Mrs. Turner's racism, which Hurston develops in episodes of her attempts at sisterly bonding with Janey, is repellent, but Tea Cake's violently macho response to it is equally so, to the reader if not (consciously) to Janey. Tea Cake's friends come to blame his death on Mrs. Turner's brother, and Janey, on the witness stand, says "Tea Cake couldn't come back to himself until he had got rid of that mad dog that was in him and he couldn't get rid of the dog and live. He had to die to get rid of the dog" (278). Tea Cake literally has rabies, having been bitten by a mad dog, and he is trying to kill Janey when she shoots him in self-defense. He dies with his teeth buried in her forearm. But the "mad dog" is also symbolic, I would argue, of Tea Cake's violent macho response to his unfounded jealousy, and his death is a (rather extreme) punishment for it. In a sense Hurston has rewritten *Othello* with a black feminist Desdemona triumphing in the end.

The circumstances of Tea Cake's infection with rabies by the bite of the mad dog are highly suggestive for my argument in this book. Tea Cake and Janey are fleeing a devastating hurricane, an unleashing of the great (mother) flood that Tea Cake has failed to take seriously. (Janey wanted to follow the example of the local Indians, evidently more in tune with the great mother, and evacuate sooner to high ground, but Tea Cake refused.) Janey has been blown from the road into the rising water next to it (water described as a "great expanse . . . full of things living and dead": quintessential modernist maternal-feminine *sous-rature*) while trying to get a piece of roof to cover the resting Tea Cake. Tea Cake wakes and sees Janey "fighting water too hard," a phrase reminiscent of the description Conrad's Stein gives of the drowning nonmodernist. He sees a cow swimming toward her with a "massive built dog . . . sitting on her shoulders and shivering and growling" (245)—the reader is thereby warned to fear the dog.

I see the cow as the maternal feminine, swimming calmly at one with this rising water; the rabid dog literally on her back is vicious, moribund patriarchy, in a wonderful use of metaphoric specificity hydrophobic, dreading this water. When Janey grabs the cow's tail, the dog moves to attack her. Tea Cake then jumps in and attacks the dog, but

> he was a powerful dog and Tea Cake was over-tired. So he didn't kill the dog with one stroke as he had intended. But the dog couldn't free himself either. They fought and somehow he managed to bite Tea Cake high up on his cheek-bone once. Then Tea Cake finished him and sent him to the bottom to stay there. The cow relieved of a great weight was landing on the fill with Janie before Tea Cake stroked in and crawled weakly upon the fill again. (246)

Tea Cake is certainly better than Janey's other men, as close as any in this novel to being the new man suitable for the new woman. But even Tea Cake cannot kill that very strong dog in one stroke before it manages to bite him fatally. The new order of the flooding maternal feminine both preserves women like Mrs. Turner and still carries on its back that rabid dog.

I would like to finish this chapter, and in a sense therefore the proper matter of this book, with two Virginia Woolf endings. The final moment of *The Waves* of 1931 gives us first the defiance of capital D-ified Death offered by Bernard (who is in some ways the best version Woolf can imagine of the patriarchal literary-cultural tradition):

> And in me too the wave rises. It swells; it arches its back. I am aware once more of a new desire, something rising beneath me like the proud horse whose rider first spurs and then pulls him back. What enemy do we now perceive advancing against us, you whom I ride now, as we stand pawing this stretch of pavement? It is death. Death is the enemy. It is death against whom I ride with my spear couched and my hair flying back like a young man's, like Percival's, when he galloped in India. I strike spurs into my horse. Against you I will fling myself, unvanquished and unyielding, O Death![38]

Unlike many others, I have always read this passage as ironic at Bernard's expense, in its megalomania, its childish heroic fantasizing, its conversion of the reader ("you whom I ride now") into a mastered horse, and, most tellingly, its idealization of Percival, that absent patriarchal-mythic center of this feminist modernist novel, who in fact dies absurdly before having a chance to live out his archaic upper-class masculine imperialist destiny in India.[39] The structuring of the lives of this novel, and of the novel itself, around the attachment to Percival, *is* the persistence of the residual cultural-literary past that is in unresolved contradiction with everything else in the novel, particularly with its formal technique, that defines and inhabits the utterly changed present/future.

But to those who read authentic life-affirming death-defiance in this passage, who do not see it as primarily or even at all ironic, the novel presents its closing line: "*The waves broke on the shore.*" Bernard may feel the wave triumphantly rising erect within him as he rides on patriarchal horseback, but the last word is given to that narrative position of modernist symbolic representation and of feminine-oceanic cyclic time that is equally with Percival a structuring force in the novel. From that position, the last thing we see is the wave that Bernard rides breaking on the shore. That breaking wave recalls Rhoda, the feminine modernist suicide: "The wave breaks. I am the foam that sweeps and fills the uttermost rims of the rocks with whiteness; I am also a girl, here in this room" (107). Transcendence, linked inextricably to defeat by excruciating limitation ("I am also a girl, here in this room"), comes not in the glory or inevitable failure of Bernard-Percival's heroic horseback ride but in Rhoda's death-leap into maternal-oceanic leveling sweep and revivifying fill.

To the Lighthouse (1927) ends, to similar purpose but more overtly, just as Lily Briscoe finishes her painting, with a very famous "line there, in the centre" (310).[40] The closing "line" of Lily's and the novel's final "vision" is a line of simultaneous separation and union: separation and union of the (devastated/freed) postwar modernist present and the (murderous/fructifying) Victorian-Edwardian realist past; separation and union of disillusioned but freer adulthood and idealized but oppressed childhood; separation and union of empowered/enchained, inspiring/inhibiting Victorian mother, Mrs. Ramsay, and cramped/autonomous modernist daughter, Lily; separation and union of tyrannical/visionary patriarchal male, Mr. Ramsay, and fecund/murdered patriarchal female, Mrs. Ramsay.

It would be impossible, and a serious distortion of the text, to claim that Woolf resolves any of those myriad interconnected gendered dualisms in favor of one term over the other. Instead, the text represents more clearly perhaps than any other the modernist moment of *sous-rature*, of the simultaneity of the impossible dialectic, of dualism that seeks neither unitary resolution in the dominance of one term over the other or in the spurious third term of dialectical synthesis, but rather the two-way passage, difference without hierarchy, never the one without the other. Lily finishes her painting by going back and forth between the canvas and her view of Mr. Ramsay and the two children, boy and girl, resisting tyranny and loving the man who imposes it, out over the maternal bay: she achieves "that razor edge of balance between two opposite forces; Mr. Ramsay and the picture" (287). Mr. Ramsay, Cam, and James are, of course, on their way to the lighthouse, which is simultaneously a stark Mr. Ramsayan phallus and a soft Mrs. Ramsayan glow:

The Lighthouse was then a silvery, misty-looking tower with a yellow eye, that opened suddenly, and softly in the evening. Now—

James looked at the Lighthouse. He could see the white-washed rocks; the tower, stark and straight; . . . So that was the Lighthouse, was it?

No, the other was also the Lighthouse. For nothing was simply one thing. The other Lighthouse was true too. (276–77)

Lily has her vision and paints her line there in the centre just as the man, the girl, and the boy, acting under the sign of the mother, at last reach that modernist lighthouse.

Chapter 7

AFTER MODERNISM

B Y CURRENT critical consensus, or at least according to the rough periodization I have been employing, modernism, having been petering out (with some notable exceptions) in the thirties, ended definitively with World War II; sometime in the two decades after that historical rupture, postmodernism began. I am not interested in entering here the debates currently raging around the term "postmodernism." The amorphousness, heterogeneity, and undefinability of "postmodernism" make "modernism" seem, by contrast, a coherent, homogeneous, consensually defined and periodized movement. No two people who write about postmodernism seem to have the same works, general periodization, or even media in mind (no doubt that is part of what characterizes it as a cultural formation). For my purposes here, I find most useful Andreas Huyssen's distinction between an earlier postmodernism of the sixties and early seventies and a different, contemporary postmodernism that began to appear in the late seventies. I also agree with Huyssen that postmodernism is predominantly an American phenomenon—both texts I discuss in this chapter are American—and that the late forties and fifties, when modernism was no longer really alive yet neither was it quite dead, were characterized most importantly by the institutionalization of New Critical modernism.[1]

In characteristic works of early postmodernism, I find that modernist *sous-rature* has disappeared. Gender war has returned with a vengeance. In the sixties and early seventies, gender once again, and perhaps as exaggeratedly as at any other time in history, became drastically polarized, with gender ideologies correspondingly dominated by antagonism.[2] That antagonism is generally either out in the open, unabashedly represented, or covered over by some version of the third term of the old dialectical synthesis, claiming to annihilate gender dualism while actually annihilating only the fact of difference. As exemplified in the texts I am about to discuss, works by men (when they do not see women as debased, trivial sex objects) damn women as authoritarian and murderously emasculating—Ken Kesey's Big Nurse in *One Flew Over the Cuckoo's Nest* (1962) is the defining instance of that representation—while works by women affirm the feminine as the only force that can save culture, civilization, the planet, from destruction by the violence and aggression of the masculine.

A juxtaposition of a canvas from Willem de Kooning's "Woman" series with one of Judy Chicago's "Dinner Party" place settings would make this configuration painfully clear. In de Kooning, the liberating, frightening power of Picasso's bathers in "Les demoiselles" has become purely horrific and alienated. We no longer have the sense that the feminine *is* the new aesthetic practice, a practice invented in the process of representing the feminine in modernist terms. Rather, we have the sense that the techniques of abstract expressionism, so derivative from cubism, are being used to convince us of the disgusting, deathly horror of woman. In Chicago, we again have the use of an already-achieved aesthetic technique, this time to convince us of the beauty and deeply resonant nature-power of sexuate female body shapes.

I find exemplary of this early postmodern paradigm Adrienne Rich's poem "Diving into the Wreck," 1972, and John Barth's story "Night-Sea Journey," 1966, from *Lost in the Funhouse*, 1968.[3] "Diving into the Wreck" is a self-conscious, ambitious, literate poem about what Rich calls elsewhere "a whole new poetry beginning here."[4] Rich in this period was the preeminent poet of the feminine as salvation from masculine aggression:[5]

Meanwhile, another kind of being
was constructing itself, blindly

—a mutant, some had said:
the blood-compelled exemplar

of a "botched civilization"
as one of them called it

children picking up guns
for that is what it means to be a man

.　.　.　.　.　.　.　.　.　.　.　.

and that kind of being has lain in our beds
declaring itself our desire

requiring women's blood for life
a woman's breast to lay its nightmare on

.　.　.　.　.　.　.　.　.　.　.　.

My heart is moved by all I cannot save:
so much has been destroyed

I have to cast my lot with those
who age after age, perversely,

with no extraordinary power,
reconstitute the world.[6]

"Those who . . . reconstitute the world" are women—the mothers and weavers. The earth is the birth-mother who delivers us, and must deliver us from male destruction—in section 13 of the poem, the speaker sees the discarded weaving of anonymous women as "still urging us, urging on / our work . . . to help the earth deliver" (67). It is characteristic of the feminist position Rich represents here that Pound is for her "one of them," a "blood-compelled exemplar" of the "botched civilization" that Pound, his modernist ironies and complexities of persona overriden, is seen to have equated simplistically with woman.[7] The straightforward, uncomplicated condemnation of the masculine and affirmation of the feminine in "Natural Resources" are also characteristic.

"Diving into the Wreck" directly engages the themes and motifs of this study.[8] The first stanza has the speaker donning the stiff, waterproof "body-armor," the "absurd flippers," the "grave and awkward mask" of the scuba diver, protective gear surrounded by negative adjectives. She is putting on as alien costume the persona of masculine culture represented in "*the* book of myths":

> First having read the book of myths,
> and loaded the camera,
> and checked the edge of the knife-blade,
> I put on
> the body-armor of black rubber
> the absurd flippers
> the grave and awkward mask.

The camera and knife are masculine culture's tools/weapons of knowledge as violent domination, knowledge of the sort recorded in the book of myths.

This speaker, however, is not supported by the culture whose representative persona she has (perforce) adopted:

> I am having to do this
> not like Cousteau with his
> assiduous team
> aboard the sun-flooded schooner
> but here alone.

"Cousteau" invokes successful, well-paid, well-advertised, masculine-scientific adventure; the "assiduous team" invokes both male bonding and masculine hierarchy; the "sun-flooded" schooner invokes logos. "Here alone," on the other hand, is the naked and revealed female speaker, present, in the poem, with her reader.

In the second, third, and fourth stanzas, the speaker somewhat self-pityingly descends: "My flippers cripple me, / I crawl like an insect down the ladder / and there is no one / to tell me when the ocean / will begin." But as she enters the blackness of the sea, leaving behind the paternal sun, she begins to feel a kind of sea-mobility reminiscent of the instructions Conrad's Stein gives about immersing in the destructive element: "the sea is another story / the sea is not a question of power / I have to learn alone / to turn my body without force / in the deep element." Turning her body without force in the deep element, in the fifth stanza, she meets "so many who have always / lived here / swaying their crenellated fans / between the reefs / and besides / you breathe differently down here." She has entered, or returned to, and knows it, the realm of feminine sea-change.

The speaker's pleasure at turning her body in the maternal element has almost made her "forget / what [she] came for," but in the sixth stanza, exactly midway through the poem, she reminds herself: "I came to explore the wreck. / The words are purposes. / The words are maps." The referent of "the words" is ambiguous. "The words" might be "I came to explore the wreck," and/or the words in the crucial book of myths, and/ or the words of this poem as it is being written. Generally, I would argue, "the words" refers to the poem's project of reclaiming for language the truth of the wreck, which involves seeing "the damage that was done / and the treasures that prevail":

> the thing I came for:
> the wreck and not the story of the wreck
> the thing itself and not the myth
> the drowned face always staring
> toward the sun
> the evidence of damage
> worn by salt and sway into this threadbare beauty
> the ribs of the disaster
> curving their assertion
> among the tentative haunters.

The speaker sees herself as poet of an essential, unmediated truth—the truth of the wreck—that has been distorted by the patriarchal book of myths. "The drowned face always staring / toward the sun" suggests that this wreck is the death of patriarchal culture, dead because its eyes can turn only toward the sun. Later, the speaker, in an effort to subsume all gender positions in her voice, says "I am he / whose drowned face sleeps with open eyes." The "open eyes" allude to "those are pearls that were his eyes," the great sea-change undergone by the dead father. That drowned face always staring toward the paternal sun, just as in Ariel's song and in *The Waste Land*, to both of which this poem alludes, is "evidence of damage / worn by salt and sway into this threadbare beauty." The truth of the wreck distorted by masculine myth, in other words—the wreck and not the story of the wreck—is that sea-change is a good thing. The "ribs of the disaster" are "curving their assertion": out of "disaster," the (self-)destruction of patriarchal culture, comes the "assertion" of the female "treasures that prevail" in the "deep element," the swayers of "crenellated fans," for example—an image reminiscent of Rachel Vinrace's initial, hopeful daughter-vision of the ocean's maternal legacy.

In the next two stanzas, the speaker becomes an androgynous mermaid/merman ("I am here, the mermaid whose dark hair / streams black, the merman in his armored body . . . I am she: I am he"). The speaker goes on to *become*, in order to tell the truth about them, the wreck's sea-changed paternal owner, its rotten cargo of semiprecious exploited goods, taken for profit out of colonized mother earth by men, and its useless, "fouled" instruments of (patriarchal) navigation, that, tellingly, "once held to a course." These are not the "treasures that prevail."

The last stanza seems to suggest that the act itself of encountering the wreck, the project enunciated *in this poem* of rewriting the story of the wreck, the story of sea-change, as a book of feminine truth rather than a book of false patriarchal myth, is the treasure that prevails:

We are, I am, you are
by cowardice or courage
the one who find our way
back to this scene
carrying a knife, a camera
a book of myths
in which
our names do not appear.

"We are, I am, you are / . . . the one who find our way" includes the androgynous position staked out in the eighth stanza and also refers to the joint identity of (female) speaker and reader suggested in the opening stanza. It is the leveling-transcendent, too easily claimed third term of dialectical synthesis, taking care of difference by means of a few pronouns and an altered conjugation.

"*Back* to this scene" suggests the womb-return metaphor that underlies the entire poem. The last four lines make explicit the poem's feminist position: the book of myths' distortion of the truth of the wreck is a result of its deletion of "our" names, women's names, from the cultural record. The maternal feminine element in which we have immersed in this poem is destructive only to moribund patriarchy. For women (and mermen) it is the site and enabler of culture's new truth-telling, womb for a whole new poetry "beginning here," in this poem (stanza eight begins "This is the place").

In John Barth's "Night-Sea Journey," the first-person story of one sperm cell's heroic swim to the ovum, the maternal feminine element is, diametrically opposite to Rich's, purely destructive, a murderous engine of cruel love. (Destruction of the echt-masculine speaker and his comrades-in-swim is assumed without question to be the same as destruction in general.) The tone and style of this story are also radically different from those of Rich's poem, not merely of course because it is a story and not a poem or because it is comic, but because it is excessive, outrageous, absurd, mock-heroic, and self-satirical, while Rich's poem is spare, compact, and earnest. But in addition to those differences, there are also surprising similarities between the two works in purpose, vision, structure, representation of gender, and literary self-positioning.

Barth opens his story (the first in *Lost in the Funhouse*) with characteristic self-reflexivity: "One way or another, no matter which theory of our journey is correct, it's myself I address; to whom I rehearse as to a stranger our history and condition, and will disclose my secret hope though I sink for it" (3). As in "Diving," the speaker claims an inclusive, universal position ("our journey," with its vast metaphysical ramifications) while in fact speaking exclusively for one gender. Also as in "Diving," "it's myself I address": despite these claims to universality, despite invocations to "our journey" or "We are, I am, you are," these works are solipsistic and megalomaniacal, their first-person voices announcing themselves as prophets of a new consciousness. Barth's sperm cell is the only swimmer of millions to reach the Shore, to tell the story of the swim, and, if he is lucky, to rewrite that story ("my secret hope"); Rich's speaker is "here alone," first diver into the hold, sole new consciousness capable of rejecting the book of myths and telling for the first time the truth of the wreck. Barth's sperm cell and Rich's speaker both become estranged from themselves (Barth's sperm cell speaks to himself "as to a stranger"; Rich's speaker dons alien mask and costume, then becomes mermaid/merman) in order to "rehearse our history and condition," and then to imagine changing it.

The most evident similarity between the two works is that both are structured as journeys toward the womb (or, in Barth's case, the fallopian tube), with the moment of arrival serving as the climax of the piece. Both simultaneously use and undercut the tradition of the sea journey as heroic quest: Barth by satire, Rich by the rejection of "myth" and by the motif of return. Both connect the maternal feminine explicitly to Arielian sea-change (the sperm cell describes his nearing approach to the ovum as "the recent sea-change" [9]); of course, the crusade of Barth's sperm cell is against this sea-change, while Rich's speaker has come to salvage and be saved by it.

At the end of his terrible journey, when he is about to succumb in spite of himself to the lure of the siren-ovum, the sperm cell addresses his possible offspring, assumed to be masculine:

I am he who abjures and rejects the night-sea journey! I. . . .
   I am all love. "Come!" She whispers, and I have no will.
   You who I may be about to become, whatever You are: with the last twitch of my real self I beg You to listen. It is *not* love that sustains me! No; though Her magic makes me burn to sing the contrary, and though I drown even now for the blasphemy, I will say truth. What has fetched me across the dreadful sea is a single hope, gift of my poor dead comrade [a sceptical philosopher-sperm who did not finish the swim]: that You may be stronger-willed than I, and that by sheer force of concentration I may transmit to You, along with Your official Heritage, a private legacy of awful recollection and negative resolve. Mad as it may be, my dream is that some unimaginable embodiment of myself (or myself plus Her if that's how it must be) will come to find itself expressing, in however garbled or radical a translation, some reflection of these reflections. If against all odds this comes to pass, may You to whom, through whom I speak, do what I cannot: terminate this aimless, brutal business! Stop Your hearing against Her song! Hate love! (11–12)

The hatred of the maternal feminine as locus of sexuate destruction could not be more clearly (if self-mockingly) expressed. Not only is the offspring assumed to be male, but the sperm-narrator hopes that offspring might be purely "embodiment of myself": Irigaray's account of the masculine fantasy of self-generation. While Rich hopes to retrieve the maternal feminine truth from the distortion of masculine myth, Barth hopes for a terminal "end to night-sea journeys! Make no more!" (12).

Both works couch their hatred of the other gender (the sperm calls "She" "other-than-a-he" [10]) in facile ideals of gender fusion that the predominant agenda of the work undercuts. We have seen Rich's gestures toward androgyny and communal identity; Barth (through the theories of the sperm cell's philosophical dead friend) describes the "purpose of the night-sea journey" as "*consummation, transfiguration, union of contraries, transcension of categories* . . . She and Hero, Shore and Swimmer, 'merged identities' to become something both and neither" (10). But he also uses a prime patriarchal cliché to describe the difference between the two "complementary" genders: the male as "destiny" and the female as "destination."[9]

The speakers in these texts hope, through anti-heroic or mock-heroic discovery and transmission of new knowledge to same-gender inheritors utterly changed by this knowledge, to defeat the other gender, the Enemy. A vision of the two genders as irretrievably sundered, of gender relations as irretrievably antagonistic, coated over by a vision of third-term synthetic transcendence of difference, underlies these works. Both the literature and the politics of the radical, countercultural sixties and early seventies, redeemingly progressive though they were in many ways, proved to be contaminated by this gender ideology.

NOTES

INTRODUCTION

1. William Shakespeare, *The Tempest*, ed. Northrop Frye (Baltimore: Penguin, 1959), I.ii.397–402. Subsequent quotations from this source will hereafter be cited parenthetically in the text by act, scene, and line number.

Cora Kaplan begins the Introduction to her *Sea Changes: Essays on Culture and Feminism* (London: Verso, 1986), with Ariel's song. Like her, I am interested in the possibility of "political transformation" (1) it suggests.

2. Virginia Woolf describes the appeal to the modernist sensibility of Elizabethan richness and strangeness in her essays "The Elizabethan Lumber Room" and "Notes on an Elizabethan Play," in *The Common Reader, First Series* (New York: Harcourt, Brace & World, 1925), 40–58. In reading Hakluyt, for example, "One is for ever untying this packet here, sampling that heap over there, wiping the dust off some vast map of the world, and sitting down in semi-darkness to snuff the strange smells of silks and leathers and ambergris, while outside tumble the huge waves of the uncharted Elizabethan sea" (40).

3. Modern drama lies outside the provenance of this study. There is no question that it evolved in conjunction with late nineteenth-century class and gender politics—that case need not be made. See, for example, Bernard Shaw, *The Quintessence of Ibsenism* (1913; reprint, New York: Hill and Wang, 1957). Most relevantly for this study, Ibsen's *The Lady From the Sea* (1888) opposes an oppressive masculine hierarchical, patriarchal order to a powerful sexuate feminine sea-force of dangerously anarchic freedom. The former prevails at the end of the play by modifying itself according to the tenets of feminism.

For work on concatenations of gender, class, and race in turn-of-the-century politics, history, and narrative as well as drama, see Elaine Showalter, *Sexual Anarchy: Gender and Culture at the Fin de Siècle* (New York: Viking, 1990), and Jane Marcus, "The Feminist Critic Reads Men: Wilde, Meredith, Ibsen," in *Art and Anger: Reading Like a Woman* (Columbus: Ohio State University Press, 1988), 3–70.

Steven Marcus makes clear, in a synthesis profoundly relevant to this study, Freud's centrality to this concatenation of modern drama and modernist narrative form in his essay "Freud and Dora: Story, History, Case History," from *In Dora's Case: Freud-Hysteria-Feminism*, ed. Charles Bernheimer and Claire Kahane (New York: Columbia University Press, 1985), 56–91:

> The general form of what Freud has written bears certain suggestive resemblances to a modern experimental novel. Its narrative and expository course, for example, is neither linear nor rectilinear; instead its organization is plastic, involuted, and heterogeneous and follows spontaneously an inner logic that seems frequently to be at odds with itself; it often loops back around itself and is multidimensional in its representation of both its material and itself. *Its continuous innovations in formal structure seem unavoidably to be dictated by its*

substance, by the dangerous, audacious, disreputable, and problematical char-acter of the experiences being represented and dealt with ... In content, how-ever, what Freud has written is in parts rather like a play by Ibsen, or more precisely like a series of Ibsen's plays. (64, italics added)

4. Julia Kristeva, *About Chinese Women*, trans. Anita Barrows (London: Marion Boyars, 1977), 38.

5. Perry Anderson, in "Modernity and Revolution," *New Left Review* 144 (March–April 1984): 96–113, refers to "the haze of social revolution drifting across the horizon of this epoch" (104). Subsequent quotations from this source will hereafter be cited parenthetically in the text by page number.

6. In *The Political Unconscious: Narrative as a Socially Symbolic Act* (Ithaca: Cornell University Press, 1981), Fredric Jameson, using Conrad as exemplary writer, focuses on the historical moment of the emergence of modernist narrative. This study is greatly influenced by Jameson's book, in that focus and in many other ways. Subsequent quotations from this source will hereafter be cited paren-thetically in the text by page number.

7. Michael Levenson, *A Genealogy of Modernism* (Cambridge: Cambridge University Press, 1984), vii.

8. Marshall Berman, *All That Is Solid Melts Into Air* (New York: Simon & Schuster, 1982).

9. Alice Jardine, *Gynesis: Configurations of Woman and Modernity* (Ithaca: Cornell University Press, 1985). Jameson, *Political Unconscious*, works by Luce Irigaray and Klaus Theweleit to be discussed in chapter 1, and *Gynesis* have had the greatest influence on this study. Subsequent quotations from this source will hereafter be cited parenthetically in the text by page number.

10. Malcolm Bradbury and James McFarlane, *Modernism* (Harmondsworth: Penguin, 1976), 30.

11. Ricardo J. Quinones, *Mapping Literary Modernism* (Princeton: Princeton University Press, 1985).

12. Eugene Lunn, *Marxism and Modernism: A Historical Study of Lukács, Brecht, Benjamin and Adorno* (Berkeley: University of California Press, 1982). Subsequent quotations from this source will hereafter be cited parenthetically in the text by page number. For documents in the modernism debates Lunn analyzes, see *Aesthetics and Politics*, ed. Perry Anderson et al. (London: New Left Books, 1977).

13. Naomi Schor considers close reading, or "reading in detail," a *feminist* act of reading, because the detail is gendered feminine in modern Western culture. See *Reading in Detail: Aesthetics and the Feminine* (New York: Methuen, 1987).

My method of reading here assumes not just textual disjunction but also a text that continually, moment by moment, reassesses and recreates itself, often with one moment of the text being produced in reaction *against* the previous moment.

14. In addition to Bradbury and McFarlane's *Modernism*, the two most useful anthologies are *The Idea of the Modern in Literature and the Arts*, ed. Irving Howe (New York: Horizon Press, 1967), and *The Modern Tradition*, ed. Richard Ellmann and Charles Feidelson (New York: Oxford University Press, 1965). Some of the recent general works on modernism I have also found useful: Matei Calinescu, *Faces of Modernity: Avant-Garde, Decadence, Kitsch* (Bloomington:

Indiana University Press, 1977); Mark Conroy, *Modernism and Authority: Strategies of Legitimation in Flaubert and Conrad* (Baltimore: Johns Hopkins University Press, 1985); Astradur Eysteinsson, *The Concept of Modernism* (Ithaca: Cornell University Press, 1991); Andreas Huyssen, *After the Great Divide: Modernism, Mass Culture, Postmodernism* (Bloomington: Indiana University Press, 1986); Hugh Kenner, *A Homemade World: The American Modernist Writers* (New York: Morrow, 1975); Kenner, *The Mechanic Muse* (New York: Oxford University Press, 1986); Kenner, *The Pound Era* (Berkeley: University of California Press, 1971); Frank Lentricchia, *Ariel and the Police* (Madison: University of Wisconsin Press, 1988); James Longenbach, *Modernist Poetics of History: Pound, Eliot, and the Sense of the Past* (Princeton: Princeton University Press, 1987); Perry Meisel, *The Myth of the Modern* (New Haven: Yale University Press, 1987); Louis Menand, *Discovering Modernism: T. S. Eliot and His Context* (New York: Oxford University Press, 1987); *Modernism: Challenges and Perspectives*, ed. Monique Chefdor, Ricardo Quinones, and Albert Wachtel (Urbana: University of Illinois Press, 1986); *Modernism Reconsidered*, ed. Robert Kiely (Cambridge: Harvard University Press, 1983); Jeffrey M. Perl, *The Tradition of Return: The Implicit History of Modern Literature* (Princeton: Princeton University Press, 1984); Marjorie Perloff, *The Poetics of Indeterminacy: Rimbaud to Cage* (Princeton: Princeton University Press, 1981); Richard Poirier, *The Renewal of Literature: Emersonian Reflections* (New York: Random House, 1987), especially chapter 2, "Modernism and Its Difficulties," 95–113; Timothy J. Reiss, *The Discourse of Modernism* (Ithaca: Cornell University Press, 1982); Andrew Ross, *The Failure of Modernism: Symptoms of American Poetry* (New York: Columbia University Press, 1986).

15. Herbert Marcuse, *The Aesthetic Dimension: Toward a Critique of Marxist Aesthetics* (Boston: Beacon, 1978).

16. Edward Said, *Beginnings: Intention and Method* (Baltimore: Johns Hopkins University Press, 1975).

17. See "Selected Bibliographies" of modernist women writers in *The Norton Anthology of Literature by Women: The Tradition in English*, ed. Sandra Gilbert and Susan Gubar (New York: Norton, 1985), 2391–2430. For general works on women modernists and experimentalists, see Shari Benstock, *Women of the Left Bank: Paris, 1900–1940* (Austin: University of Texas Press, 1986); *Breaking the Sequence: Women's Experimental Fiction*, ed. Ellen Friedman and Miriam Fuchs (Princeton: Princeton University Press, 1989); Rachel Blau DuPlessis, *Writing Beyond the Ending: Narrative Strategies of Twentieth-Century Women Writers* (Bloomington: Indiana University Press, 1985); *The Gender of Modernism*, ed. Bonnie Kime Scott (Bloomington: Indiana University Press, 1990); Sandra Gilbert and Susan Gubar, *No Man's Land: The Place of the Woman Writer in the Twentieth Century* (New Haven: Yale University Press), vol. 1, *The War of the Words*, 1988, vol. 2, *Sexchanges*, 1989, and vol. 3, *Letters From the Front*, forthcoming; Susan Rubin Suleiman, *Subversive Intent: Gender Politics and the Avant-Garde* (Cambridge: Harvard University Press, 1990); also, *Women's Studies* 13 (December 1986), special issue on *The Female Imagination and the Modernist Aesthetic*, and *Tulsa Studies in Women's Literature* 8, no. 1 (Spring 1989), special issue, *Toward a Gendered Modernity*.

18. The most powerful arguments of this type have been made by Virginia Woolf, explicitly in *A Room of One's Own* (New York: Harcourt, Brace & World, 1929), and implicitly in "Modern Fiction," in *The Common Reader*, and in "Mr. Bennett and Mrs. Brown," in *The Captain's Death Bed and Other Essays* (New York: Harcourt, Brace & World, 1950). Some American works of diverse provenance: *Breaking the Sequence*, ed. Friedman and Fuchs; Carolyn Burke, "Getting Spliced: Modernist Poetry and Sexual Difference," *American Quarterly* 39, no. 1 (Spring 1987): 98–121; DuPlessis, *Writing Beyond the Ending*; Kathleen Fraser, "The Tradition of Marginality," unpublished essay, The Poetry Project, St. Mark's Church, New York, June 6, 1985; Suzette Henke, *James Joyce and the Politics of Desire* (New York: Routledge, 1990); Margaret Homans, "'Her Very Own Howl': The Ambiguities of Representation in Recent Women's Fiction," *Signs* 9, no. 2 (1983): 186–205; Jardine, *Gynesis*; E. Ann Kaplan, *Women and Film: Both Sides of the Camera* (New York: Methuen, 1983); Laura Mulvey, "Feminism, Film and the *Avant-Garde*," in *Women Writing and Writing About Women*, ed. Mary Jacobus (London: Croom Helm, 1979); Anaïs Nin, *The Novel of the Future* (New York: Macmillan, 1970); Suleiman, *Subversive Intent*.

Jardine's notion of "gynesis" does not connect modernist form with écriture féminine. Instead, it sees the discourse-disruptions of modernity *as* the cultural feminine itself. Gynesis is "the putting into discourse of 'woman' as that *process* diagnosed in France as intrinsic to the condition of modernity; indeed, the valorization of the feminine, woman ... as somehow intrinsic to new and necessary modes of thinking, writing, speaking" (25). This notion of the *valorization* of woman, or the feminine, reiterated several times throughout Jardine's book (26, 73, 200), is different from my notion of modernist *sous-rature*.

19. Rachel Blau DuPlessis and the Members of Workshop 9, "For the Etruscans: Sexual Difference and Artistic Production—The Debate Over a Female Aesthetic," in *The Future of Difference*, ed. Hester Eisenstein and Alice Jardine (Boston: G. K. Hall, 1980), 150.

20. Julia Kristeva, "Oscillation Between Power and Denial," trans. Marilyn A. August, in *New French Feminisms*, ed. Elaine Marks and Isabelle de Courtivron (Amherst: University of Massachusetts Press, 1980), 165.

21. Poirier, "Modernism and Its Difficulties," is particularly helpful on the issue of difficulty. On these debates in general, see Lunn, *Marxism and Modernism*, and Anderson, ed., *Aesthetics and Politics*.

22. Kenner, *A Homemade World*, xi–xii.

23. See Houston A. Baker, *Modernism and the Harlem Renaissance* (Chicago: University of Chicago Press, 1987).

24. Leslie Fishbein, *Rebels in Bohemia: The Radicals of The Masses* (Chapel Hill: University of North Carolina Press, 1982).

25. Daniel Aaron, *Writers on the Left* (New York: Oxford University Press, 1961), 271–72.

26. For an account of the difference between New Critical close reading and its contemporary at Harvard, a different sort of close reading predictive in some ways of deconstruction, see Richard Poirier, "Hum 6, or Reading before Theory," *Raritan* 9, no. 4 (Spring 1990): 14–31.

27. Needless to say, a great deal of nonmodernist fiction and poetry was writ-

ten in the modernist period, even by writers I would associate with modernism. For example, in Kate Chopin's "The Storm," 1898, a deluge brings about an unambiguously positive release of illicit female desire, and in Stephen Crane's "The Open Boat," also of 1898, the raging ocean is an unambiguously negative locus of alienation and death. Later, Robert Graves revived the Romantic, sea-linked "femme fatale" in his *White Goddess* mythologies, the "Virgin" of "silver beauty" whose "brow was creamy as the crested wave," but who is *really* "the undying snake from chaos hatched, / Whose coils contain the ocean," ("To Juan at the Winter Solstice," 1945), to whom the Sun-Hero inevitably falls prey.

Versions of nineteenth-century realism continue now, in fact, to dictate the formal conventions of commercially successful fiction, since the middle class dominates the fiction market. Much nonmodernist fiction (utopian fantasy as well as standard realism) written in the modernist period provided straightfor-ward, nonsuppressed representations of aspects of socialism and feminism. I would argue that these fictions (see, for example, Howells's *A Hazard of New Fortunes*, 1890, or Gilman's *Herland*, 1915), lack the subversive, destabilizing power of the modernist suppressed and reinscribed representations, which enact at the deep level of form modernist culture's ambivalence (frightened desire, de-siring fear) toward the revolutionary horizon. See my "History as Suppressed Referent in Modernist Fiction," *ELH* 51, no. 1 (Spring 1984): 137–52, which is indebted to Jameson's analysis of *Nostromo* in *The Political Unconscious*.

See also George Levine, *The Realistic Imagination: English Fiction from Frank-enstein to Lady Chatterley* (Chicago: University of Chicago Press, 1987), for a very different view of the relationship between nineteenth-century realism and twentieth- century modernism, with the former seen as already containing many of the latter's most important attributes: "realism is itself intimately and authori-tatively connected to the modernist position" (3).

28. Henry James, *The Portrait of a Lady* (1881; reprint, New York: Signet, 1963), 544. Subsequent quotations from this source will hereafter be cited par-enthetically in the text by page number. For an analysis of the occulted maternal in this novel, see Beth Sharon Ash, "Frail Vessels and Vast Designs: A Psycho-analytic Portrait of Isabel Archer," in *New Essays on "The Portrait of a Lady,"* ed. Joel Porte (Cambridge: Cambridge University Press, 1990), 123–62.

29. Grace Paley, "A Conversation With My Father," in *Enormous Changes at the Last Minute* (1974; reprint, New York: Dell, 1975), 167.

30. George Eliot, *The Mill on the Floss* (1860; reprint, New York: Signet, 1965), 545–46. Subsequent quotations from this source will hereafter be cited parenthetically in the text by page number. Note, for future reference, the contrast between Eliot's "daisied fields" and the perfectly ambiguous flowered field that closes the climactic drowning in *The Awakening*.

31. Charles Dickens, *Our Mutual Friend* (1864–65; reprint, Harmondsworth: Penguin, 1971), 585. Subsequent quotations from this source will hereafter be cited parenthetically in the text by page number.

32. For a discussion of homoeroticism in this novel, see Eve Kosofsky Sedgwick, *Between Men: English Literature and Male Homosocial Desire* (New York: Columbia University Press, 1985), chapter 9: "Homophobia, Misogyny, and Capital: The Example of *Our Mutual Friend*," 161–79.

33. Even the American deconstructionist reader, committed to ferreting out undecidability, would have to acknowledge that these texts construct themselves as decidable, with positive-negative dualisms at least ostensibly intact.

CHAPTER 1
MODERNISM UNDER ERASURE

1. Perry Anderson, "Modernity and Revolution," *New Left Review* 144 (March–April 1984): 96–113 (reprinted in *Marxism and the Interpretation of Culture*, ed. Cary Nelson and Lawrence Grossberg [Urbana: University of Illinois Press, 1988], 317–33). Subsequent quotations from this source will hereafter be cited parenthetically in the text by page number.

2. See Raymond Williams, *Marxism and Literature* (Oxford: Oxford University Press, 1977).

3. For a definitive treatment of this phenomenon, see Marjorie Perloff, *The Futurist Moment: Avant-Garde, Avant-Guerre, and the Language of Rupture* (Chicago: University of Chicago Press, 1986).

4. I am using the term "feminism" here anachronistically. For a history of the emergence of twentieth-century feminism from the nineteenth-century woman movement in the United States, see Nancy F. Cott, *The Grounding of Modern Feminism* (New Haven: Yale University Press, 1987).

5. Joseph Conrad, *Lord Jim*, ed. Thomas C. Moser (1900; reprint, New York: Norton, 1968), 5. Jameson, *The Political Unconscious*, 210–11. Subsequent quotations from these sources will hereafter be cited parenthetically in the text by page number.

6. "At once inside and outside a certain Hegelian and Heideggerian tradition, Derrida, then, is asking us to change certain habits of mind: the authority of the text is provisional, the origin is a trace; contradicting logic, we must learn to use and erase our language at the same time." Gayatri Chakravorty Spivak, Translator's Preface, in Jacques Derrida, *Of Grammatology* (Baltimore: Johns Hopkins University Press, 1976), xviii. See, for example, "The Outside Is the Inside," *Of Grammatology*, 44. My appropriation of this term here is, again, loose, emblematic, not in strict adherence to its rigorous Heideggerian-Derridean philosophical signification—inspired by rather than scrupulously faithful to Derrida.

Theodor Adorno's formulations of the "negativity" of "autonomous"—i.e., certain modes of modernist and avant-garde—art are highly relevant to my work here. He sees in some (rather select) forms of modernist and avant-garde art a version of the unresolved dialectic, between the hegemonic "culture industry" and its critical subversions in an "autonomous" art that is determined by reaction to that "industry" at the same time that it is subversive of it. See Theodor Adorno and Max Horkheimer, *Dialectic of Enlightenment*, trans. John Cumming (New York: Herder and Herder, 1972), and Adorno, *Aesthetic Theory*, trans. C. Lenhardt (London: Routledge & Kegan Paul, 1984). For a very helpful analysis of Adorno's ideas in relation to his debate with Walter Benjamin over the subversive potential of popular culture, see Lunn, *Marxism and Modernism*.

7. Derrida, *Of Grammatology*, 87.

8. Needless to say, this quality of self-contradiction is not exclusive to the modernist text. It appears throughout literary history, but most notably, I would

argue, at times of historical transition comparable to the advent of modernity; for example, in Shakespeare, Milton, and Blake. Unsynthesized dialectic characterizes modernist texts more pervasively, however, than it does works of other periods. As Marcia Ian says in her unpublished essay, "Two's Company, Three's a Construction: Psychoanalysis and the Failure of Identity," "early modernist art . . . went out of its way to declare its allegiance to the law of contradiction, to announce that it found the law of non-contradiction a bore" (6).

9. Terry Eagleton, *William Shakespeare* (Oxford and New York: Basil Blackwell, 1986), ix, emphasis added.

10. Eugene Lunn, *Marxism and Modernism*, 34–37.

11. Cleanth Brooks, "The Language of Paradox," in *The Well Wrought Urn* (New York: Harcourt, Brace & World, 1947), 3–21; William Empson, *Seven Types of Ambiguity* (New York: New Directions, 1947), 192.

12. F. Scott Fitzgerald, *The Crack-Up*, ed. Edmund Wilson (New York: Scribner's, 1945), 69.

13. Maurice Merleau-Ponty, "Cézanne's Doubt," in *Sense and Non-sense*, trans. Hubert L. Dreyfus and Patricia Allen Dreyfus (Evanston: Northwestern University Press, 1964), 12.

14. *Complete Works of Oscar Wilde* (New York: The Pearson Publishing Co., 1909), 1078.

15. Wallace Stevens, *The Necessary Angel: Essays on Reality and the Imagination* (New York: Random House, 1942); for example, "unreal things have a reality of their own" ("The Noble Rider and the Sound of Words," 4); or, "Let be be finale of seem," line 7 of "The Emperor of Ice Cream," *Harmonium*, 1923. Marianne Moore, "imaginary gardens with real toads in them," line 32 of "Poetry," 1921 version, *Poems*, 1921. William Carlos Williams, "No ideas / but in things," lines 9–10 of "A Sort of a Song," *The Wedge*, 1944. William Butler Yeats, *A Vision*, 1925, 1937.

16. I am aware of the vastness of this issue and also aware that I am treating the massiveness of its presence in the history of Western philosophy rather casually here. Binary and tripartite structures pervade Western thought and culture at every level.

17. Jacques Derrida, *Positions*, trans. Alan Bass (Chicago: University of Chicago Press, 1981), 41–44, no italics added. Subsequent quotations from this source will hereafter be cited parenthetically in the text by page number.

18. Julia Kristeva, *About Chinese Women*, 38.

19. Luce Irigaray, *Speculum of the Other Woman*, trans. Gillian C. Gill (Ithaca: Cornell University Press, 1985). Subsequent quotations from this source will hereafter be cited parenthetically in the text by page number.

20. See, for example, Jardine, *Gynesis*, 32–34; Jane Gallop, *The Daughter's Seduction: Feminism and Psychoanalysis* (Ithaca: Cornell University Press, 1982); Margaret Homans, *Bearing the Word* (Chicago: University of Chicago Press, 1986); *In Dora's Case*, ed. Charles Bernheimer and Claire Kahane, especially Jacqueline Rose, "Dora: Fragment of an Analysis," 128–48; or *Feminine Sexuality: Jacques Lacan and the école freudienne*, ed. Juliet Mitchell and Jacqueline Rose (New York: Norton, 1983).

21. *Speculum* 20; this is a direct quote from Freud, "Femininity," in *New Introductory Lectures on Psycho-Analysis*, vol. 22 of *The Standard Edition of the*

Complete Psychological Works of Sigmund Freud, ed. and trans. James Strachey (London: Hogarth Press, 1953–74), 102.

22. See Sedgwick, *Between Men*.

23. On the exchange of women or the traffic in women, see most notably Claude Lévi-Strauss, *The Elementary Structures of Kinship* (Boston: Beacon, 1969), and Gayle Rubin, "The Traffic in Women: Notes Toward a Political Economy of Sex," in *Toward an Anthropology of Women*, ed. Rayna Reiter (New York: Monthly Review Press, 1975), 157–210. Sedgwick, *Between Men*, is a definitive extension of these ideas and articulation of them in relation to English literature.

24. See Sarah Kofman, *The Enigma of Woman: Woman in Freud's Writings*, trans. Catherine Porter (Ithaca: Cornell University Press, 1985), for a brilliant analysis of Freud's recognition, and therefore subsequent misogynist suppression, of the power of the mother. See also Madelon Sprengnether, *The Spectral Mother: Freud, Feminism, and Psychoanalysis* (Ithaca: Cornell University Press, 1991).

As Gilbert and Gubar point out in *No Man's Land*, vol. 2: *Sexchanges*, Freud, and the male modernists as well, were responding to the turn-of-the-century derepression of the mother in anthropological theories of "matriarchy" that emerged in the wake of J. J. Bachofen's *Mother Right* of 1861.

25. See Sigmund Freud, *Moses and Monotheism*, trans. Katherine Jones (New York: Vintage, 1939), for the most detailed modern elaboration of this patriarchal myth.

26. See Friedrich Engels, *The Origin of the Family, Private Property, and the State* (New York: Pathfinder, 1972); see *Speculum* 125–26 and 140 for Irigaray's elaborations of these connections.

27. *Republic* VII, 514–18.

28. The echo of Part I here ("The Blind Spot of an Old Dream of Symmetry") is characteristic of Irigaray's self-echoing prose.

29. Irigaray is making use, of course, here and throughout this section, of the derivation of "hysteria" from the Greek "hystera," or womb.

30. The Sixth Tractate, "The Impassivity of the Unembodied," *Plotinus' Enneads*, trans. Stephen MacKenna, 2d ed., rev. by B. S. Page (London: Faber & Faber, 1956), 201–22.

31. See also "Volume-Fluidity," *Speculum* 227–40; and "The 'Mechanics' of Fluids," Irigaray, in *This Sex Which Is Not One*, trans. Catherine Porter with Carolyn Burke (Ithaca: Cornell University Press, 1985), 106–18.

32. There are, of course, crucial and numerous exceptions—Poseidon comes readily to mind. Generally, bodies of water on earth, particularly oceans, lakes, or ponds (rivers can go either way), lend themselves most readily to use as feminine iconography, rain to masculine. See *Encyclopedia Britannica*, 15th ed., vol. 26, 574.

33. Plotinus's rejection of the maternal analogy at the end of "Une Mère de Glace" has a quality of embarrassment, a product of his having realized where his argument tended and decided it would not do. Its effect, I would argue, is to reinforce the maternal analogy.

34. *Noblest of the Elements: A New Art Book and Engagement Book for 1987*, ed. Sally Fisher, design by Peter Oldenburg (New York: The Metropolitan Museum of Art, 1987).

35. Klaus Theweleit, *Women, Floods, Bodies, History*, vol. 1 of *Male Fantasies* (Minneapolis: University of Minnesota Press, 1987).

36. Gilles Deleuze and Félix Guattari, *Anti-Oedipus*, trans. Robert Hurley, Mark Seem, and Helen R. Lane (Minneapolis: University of Minnesota Press, 1983). Jardine, *Gynesis*, also makes use of this work.

37. The fountain is a good metaphor here, but, like a river, it can also go the other way. For example, the fountain is a figure of the maternal fecundity and life-force of Mrs. Ramsay in *To the Lighthouse* (while Mr. Ramsay is a "beaker of brass, barren and bare"); the fountain is also a feminine figure in Gertrude Stein's *Tender Buttons*.

38. Marcia Ian, "Two's Company": "in [Freudian] psychoanalysis, unlike in any other science, the law of noncontradiction does not apply. . . . in *The Interpretation of Dreams*, Freud was making a hermeneutical science out of the law of contradiction" (6).

39. Irigaray, *This Sex*. Many defend Irigaray against the charge of "biologism" in her rhetoric of writing the female body in *This Sex*. See, for example, Meaghan Morris, "The Pirate's Fiancée," in *The Pirate's Fiancée: Feminism, Reading, Postmodernism* (London: Verso, 1988), 64–65, where she argues that the "two lips" are cultural rather than biologist or essentialist.

CHAPTER 2
A DIFFERENT STORY

1. Henry James, *The Turn of the Screw*, 1898, in *The Turn of the Screw and Other Stories* (Harmondsworth: Penguin, 1969), 7–121. Subsequent quotations from this source will hereafter be cited parenthetically in the text by page number.

The initiatory and still important work of psychoanalytic criticism was Edmund Wilson, "The Ambiguity of Henry James," 1930, reprinted in *A Casebook on Henry James's The Turn of the Screw*, ed. Gerald Willen (New York: Krowell, 1960), 115–53. Analyses of *The Turn of the Screw* also appear in these influential psychoanalytically oriented books: Leo Bersani, *A Future for Astyanax: Character and Desire in Literature* (Boston: Little, Brown, 1976); Peter Brooks, *The Melodramatic Imagination* (New Haven: Yale University Press, 1976); Shoshana Felman, "Henry James: Madness and the Risks of Practice (Turning the Screw of Interpretation)," in *Writing and Madness*, trans. Martha Noel Evans, Shoshana Felman, with Brian Massumi (Ithaca: Cornell University Press, 1985), 141–247. It would be impossible to provide a representative, let alone inclusive, list of psychoanalytic works on this text. See n. 22, below.

2. Framing narration is a device as old as narrative itself, but it becomes a hallmark of modernist and postmodernist narrative.

3. Charlotte Perkins Gilman, "The Yellow Wallpaper" (1892; reprint, Old Westbury, NY: The Feminist Press, 1973). Subsequent quotations from this source will hereafter be cited parenthetically in the text by page number.

For other (partly congruent, partly divergent) feminist analyses of "The Yellow Wallpaper," see Gillian Brown, "The Empire of Agoraphobia," *Representations* 20 (Fall 1987): 134–57; Sandra Gilbert and Susan Gubar, *The Madwoman in the Attic: The Woman Writer and the Nineteenth-Century Literary Imagination* (New Haven: Yale University Press, 1979); Gilbert and Gubar, *No Man's Land*, vol. 2, *Sexchanges*; Janice Haney-Peritz, "Monumental Feminism and Literature's Ancestral House: Another Look at 'The Yellow Wallpaper,'" *Women's Studies* 12, no. 2 (1986): 113–28; Elaine R. Hedges's Afterword, in Gilman, "The Yellow Wallpaper"; Mary Jacobus, "An Unnecessary Maze of Sign-Reading," in *Reading Woman: Essays in Feminist Criticism* (New York: Columbia University Press, 1986), 229–48; Jean E. Kennard, "Convention Coverage or How to Read Your Own Life," *New Literary History* 8, no. 1 (1981): 69–88; Annette Kolodny, "A Map for Rereading: Or, Gender and the Interpretation of Literary Texts," *New Literary History* 11, no. 3 (1980): 451–67; Susan S. Lanser, "Feminist Criticism, 'The Yellow Wallpaper,' and the Politics of Color in America," *Feminist Studies* 15, no. 3 (Fall 1989), 415–41; William Veeder, "Who is Jane? The Intricate Feminism of Charlotte Perkins Gilman," *Arizona Quarterly* 44, no. 3 (1988), 40–79.

4. For a discussion of "The Yellow Wallpaper" as a work of modernist origination, see Marianne DeKoven, "Gendered Doubleness and the 'Origins' of Modernist Form," *Tulsa Studies in Women's Literature* 8, no. 1 (Spring 1989): 19–42.

5. See Veeder, "Who Is Jane?", and Jacobus, "Unnecessary Maze," on the presence of *Jane Eyre* in "The Yellow Wallpaper."

6. See Gilman's socialist-feminist *Women and Economics* (1898; reprint, New York: Harper & Row, 1966), and her feminist utopian novel *Herland* (1915; reprint, New York: Pantheon, 1979). See James's antifeminist novel *The Bostonians* (1886; reprint, Harmondsworth: Penguin, 1966) and his antisocialist, antianarchist novel *The Princess Casamassima* (1886; reprint, Harmondsworth: Penguin, 1977).

7. See Jacobus, "Unnecessary Maze," on the connection of the female gothic to the Freudian uncanny in "The Yellow Wallpaper."

8. This choice of a name for the master's country seat is highly significant. "Nellie Bly" was the pseudonym of Elizabeth Cochrane, 1867–1922, who took the name from a popular Stephen Foster love song. Cochrane was a "U.S. newspaper writer whose around-the-world race against a theoretical record made the name celebrated and a synonym for the feminine star reporter" (*Encyclopedia Britannica*, 15th ed., vol. 2, 304). In 1889–90, she beat Phileas Fogg's record. She was also a leftist-feminist muckraker: "Feigning insanity to get into the asylum on Blackwell's Island, she wrote an exposé that brought about needed reforms. Later she exposed tenement conditions, the techniques of 'mashers,' the Albany lobby, and the like" (304).

9. See John Carlos Rowe's chapter on *The Turn of the Screw*, "The Use and Abuse of Uncertainty," in his *The Theoretical Dimensions of Henry James* (Madison: University of Wisconsin Press, 1984), 120–46: "The transference of authority from ruler to ruled in James's writings is especially interesting because it seems regularly to result in the displacement of political and economic issues into psychological concerns of individual characters. Both *The Turn of the Screw* and the history of its interpretations are excellent illustrations of this sort of transference; both the narrative structure and diverse critical views of this work seem to concentrate on the psychology of the Governess to the significant exclusion of the work's wider social implications" (123).

10. See Hedges, Afterword, 46–47, for an account of Gilman's own disastrous rest cure.

11. See Gilbert and Gubar, *Madwoman*, 90.

12. See Jacobus, "Unnecessary Maze," 236, on John's repression of the unconscious. The entire essay concerns itself with an analysis of "The Yellow Wallpaper" as representation of, and rebellion against, patriarchal repression of the feminine/unconscious.

13. Lanser, "Feminist Criticism," sees "yellow" as the turn-of-the-century American racial other, whose inroads into American "racial purity" Gilman feared and detested just as much as she desired racial equality. This important reading adds to, rather than changes, the connection of yellow to feminine sexuality and its repression. Again, we see here a characteristic modernist conflation of racial otherness and the sexuate maternal feminine.

14. Jacobus, in "Unnecessary Maze," cites Jane Gallop's claim in *The Daughter's Seduction* that "smell in the Freudian text may have a privileged relation to female sexuality" (243).

15. Lanser's quotes from Gilman's pronouncements on race actually point to irreducible contradiction in her racial attitudes rather than the straightforward racism Lanser emphasizes. She argues that Gilman only *seems* egalitarian in her racial attitudes and that these quotes reveal her underlying racism. I would say, again, that her opinions are irreducibly contradictory.

16. For an account of this critical history, and particularly of the "apparitionist" versus "antiapparitionist" debate, see Charles Thomas Samuels, *The Ambiguity of Henry James* (Urbana: University of Illinois Press, 1971). See also Felman, "Henry James," and Rowe, "The Use and Abuse of Uncertainty." As Shlomith Rimmon says in *The Concept of Ambiguity* (Chicago: University of Chicago Press, 1977): "*The Turn of the Screw* has been so firmly linked with ambiguity that even people who have not read it know that it is somehow supposed to be ambiguous" (116).

17. See n. 1.

18. Note the marked beauty of her opening line: "I remember the whole beginning as a succession of flights and drops, a little see-saw of the right throbs and the wrong" (14).

See also James's letter of 1898 to H. G. Wells: "Therefore I had to rule out subjective complications of her own—play of tone etc; and keep her impersonal save for the most obvious and indispensable little note of neatness, firmness and courage." In *Selected Letters of Henry James*, ed. Leon Edel (New York: Farrar, Straus & Cudahy, 1960), 146; also in *The Turn of the Screw: Authoritative Text, Backgrounds and Sources, Essays in Criticism*, ed. Robert Kimbrough (New York: Norton, 1966), 111.

James is equally explicit in his 1908 New York Edition preface: "To knead the subject of my young friend's, the supposititious narrator's, mystification thick, and yet strain the expression of it so clear and fine that beauty would result: no side of the matter so revives for me as that endeavour" (120 in Kimbrough, ed., *Authoritative Text*).

19. See for example Samuels, *Ambiguity* (he accuses her of "vanity" [13]). He also calls her "a snob and a prude, conceited and self-justifying" (16), "murder-

ously ruthless in expression of her ideals" (20), and attacks her "moral pretensions and class envy" (21). Thomas M. Cranfill and Robert L. Clark, Jr., in *An Anatomy of The Turn of the Screw* (Austin: University of Texas Press, 1965), portray her in almost hysterical terms as a sort of monstrous Big Nurse, referring to her "concentration-camp surveillance" (158).

20. The evidence against the apparitions' existence is that no one else beside the narrator sees them and that Mrs. Grose and Flora in one episode, and Miles in another, explicitly fail to see them while they are appearing to the narrator. The evidence in favor of their existence is, first, that the narrator sees them in appropriate embodiment before she finds out from Mrs. Grose who they are or what they should look like. She describes Peter Quint so accurately after her first encounter with him that Mrs. Grose immediately knows it is he (36–37). (I would say that is the strongest piece of evidence in the text on either side of the debate.) Also, Flora does go to the spot across the pond where Miss Jessel first appeared to the narrator (95). Finally, Miles, when he fails to see Peter Quint in the final episode, asks whether it is Miss Jessel at the window (120–21).

That James himself was a convinced apparitionist is quite clear in the Preface: "I recognise again, that Peter Quint and Miss Jessel are not 'ghosts' at all, as we now know the ghost, but goblins, elves, imps, demons as loosely constructed as those of the old trials for witchcraft" (122).

21. Leo Bersani, *A Future for Astyanax*, 139. Subsequent quotations from this source will hereafter be cited parenthetically in the text.

22. Not, of course, an exhaustive list of contemporary critical approaches to James. As Richard A. Hocks says in *American Literary Scholarship 1986* (Durham: Duke University Press, 1988): "Like a huge magnet James continues to attract massive scholarship of every stripe and hue, from Adeline Tintner's 'old-fashioned' source/analogue studies (a banner year, even for her) to the most theoretical day-after-tomorrow analysis. I detect a new thematic interest in James's 'aestheticizing of capitalism,' as James Cox puts it, and more new psychoanalytic readings abound" (93).

23. See Felman, "Henry James," and Rowe, "Uses and Abuses," on the significance of the master's power. For a Foucauldian reading of issues of power in James, see Mark Seltzer, *Henry James and the Art of Power* (Ithaca: Cornell University Press, 1984).

24. See Nina Auerbach, *Woman and the Demon: The Life of a Victorian Myth* (Cambridge: Harvard University Press, 1982).

25. The evidence that Quint appears to the narrator on the old tower comes during her conversation with Mrs. Grose following her second confrontation with him: " 'Have you seen him before?' 'Yes—once. On the old tower' " (34).

26. This particular fact about Peter Quint is emphasized by reiteration: "She thought a minute. 'Was he a gentleman?' I found I had no need to think. 'No.' She gazed in deeper wonder. 'No' " (35). Again: " 'He's tall, active, erect,' I continued, 'but never—no, never!—a gentleman' " (36).

27. Miss Jessel is very close here to the "blazing" Victorian madwoman, type of displaced feminist rage, discussed by Gilbert and Gubar in *Madwoman*. Bertha Rochester of *Jane Eyre* is the locus classicus of this phenomenon. James's depiction of Miss Jessel in this scene is very similar (and perhaps indebted) to Brontë's

of Bertha. *Jane Eyre* echoes through this tale of an ambitious governess as it does through "The Yellow Wallpaper."

CHAPTER 3
DARKER AND LOWER DOWN

1. Joseph Conrad, *The Nigger of the "Narcissus"*, in *Three Great Tales* (New York: Vintage-Random House, n.d.); Gertrude Stein, "Melanctha," in *Three Lives* (New York: Vintage-Random House, 1936). Subsequent quotations from these sources will hereafter be cited parenthetically in the text by page number.

2. The argument of this chapter is indebted to Lisa Ruddick's "'Melanctha': The Costs of Mind-Wandering," in *Reading Gertrude Stein: Body, Text, Gnosis* (Ithaca: Cornell University Press, 1990), 12–54. Ruddick does not deal directly with the issue of race, but treats Melancthan mind-wandering as a subversive, destabilizing, ambiguous force in the text, discussing it in relation to Stein's constructions of gender and to William James's work on modes of attention.

3. Gertrude Stein, *The Autobiography of Alice B. Toklas* (New York: Vintage-Random House, 1933), 54.

4. The relevance of the issue of race to Stein's work, however, also comes to mind in relation to the original production of *Four Saints in Three Acts*, which used a black cast.

5. Gertrude Stein, *Q.E.D.*, in *Fernhurst, Q.E.D., and Other Early Writings* (New York: Liveright, 1971). For an illuminating account of the transformation of *Q.E.D.* into "Melanctha," see Leon Katz's introduction to this volume.

6. I discuss Gertrude Stein's complex relationship to the modernist and avant-garde traditions in "Gertrude Stein and the Modernist Canon," in *Gertrude Stein and the Making of Literature*, ed. Shirley Neuman and Ira B. Nadel (London: Macmillan; Boston: Northeastern University Press, 1988), 8–20, and in "Half In and Half Out of Doors: Gertrude Stein and Literary Tradition," in *A Gertrude Stein Companion: Content with the Example*, ed. Bruce Kellner (New York: Greenwood, 1988), 75–83.

7. And also, of course, in *Nostromo*. Some books and articles focusing on imperialism in Conrad: Patrick Brantlinger, "*Heart of Darkness*: Anti-Imperialism, Racism, or Impressionism?" *Criticism* 27, no. 4 (Fall 1985): 363–85; Hunt Hawkins, "Conrad and the Psychology of Colonialism," in *Conrad Revisited: Essays for the Eighties*, ed. Ross C. Murfin (University: University of Alabama Press, 1985), 71–87; Robert F. Lee, *Conrad's Colonialism* (The Hague: Mouton, 1969); John McClure, *Kipling and Conrad: The Colonial Fiction* (Cambridge: Harvard University Press, 1981); Benita Parry, *Conrad and Imperialism: Ideological Boundaries and Visionary Frontiers* (London: Macmillan, 1983); Alan Sandison, *The Wheel of Empire: A Study of the Imperial Idea in Some Late Nineteenth and Early Twentieth Century Fiction* (London: Macmillan, 1967).

8. Conrad is ostensibly conservative, like James; Stein is ostensibly "neutral," as in naturalism. See n. 14, below, for references to discussions of Conrad's politics.

9. I am guilty of that oversight in *A Different Language: Gertrude Stein's Experimental Writing* (Madison: University of Wisconsin Press, 1983). In my

case, and I suspect in many others, it is a result of mortified denial rather than indifference.

10. This projection of repressed sexuality onto blacks is a staple of racism. The difference in "Melanctha," as in *The Nigger of the "Narcissus,"* is that Stein and Conrad enter into the subjectivity of their racially other characters.

11. Wonderfully, "solidarity" continues to be a crucial Polish word.

As Ian Watt says in *Conrad in the Nineteenth Century* (Berkeley: University of California Press, 1979), "The word solidarity came into English in 1848, the Year of Revolutions and of the Communist Manifesto . . . Conrad's conservative tendencies, however, were in uneasy conflict both with his sceptical realism about human history, and with his basic social attitudes which, though certainly not democratic, were in many ways deeply egalitarian and individualist" (109–10).

Webster's Second International quotes the Preface to *The Nigger of the "Narcissus"* as its only instance of usage in its definition of "solidarity."

12. Watt is not alone in finding political tendencies in Conrad that are in "uneasy conflict" with his overt conservatism. Ford Madox Ford's account of Conrad's politics seems to have made Conrad's conservatism a given. He called Conrad "at heart an aristo-royalist apologist" and said that "the whole Left in politics was forever temperamentally suspect for him" (*Mightier Than the Sword* [London: George Allen & Unwin, 1938], 65). Gustav Morf, however, takes the opposite position in his influential *The Polish Heritage of Joseph Conrad* (New York: Haskell House, 1965), viii, seeing Conrad as "an incipient or repressed revolutionary" and his fiction "as a record of struggle with those latent tendencies." (I agree with Morf.) In *Conrad's Politics: Community and Anarchy in the Fiction of Joseph Conrad* (Baltimore: Johns Hopkins University Press, 1967), Avrom Fleishman, like Watt and also like Eloise Knapp Hay in *The Political Novels of Joseph Conrad: A Critical Study* (Chicago: University of Chicago Press, 1963), argues for the complexity and inconsistency of Conrad's politics: "Conrad was open to the prevailing political ideas of his time" (ix). Irving Howe argues that Conrad was fascinated by the anarchism he overtly discredits in his fiction, linking it to the disruptive work of the writer (as Conrad saw it) and to a subversive Dostoevskian strain in Conrad ("Conrad: Order and Anarchy," in *Politics and the Novel* [New York: Avon, 1957], 79–115). And F. R. Leavis, in *The Great Tradition* (London: Chatto & Windus, 1948), sees Conrad as a liberal humanist.

13. See Watt, *Conrad*, 88–94, for a detailed account of Conrad's fictional adaptation of his 1884 voyage as second mate on the *Narcissus*.

14. See Albert Guerard's insight, crucial to this chapter, in *Conrad the Novelist* (Cambridge: Harvard University Press, 1958; New York: Atheneum, 1970): "The actual rescue is presented as a difficult childbirth" (112).

15. I am indebted to Chris Goulian for this insight.

16. But, as Stephen Murdock notes in his unpublished paper "Racial Taxonomies and (post-)Modern Language in Conrad's *The Nigger of the 'Narcissus'*," Donkin is also the most racist character in the novella. Again, race is chaotically, undecidably articulated in this text.

17. For an analysis of the contradiction in *Three Lives* between painful content and cool, flat narrative tone, see DeKoven, *A Different Language*, 29–35.

18. That new story was very purposefully written by Toni Morrison in *The Bluest Eye* (New York: Simon & Schuster, 1970).

19. A great deal of work has been done on narrative point of view in *The Nigger of the "Narcissus,"* the most influential and liberating of which is by Guerard, in *Conrad*. Of the "waverings of point of view" that "disturb logicians," Guerard says "the best narrative technique is the one which, however imperfect logically, enlists the author's creative energies and fully explores his subject" (107). For more recent work on this issue, some of it incorporating the evidently relevant ideas of deconstruction, see Jeremy Hawthorn, "The Incoherences of *The Nigger of the 'Narcissus'*," *Conradiana* 11, no. 2 (Spring 1979): 98–115; Jakob Lothe, "Variations of Narrative in *The Nigger of the 'Narcissus'*," *Conradiana* 16, no. 3 (Fall 1984): 215–24; David Manicom, "True Lies/False Truths: Narrative Perspective and the Control of Ambiguity in *The Nigger of the 'Narcissus'*," *Conradiana* 18, no. 2 (Spring 1986): 105–18; Marion C. Michael, "James Wait as Pivot: Narrative Structure in *The Nigger of the 'Narcissus'*," in *Joseph Conrad: Theory and World Fiction*, ed. Wolodymyr T. Zyla and Wendell M. Aycock (Lubbock: Texas Tech Press, 1974), 89–115; and Werner Senn, *Conrad's Narrative Voice: Stylistic Aspects of his Fiction* (Berne: Franche, 1980).

20. There are of course much more radical, and extensively discussed, stylistic innovations in "Melanctha"; innovations virtually all of Stein's critics have felt obligated to account for. In *A Different Language*, I argue that these innovations belong to the avant-garde rather than the modernist tradition.

21. Stein was obviously not only aware of her sexual preference but a sexually active lesbian when she wrote *Q.E.D.* in 1903, yet, as that novel makes clear, she was still plagued by guilt and inhibition. See Richard Bridgman, *Gertrude Stein In Pieces* (New York: Oxford University Press, 1970), on the profound effects of that guilt and inhibition on her career.

22. The American title of the first edition was *The Children of the Sea* (Watt, *Conrad*, 105, n. 7).

23. Julia Kristeva, "Women's Time," trans. Alice Jardine and Harry Blake, *Signs* 7, no. 1 (Autumn 1981): 13–35; reprinted in *The Kristeva Reader*, ed. Toril Moi (New York: Columbia University Press, 1986), 187–213.

CHAPTER 4
THE VAGINAL PASSAGE

1. Joseph Conrad, *Heart of Darkness* (1899; reprint, Harmondsworth: Penguin, 1973); Virginia Woolf, *The Voyage Out* (1915; reprint, New York: Harcourt Brace Jovanovich, 1948). Subsequent quotations from these sources will hereafter be cited parenthetically in the text by page number.

Although the publication date of *The Voyage Out* would seem to make it a work of high rather than early modernism, Woolf began work on the novel in 1906 (the year Stein wrote "Melanctha") and clearly invented modernist narrative for herself in the course of writing (and rewriting, and rewriting) it. Woolf's original title was *Melymbrosia*; the novel evolved into *The Voyage Out*.

2. For feminist criticism of *The Voyage Out*, see Elizabeth Abel, *Virginia Woolf and the Fictions of Psychoanalysis* (Chicago: University of Chicago Press, 1990); Louise DeSalvo, *Virginia Woolf's First Voyage: A Novel in the Making* (Totowa, NJ: Rowman and Littlefield, 1980), a detailed treatment of the lengthy, arduous composition of this novel (see n. 1), including analysis of the feminist

material Woolf suppressed in those revisions (see also Mitchell Leaska, *The Novels of Virginia Woolf: From Beginning to End* [New York: John Jay Press, 1977], for analysis of earlier drafts and revisions); Rachel Blau DuPlessis, *Writing Beyond the Ending*; Christine Froula, *Joyce and Woolf: Gender, Culture, and Literary Authority* (University of Chicago Press, forthcoming) and Madeline Moore, *A Short Season Between Two Silences: The Mystical and Political in Virginia Woolf* (Boston: Allen and Unwin, 1983). For an analysis of the complex representations of London in Woolf's fiction that include enabling, liberating manifestations not apparent in *The Voyage Out*, see Susan Squier, *Virginia Woolf: A Feminist Politics of the City* (Chapel Hill: University of North Carolina Press, 1985).

3. Joseph Conrad, "The Return," in *Tales of Unrest* (1898; reprint, Harmondsworth: Penguin, 1977), 111–70. Subsequent quotations from this source will hereafter be cited parenthetically in the text by page number.

4. In *Joseph Conrad: A Psychoanalytical Biography* (Princeton: Princeton University Press, 1967), Bernard C. Meyer finds in Conrad a "mother fixation" (114) attributable to the early death of his mother (she died in 1865, when Conrad was only seven; Julia Stephen died when Virginia was thirteen) and argues that "the re-establishment of a blissful intimacy between mother and child seems to represent the deepest significance of the conception of love in many of Conrad's stories." The ultimate figure of this "blissful intimacy" is "the child at the mother's breast" (182). Meyer does not make the connection of the maternal to the wilderness in *Heart of Darkness*. Albert Guerard does, in *Conrad the Novelist*, connect the fear of darkness, of "the smell of the damp earth" and "the menace of vegetation," to the fear of the feminine (47). Guerard's first chapter, "The Journey Within," was crucial in establishing the allegiance of Conrad's narrative practice to the dream and the unconscious.

5. Meyer, *Conrad*, notes that Conrad's heroines are "dentally superb" (171). He finds in the association of teeth and the maternal feminine a projected wish to be devoured and a desire to devour (182), and considers *Heart of Darkness* to be "about" cannibalism as figure of infantile orality (334).

6. See Klaus Theweleit, *Women, Floods, Bodies, History*, on class, sexuality, and the feminine in relation to rigid/liquid figuration.

7. Woolf greatly admired Conrad—see, for example, "Joseph Conrad" in *The Common Reader*, 228–35, and "Mr. Conrad: A Conversation," in *The Captain's Death Bed*, 76–81. T. S. Eliot remarked that "Of all contemporary authors, Mrs. Woolf is the one who reminds me most of Joseph Conrad" ("*Le roman anglais contemporain*," *Nouvelle revue française* 28 [May 1927], 672–74). Rosemary Pitt discusses the common theme of "exploration of the self" or "voyage into the self" in the two works in "The Exploration of Self in Conrad's *Heart of Darkness* and Woolf's *The Voyage Out*," *Conradiana* 10, no. 2 (Spring 1978): 141–54, and also notes that both works "begin with ships leaving the Thames in London and entering far-off areas, associated with darkness, and remote from civilization" (151). Pitt argues that "the influence of Conrad on Virginia Woolf and the debt she owes to him are considerable and seem to have been indirect" (141). James Naremore, in *The World Without a Self: Virginia Woolf and the Novel* (New Haven: Yale University Press, 1973) says, of a passage in *The Voyage Out*: "here there is not only Conrad's insistence on mood but even images that seem to owe

vaguely to his story" (45). See also Shirley Neuman, *"Heart of Darkness,* Virginia Woolf and the Spectre of Domination," in *Virginia Woolf: New Critical Essays,* ed. Patricia Clements and Isobel Grundy (Totowa, NJ: Barnes & Noble, 1983), 57–76.

8. Note the similarity to this passage of Woolf's famous formulation in "Modern Fiction": "Life is not a series of gig lamps symmetrically arranged; but a luminous halo, a semi-transparent envelope surrounding us from the beginning of consciousness to the end" (*Common Reader,* 154). It is also in this essay that she says "we reserve our unconditional gratitude for Mr. Hardy, for Mr. Conrad" (151).

9. Some other feminist readers of Conrad have assumed that the heart of darkness is gendered feminine. Gilbert and Gubar entitle the first chapter of *Sexchanges* "Heart of Darkness: The Agon of the Femme Fatale" (3–46). Although this chapter is primarily about Rider Haggard's *She,* 1887, Gilbert and Gubar say that "Conrad's *Heart of Darkness* (1899) . . . penetrates more ironically and thus more inquiringly into the dark core of otherness that had so disturbed the patriarchal, the imperialist, and the psychoanalytic imaginations. . . . Conrad designs for Marlow a pilgrimage whose guides and goal are . . . eerily female" (44). See also Johanna M. Smith, " 'Too Beautiful Altogether': Patriarchal Ideology in *Heart of Darkness,*" in *Heart of Darkness: A Case Study in Contemporary Criticism,* ed. Ross C. Murfin (New York: St. Martin's Press, 1989), 179–95. Smith's epigraph is a quote from Hélène Cixous's "The Laugh of the Medusa," trans. Keith Cohen and Paula Cohen, *Signs* 1 (1976): 875–94, that plays on the obvious link to imperialism in the Freudian notion of woman as "dark continent": "What (men) have said so far, for the most part, stems from the opposition activity/passivity, from the power relation between a fantasized obligatory virility meant to invade, to colonize, and the consequential phantasm of woman as a 'dark continent' to penetrate and to 'pacify.' " As that epigraph and her title imply, Smith argues that *Heart of Darkness* primarily perpetuates patriarchal ideology (most feminist analyses of *Heart of Darkness* agree with her), though she acknowledges the complexity of the position of patriarchal as well as imperialist ideologies in this text. See also Anne McKlintock, " 'Unspeakable Secrets': The Ideology of Landscape in Conrad's *Heart of Darkness,*" BMMLA 17, no. 1 (Spring 1984) 38–53; Bruce R. Stark, "Kurtz's Intended: The Heart of *Heart of Darkness,*" *Texas Studies in Literature and Language* 16 (Fall 1974): 535–55; Henry Staten, "Conrad's Mortal Word," *Critical Inquiry* 12, no. 4 (Summer 1986): 720–40; Nina P. Straus, "The Exclusion of the Intended from Secret Sharing in Conrad's *Heart of Darkness,*" *Novel* 20, no. 2 (Winter 1987): 123–37; and Zohreh T. Sullivan, "Enclosure, Darkness, and the Body: Conrad's Landscape," *The Centennial Review* 25 (1981): 59–79.

10. Rather than reading this pronouncement and others like it elsewhere in the text in the context of Marlow's shifting relation to his story and of his varyingly intense but persistent irony, most critics seem to take them at face value, as part of what they see as the text's overall or underlying conservatism, despite acknowledging elements of the text critical of imperialism. Watt, *Conrad,* is an exception: "while Marlow nowhere retracts his views on 'efficiency' and 'a definite idea,' they play a rather minor and extremely ambiguous role in the rest of the story" (217).

11. As Watt, *Conrad*, argues, "we must register both the conciliatory intention, and the intrinsic inadequacy, of Marlow's attempt to exclude his listeners and his country from the ugliness of imperialism" (217).

12. Peter Brooks, "An Unreadable Report: Conrad's *Heart of Darkness*," in *Reading for the Plot: Design and Intention in Narrative* (New York: Knopf, 1984), 238–63, provides a brilliant analysis of the modernist narrative complexities of *Heart of Darkness*. Brooks notes that "Marlow's act of narration" occurs "at the moment of the turning of the tide on the Thames" (238–39)—a moment not only of symbolic significance in historical and narrative terms (the advent of modernity and with it modernist narrative), but also, for my purposes, the moment of the full ascendancy of the maternal.

13. See Jane Marcus, "The Niece of a Nun: Virginia Woolf, Caroline Stephen, and the Cloistered Imagination," in *Virginia Woolf and the Languages of Patriarchy* (Bloomington: Indiana University Press, 1987), 115–35, for an analysis of the virgin as positive, empowered figure in Woolf's work.

14. The Clarissa and Richard Dalloway of *Mrs. Dalloway*, 1925, are based very loosely on this couple, similar in class status but entirely different in effect and significance.

15. For an interesting analysis of the significance of the repetition in "the horror! the horror!," see Garrett Stewart, *Death Sentences: Styles of Dying in British Fiction* (Cambridge: Harvard University Press, 1984) and also his "Lying as Dying in *Heart of Darkness*," *PMLA* 95 (May 1980): 319–31.

16. I am indebted to Cornelia Spoor for her enlightening work on Helen Ambrose as an ambiguous mother figure, and also on the water imagery associated with Rachel, in her prize-winning 1985 Rutgers University English Department Senior Honors Thesis, " 'Only in Silence': Mother-Daughter Relations in the Earlier Novels of Virginia Woolf."

17. See Gilbert and Gubar, *War of the Words*, chapter 5: "Sexual Linguistics: Women's Sentence, Men's Sentencing," 227–71.

18. The wilderness here is much like Woolf's sea that might bring "death or some unexampled joy" (*The Voyage Out*, 32).

19. See Smith, "Too Beautiful," for an application to *Heart of Darkness* of the notion of female silence as a sign of patriarchal oppression/suppression of women. For an alternative analysis of the connection between silence or blankness and female empowerment, see Susan Gubar, " 'The Blank Page' and the Issues of Female Creativity," in *The New Feminist Criticism: Essays on Women, Literature and Theory*, ed. Elaine Showalter (New York: Pantheon, 1985), 292–313.

20. In "On Impressionism," 1914, in *Critical Writings of Ford Madox Ford*, ed. Frank MacShane (Lincoln: University of Nebraska Press, 1964), Ford cites as one of the "maxims, gained mostly in conversation with Mr. Conrad" (38–39): "Always consider the impressions that you are making upon the mind of the reader, and always consider that the first impression with which you present him will be so strong that it will be all that you can ever do to efface it, to alter it or even quite slightly to modify it" (39).

21. Marlow refers specifically here to the near-enough lie of allowing the "papier-mâché Mephistopheles" to imagine what he will of the powers supporting Marlow's enterprise so he can get rivets to repair his steamer. I would argue,

however, that the remark applies to the whole text, particularly in light of the large meditation on lying and on the telling of this story that follows Marlow's admission.

22. In relation to these issues, see Staten, "Conrad's Mortal Word," and Stewart, "Lying as Dying" and *Death Sentences*.

23. The consensual reading of this and similar passages focuses on the (essentially Victorian) thematic of progress versus atavism. See for example Watt, *Conrad*, "Ideological Perspectives: Kurtz and the Fate of Victorian Progress," 147–68. Guerard finds the atavism theme "rather superficial" in the narrative (38).

A significant body of criticism of *Heart of Darkness* finds it an irredeemably racist text, particularly in the treatment of Africans as subhuman or barely human that derives from the atavism theme. The most eloquent, persuasive work I know developing this position is Chinua Achebe's "An Image of Africa: Racism in Conrad's *Heart of Darkness*," *The Massachusetts Review* 18 (1977), 782–94, reprinted in *Heart of Darkness*, ed. Robert Kimbrough (New York: Norton, 1988), 251–62.

24. See "Oscillation between Power and Denial," trans. Marilyn A. August, in *New French Feminisms*, ed. Elaine Marks and Isabelle de Courtivron, 165–67, and "Women's Time," trans. Alice Jardine and Harry Blake, *Signs* 7, no. 1 (Autumn 1981): 13–35, reprinted in *The Kristeva Reader*, ed. Toril Moi, 187–213.

25. The "nihilism" of *Heart of Darkness* receives its most important contemporary treatment from American deconstructionists, most notably J. Hillis Miller—see for example his "*Heart of Darkness* Revisited," in *Heart of Darkness: A Case Study in Contemporary Criticism*, ed. Ross C. Murfin, 209–24. See also Marjorie Berger's excellent "Telling Darkness," *ELT* 25, no. 4 (1982): 199–210.

26. See Guerard, *Conrad*, 25, 40.

27. On Conrad's fear of sex ("the uncongenial subject") and the failure of most of his attempts to characterize women, the crucial work is Thomas Moser, *Joseph Conrad: Achievement and Decline* (Cambridge: Harvard University Press, 1957). Moser notes the femininity of the jungle imagery in *Heart of Darkness*, connecting it to female sexual menace, but also finding that "for the first time, Conrad has been able to use material potentially related to sex in such a way as not to ruin his story and, in fact, in some respects to strengthen it" (80).

28. See Stewart, *Death Sentences*.

29. Smith, "'Too Beautiful'," agrees: "He (Marlow) and his audience (and the reader) know that by substituting the Intended's name for 'The horror! The horror!' he equates the two," though Smith uses this insight to argue that "keeping her ignorant of this equation is a mode of humiliating her" (193).

30. "For what could be more serious than the love of man for woman, what more commanding, more impressive, bearing in its bosom the seeds of death" in Virginia Woolf, *To the Lighthouse* (New York: Harcourt, Brace & World, 1927), 151.

31. See, for example, Froula, *Joyce and Woolf*; Leaska, *Virginia Woolf*; and Stewart, *Death Sentences*. DuPlessis, *Writing*, emphasizes Woolf's feminist revisions of the romance plot.

32. For different readings of the *Comus* allusion, see Froula, *Joyce and Woolf*, and Beverly Ann Schlack, *Continuing Presences: Virginia Woolf's Use of Literary Allusion* (University Park: Pennsylvania State University Press, 1979).

33. Catherine Belsey, *John Milton: Language, Gender, Power* (London: Blackwell, 1988), 52–53. Subsequent quotations from this source will hereafter be cited parenthetically in the text by page number.

34. The circumstances of Rachel's death, particularly the inept medical care and the disastrously misleading doctor's reassurances, as well as the close link between marriage and death, parallel those of Stella Duckworth's. See Quentin Bell, *Virginia Woolf: A Biography* (New York: Harcourt Brace Jovanovich, 1972), vol. 1, 54–57.

35. See DeSalvo, *First Voyage*. See also Stewart, *Death Sentences*, on the drowning figuration in Rachel's death sequence. He sees it as "an unconscious journey toward womblike retreat serving to reverse the trauma of passage through the original birth canal, with the whole ordeal encoding her need to flee the enforced maturity of sexual embrace" (260). Drowning is also "an embrace of incoherence, dissolution of the self" (260), linked to Woolf's "fluid prose style" (258).

36. See Gilbert and Gubar's vastly influential analysis of *Jane Eyre* in *Madwoman*, chap. 10, "A Dialogue of Self and Soul: Plain Jane's Progress," 336–71.

37. This image recalls the jungle scene where Helen, perhaps with Terence's help, "rolled" Rachel "this way and that."

CHAPTER 5
THE DESTRUCTIVE ELEMENT

1. Kate Chopin, *The Awakening*, in *The Awakening: An Authoritative Text, Contexts, Criticism*, ed. Margaret Culley (New York: Norton, 1976); Joseph Conrad, *Lord Jim*, in *Lord Jim: An Authoritative Text, Backgrounds and Sources, Essays in Criticism*, ed. Thomas C. Moser (New York: Norton, 1968). Subsequent quotations from these sources will hereafter be cited parenthetically in the text by page number.

2. See Jameson, *The Political Unconscious*, chap. 5, "Romance and Reification: Plot Construction and Ideological Closure in Joseph Conrad," 206–80, particularly his analysis of history and form in *Nostromo*: "in the very movement in which it represses such content and seeks to demonstrate the impossibility of such representation, by a wondrous dialectical transfer the historical 'object' itself becomes inscribed in the very form" (280). See also my application of this insight to a range of modernist texts in "History as Suppressed Referent in Modernist Fiction," 137–52.

3. For a full treatment of this issue in relation to *The Awakening* and "The Yellow Wallpaper," see my "Gendered Doubleness and the 'Origins' of Modernist Form," 19–42.

4. On the influence of Flaubert and the French novel, see Kenneth Eble, "A Forgotten Novel: Kate Chopin's *The Awakening*," *Western Humanities Review* 10, no. 4 (1956): 261–69; Lewis Leary, *Southern Excursions: Essays on Mark Twain and Others* (Baton Rouge: Louisiana State University Press, 1971); Daniel S. Rankin, *Kate Chopin and Her Creole Stories* (Philadelphia: University of Pennsylviana Press, 1932); and Larzer Ziff, *The American 1890s: Life and Times of a Lost Generation* (New York: Viking, 1966). See Leary, *Southern Excursions*, on

the influence of Whitman. On connections to American realism and naturalism, see Warner Berthoff, *The Ferment of Realism* (New York: Free Press, 1965); Per Seyersted, *Kate Chopin: A Critical Biography* (Baton Rouge, Louisiana State University Press, 1969); and Peggy Skaggs, "*The Awakening*'s Relationship with American Regionalism, Romanticism, Realism, and Naturalism," in *Approaches to Teaching Chopin's The Awakening*, ed. Bernard Koloski (New York: MLA, 1988), 80–85. On impressionism, see Eble, "A Forgotten Novel," and John R. May, "Local Color in *The Awakening*," *The Southern Review* 6, no. 4 (1970), 1031–40. On regionalism and local color, see May, "Local Color," Skaggs, "*The Awakening*," and, a persuasive analysis of Chopin's repudiation of the local color movement, Helen Taylor, *Gender, Race and Region in the Writings of Grace King, Ruth McEnery Stuart, and Kate Chopin* (Baton Rouge: Louisiana State University Press, 1989), 164–202.

5. *The Norton Anthology of Literature by Women: The Tradition in English*, ed. Sandra Gilbert and Susan Gubar, reprints *The Awakening* (as well as "The Yellow Wallpaper") in full. The only other full-length novels it reprints are *Jane Eyre* and Toni Morrison's *The Bluest Eye*. For feminist criticism of *The Awakening*, see Priscilla Allen, "Old Critics and New: The Treatment of Chopin's *The Awakening*," in *The Authority of Experience: Essays in Feminist Criticism*, ed. Arlyn Diamond and Lee R. Edwards (Amherst: University of Massachusetts Press, 1977), 224–38; Sandra Gilbert, "The Second Coming of Aphrodite: Kate Chopin's Fantasy of Desire," *Kenyon Review* 5, no. 2 (1983): 42–56; Cristina Giorcelli, "Edna's Wisdom: A Transitional and Numinous Merging," in *New Essays on The Awakening*, ed. Wendy Martin (Cambridge: Cambridge University Press, 1988), 109–48; Wendy Martin's Introduction, in *New Essays*, 1–31; Ellen Moers, *Literary Women* (Garden City: Anchor, 1977); Elaine Showalter, "Tradition and The Female Talent: *The Awakening* as a Solitary Book," in *New Essays*, 33–57; Patricia Meyer Spacks, *The Female Imagination* (New York: Avon, 1972); Carole Stone, "The Female Artist in Kate Chopin's *The Awakening*: Birth and Creativity," *Women's Studies* 13, nos. 1–2 (1986): 23–32; Taylor, *Gender, Race and Region*; Paula A. Treichler, "The Construction of Ambiguity in *The Awakening*: A Linguistic Analysis," in *Women and Language in Literature and Society*, ed. Sally McConnell-Ginet, Ruth Borkman, and Nelly Furman (New York: Praeger, 1980), 239–57; Suzanne Wolkenfeld, "Edna's Suicide: The Problem of the One and the Many," in *The Awakening*, ed. Culley, 218–24; and Joan Zlotnick, "A Woman's Will: Kate Chopin on Selfhood, Wifehood and Motherhood," *The Markham Review* (October 1968), unpaginated; also, in Koloski, ed., *Approaches*, see "Part Two: Approaches—Women's Experience," containing articles by Susan J. Rosowski, Elizabeth Fox-Genovese, Patricia Hopkins Lattin, Dale Marie Bauer and Andrew M. Lakritz, and E. Laurie George.

6. Some critics consider *The Awakening* modernist—see, for example, Michael T. Gilmore, "Revolt Against Nature: The Problematic Modernism of *The Awakening*," in *New Essays*, 59–87. Showalter, "Tradition," considers it a transitional work, in many ways predictive of modernism.

7. The ambiguities of the novel have been noted by most critics, but almost all have argued that Chopin resolves them. Threichler, "Ambiguity," for example, whose thesis is the endemic linguistic ambiguity of Chopin's prose, finds that

ambiguity resolved in the progress of the reader's response to language (256). Giorcelli, "Edna's Wisdom," Kenneth M. Rosen, "Kate Chopin's *The Awakening*: Ambiguity as Art," *Journal of American Studies* 5 (1971), 197–200, as well as Ruth Sullivan and Stewart Smith, in "Narrative Stance in Kate Chopin's *The Awakening*," *Studies in American Fiction* 1 (1973): 62–75, argue for unresolved ambiguity.

8. See Guerard, *Conrad*: "We must remember that in every chapter and on every page the double appeal to sympathy and judgment is made, though one or the other may dominate; we are not being subjected to the blunt regular swings of a pendulum."

9. See Ziff, *1890s*, 305.

10. See Rachel Blau DuPlessis's notion of "ambiguously nonhegemonic" cultural positioning, in "For the Etruscans: Sexual Difference and Artistic Production—The Debate Over a Female Aesthetic," in *The Future of Difference*, ed. Hester Eisenstein and Alice Jardine, 128–56.

11. See Moser, *Joseph Conrad: Achievement and Decline*, 46–47. In *Orientalism* (New York: Pantheon, 1978), Edward Said discusses the West's symbolic association of the East with the feminine.

12. Joseph Conrad, "Youth: A Narrative," in *"Youth" and "Gaspar Ruiz"* (1902; reprint, London: J. M. Dent, 1963), 37–38.

13. See Jameson, *Political Unconscious*, 210.

14. In the predominant symbolic configuration of this novel, the butterfly is the ideal, or logos-transcendence, while the beetle, ugly and evil but necessary, is earthbound immanence. See Tony Tanner, "Butterflies and Beetles—Conrad's Two Truths," in *Lord Jim*, ed. Moser, 447–62.

15. See, for example, Guerard, *Conrad*; Michael P. Jones, *Conrad's Heroism: A Paradise Lost* (Ann Arbor: UMI Research Press, 1985); Stephen K. Land, *Paradox and Polarity in the Fiction of Joseph Conrad* (New York: St. Martin's Press, 1984); Werner Senn, *Conrad's Narrative Voice: Stylistic Aspects of his Fiction* (Berne: Franche, 1980).

16. See Guerard, *Conrad*, 25.

17. Note here, for future reference, the glowing red side-light that Jim focuses on after he jumps—"he rolled over, and saw vaguely the ship he had deserted uprising above him, with the red side-light glowing large in the rain like a fire on the brow of a hill seen through a mist" (68)—and its similarity to the red light in the passage in "Youth" associating the East with the feminine: "A red light burns far off upon the gloom of the land, and the night is soft and warm" (37).

18. On the profound significance for Conrad of the 1848 revolutions, see, of course, *Nostromo*; also, for example, Gustav Morf, *Polish Heritage*; Eloise Knapp Hay, *The Political Novels of Joseph Conrad*; or Watt, *Conrad*. On Stein, see also Elizabeth B. Tennenbaum, "'And the woman is dead now': a Reconsideration of Conrad's Stein," *Studies in the Novel* 10 (1978): 335–45.

19. Moser, *Achievement and Decline*, argues that Conrad's "lack of creative involvement in the love story" (84) makes for relatively bad writing in the sequences featuring Jewel. Guerard, *Conrad*, and Jameson, *Political Unconscious*, among others, consider the Patusan section far weaker than the first part of the novel.

20. Though Jim describes Doramin's wife as a "little, motherly witch of a wife" with a "sharp chin," Conrad has her speak movingly and with the authority of the "vast prospect": "Without removing her eyes from the vast prospect of forests stretching as far as the hills, she asked me in a pitying voice why was it that he so young had wandered from his home, coming so far, through so many dangers? Had he no household there, no kinsmen in his own country? Had he no old mother, who would always remember his face?" (167–68).

21. Also, of course, because of what Moser calls the "uncongenial subject." See n. 19, above.

22. See for example Guerard, *Conrad*, 149–51, or Morf, *Polish Heritage*, 158. That relationship is most overtly articulated here: "And there ran through the rough talk a vein of subtle reference to their common blood, an assumption of common experience; a sickening suggestion of common guilt, of secret knowledge that was like a bond of their minds and of their hearts" (235).

23. See also Linda M. Shires, "The 'Privileged' Reader and Narrative Methodology in *Lord Jim*," *Conradiana* 17, no. 1 (Winter 1985): 19–30.

CHAPTER 6
(ANTI-)CANONICAL MODERNISM

1. For the most part, I will make no explicit reference to the vast accumulation of criticism on the texts I treat in this chapter, with the exception of some work on gender. I will assume the reader's familiarity with the major traditional critical assessments of the canonical modernist texts.

2. D. H. Lawrence, *Pansies*, 1929, reprinted in *The Complete Poems of D.H. Lawrence*, ed. Vivian de Sola Pinto and F. Warren Roberts (New York: Penguin, 1977), 428–29.

3. In this poem, *sous-rature* overrides the misogynist male-modernist ideology so well documented by Gilbert and Gubar and frequently articulated by Lawrence, as in the following (note the simplistic antifemale use of "swamped" here, contrasted to its complex development in "To Let Go"): "the modern young man is afraid of being swamped, turned into a mere accessory of bare-limbed swooping women. . . . He knows perfectly well that [man] will never be master again" (D. H. Lawrence, "Matriarchy," in *Assorted Articles, Phoenix II: Uncollected, Unpublished, and Other Prose Works*, ed. Warren Roberts and Harry T. Moore (New York: Viking, 1968), 549, quoted in Gilbert and Gubar, *Sexchanges*, 34.

4. D. H. Lawrence, *Sons and Lovers*, ed. Julian Moynahan (1913; reprint, Harmondsworth: Penguin, 1977): "Morel . . . was hewing at a piece of rock that was in the way for the next day's work. As he sat on his heels, or kneeled, giving hard blows with his pick, 'uszza—uszza!' he went. 'Shall ter finish, Sorry?' cried Barker, his fellow butty. 'Finish? Niver while the world stands!' " (30).

5. See especially *Women in Love* (1920; reprint, New York: Viking, 1960).

6. On "masculine hardness" as a male modernist strategy to redeem literature from "feminine looseness and vagueness," see Gilbert and Gubar, *War of the Words*, chap. 3: "Tradition and the Female Talent," 125–62.

7. E. M. Forster, *Howards End* (1910; reprint, New York: Vintage, 1921).

Subsequent quotations from this source will hereafter be cited parenthetically in the text by page number.

8. I am indebted to my colleague Daniel Harris for pointing out the importance of this line.

9. *A Passage to India* (New York: Harcourt, Brace & World, 1924). Subsequent quotations from this source will hereafter be cited parenthetically in the text by page number.

10. Museum of Modern Art, New York. I am assuming the reader's familiarity with this work.

11. I am most indebted to the Harvard lectures of Professor Michael Fried, in his course on twentieth-century painting, for my knowledge of "Les demoiselles" and of cubism. See also, for example, Clement Greenberg, *Art and Culture* (Boston: Beacon, 1961); Daniel Henry Kahnweiler, *The Rise of Cubism*, trans. Henry Aronson (New York: Wittenborn, Schultz, 1949); Harold Rosenberg, *Art on the Edge* (Chicago: University of Chicago Press, 1975); and Gertrude Stein, *Picasso* (1938; reprint, Boston: Beacon, 1959).

12. See Pierre Daix, "Dread, Desire, and the Demoiselles," *Artnews* 87, no. 6 (Summer 1988): 133–37, for an analysis of the painting as an expression of Picasso's "rage" at his mistress, Fernande Olivier.

13. Gertrude Stein, "Poetry and Grammar," in *Lectures in America* (New York: Random House, 1935), 237.

14. Perloff, *The Poetics of Indeterminacy*, 43.

15. Ezra Pound, "Vorticism," *Gaudier-Brzeska*, 1916; reprinted in *The Modern Tradition*, ed. Richard Ellmann and Charles Feidelson (New York: Oxford University Press, 1965), 150. Subsequent quotations from this source will hereafter be cited parenthetically in the text by page number.

16. Hugh Kenner, *The Pound Era* (Berkeley: University of California Press, 1971), 184. Subsequent quotations from this source will hereafter be cited parenthetically in the text by page number.

17. On Futurism's influence on Pound, see Perloff, *The Futurist Moment*. On the connection of modernism to technological modernity, see Hugh Kenner, *A Homemade World* and *The Mechanic Muse*.

18. For recent Eliot biography and criticism that focuses on his attitudes toward women and the feminine in his life and work (predominantly documenting his misogyny), see Calvin Bedient, *He Do the Police in Different Voices: The Waste Land and its Protagonist* (Chicago: University of Chicago Press, 1986); Ronald Bush, *T. S. Eliot: A Study in Character and Style* (New York: Oxford University Press, 1983); Gilbert and Gubar, *War of the Words*, 30–32 and 235–36; Lyndall Gordon, *Eliot's Early Years* (London: Oxford University Press, 1977); Gregory Jay, *T. S. Eliot and the Poetics of Literary History* (Baton Rouge: Louisiana State University Press, 1984); Tony Pinkney, *Women in the Poetry of T. S. Eliot: A Psychoanalytic Approach* (London: Macmillan, 1984); Elisa Kay Sparks, "Old Father Nile: T. S. Eliot and Harold Bloom on the Creative Process as Spontaneous Generation," and Stephen C. Clark, "Testing the Razor: T. S. Eliot's *Poems 1920*," in *Engendering the Word: Feminist Essays in Psychosexual Poetics*, ed. Temma F. Berg, Anna Shannon Elfenbein, Jeanne Larsen, and Elisa Kay Sparks (Urbana: University of Illinois Press, 1989), 51–80 and 167–89.

19. T. S. Eliot, "The Love Song of J. Alfred Prufrock," from *Prufrock and Other Observations*, 1917, in *T. S. Eliot: Selected Poems* (New York: Harcourt, Brace & World, 1934), 11–16.

20. T. S. Eliot, *The Waste Land*, 1922, in *Selected Poems*, 49–74, lines 290–99.

21. Eliot's note to line 218 ("I Tiresias, though blind, throbbing between two lives") (notoriously) begins "Tiresias, although a mere spectator and not indeed a 'character', is yet the most important personage in the poem, uniting all the rest" (70). On the indeterminacy of Tiresias, and of the entire poem, see Harriet Davidson, *T. S. Eliot and Hermeneutics* (Baton Rouge: Louisiana State University Press, 1986).

22. James Joyce, *A Portrait of the Artist as a Young Man*, 1916, ed. Chester G. Anderson, (Harmondsworth: Penguin, 1976), 63–64. Subsequent quotations from this source will hereafter be cited parenthetically in the text by page number. For other feminist approaches to *Portrait*, and Joyce, see Froula, *Joyce and Woolf*; Henke, *Politics of Desire*; and Bonnie Kime Scott, *Joyce and Feminism* (Bloomington: Indiana University Press, 1984); see also *Modern Fiction Studies* 35, no. 3 (Autumn 1989), a special issue on *Feminist Readings of Joyce*.

23. See "Controversy: The Question of Esthetic Distance," in *Portrait*, ed. Anderson, 446–80, for a history and summary of the debate over the question of Joyce's ironic distance from Stephen.

24. On "Circe," see Sandra Gilbert, "Costumes of the Mind: Transvestism as Metaphor in Modern Literature," *Critical Inquiry* 7, no. 2 (Winter 1980): 391–417. See also Gilbert and Gubar, in *No Man's Land*, both volume 1, *War of the Words*, and volume 2, *Sexchanges*, on Joyce's misogyny. For works on Joyce's sympathy to women and feminism, including historical as well as critical analyses (the former focusing on Joyce's contact with turn-of-the-century Irish feminists), see Scott, *Joyce and Feminism* and *Women in Joyce*, ed. Sezette Henke and Elaine Unkeless (Urbana: University of Illinois Press, 1982).

25. James Joyce, *Ulysses* (New York: Vintage, 1961). Subsequent quotations from this source will hereafter be cited parenthetically in the text by page number. For highly suggestive deconstructive-historical work on Joyce, see Derek Attridge, *Peculiar Language: Literature as Difference from the Renaissance to James Joyce* (Ithaca: Cornell University Press, 1988).

26. See Weldon Thornton, *Allusions in Ulysses: An Annotated List* (Chapel Hill: University of North Carolina Press, 1961), 12.

27. Langston Hughes, "The Negro Speaks of Rivers," in *The New Negro*, ed. Alain Locke (1925; reprint, New York: Atheneum, 1968), 141. Jean Toomer, *Cane* (1923; reprint, New York: Norton, 1975). Subsequent quotations from this source will hereafter be cited parenthetically in the text by page number.

28. Arnold Rampersad, *The Life of Langston Hughes*, vol. 1, 1902–1941, *I Too Sing America* (New York: Oxford University Press, 1986), 40. Subsequent quotations from this source will hereafter be cited parenthetically in the text by page number.

29. Gertrude Stein, *Tender Buttons*, 1914, in *Selected Writings*, 459–509. Subsequent quotations from this source will hereafter be cited parenthetically in the text by page number.

Though her work after *Three Lives* took Stein past modernism into experimentalism and the avant-garde, her ambivalence toward twentieth-century rupture remained characteristically modernist.

30. Gertrude Stein, "Poetry and Grammar," 231.

31. Gertrude Stein, "A Transatlantic Interview," in *A Primer for the Gradual Understanding of Gertrude Stein*, ed. Robert Bartlett Haas (Los Angeles: Black Sparrow, 1971), 11–35. Subsequent quotations from this source will hereafter be cited parenthetically in the text by page number.

32. "This that I have just described, the creating it without naming it, was what broke the rigid form of the noun the simple noun poetry which now was broken" ("Poetry and Grammar," 237).

33. See Richard Bridgman, *Gertrude Stein In Pieces* (New York: Oxford University Press, 1970).

34. See "Composition as Explanation," *Selected Writings*, 511–23.

35. See for example Harriet S. Chessman, *The Public is Invited to Dance: Representation, the Body, and Dialogue in Gertrude Stein* (Stanford: Stanford University Press, 1989); my *A Different Language*; Janice Doane, *Silence and Narrative: The Early Novels of Gertrude Stein* (Westport, CT: Greenwood, 1986); Gilbert and Gubar, *War of the Words* and *Sexchanges*; Lisa Ruddick, *Reading Gertrude Stein*; Catharine Stimpson's crucial work on Stein, including "Gertrude Stein and the Transposition of Gender," in *The Poetics of Gender*, ed. Nancy K. Miller (New York: Columbia University Press, 1986), "The Mind, the Body and Gertrude Stein," *Critical Inquiry* 3, no. 3 (Spring 1977): 489–506, "Reading Gertrude Stein," *Tulsa Studies in Women's Literature* 4, no. 2 (Fall 1985): 265–71, and "The Somagrams of Gertrude Stein," *Poetics Today* 6, nos. 1–2 (1985): 67–80; and Jayne Walker, *The Making of a Modernist: Gertrude Stein from 'Three Lives' to 'Tender Buttons'* (Amherst: University of Massachusetts Press, 1984).

36. H.D., "Sea Rose," in *Sea Garden*, 1916; reprinted in H.D., *Collected Poems, 1912–1944*, ed. Louis L. Martz (New York: New Directions, 1983). See Rachel Blau DuPlessis, *H.D.: The Career of That Struggle* (Bloomington: Indiana University Press, 1986); Susan Stanford Friedman, *Psyche Reborn: The Emergence of H.D.* (Bloomington: Indiana University Press, 1981); Elizabeth A. Hirsh, "Imaginary Images: 'H.D.,' Modernism, and the Psychoanalysis of Seeing," in *Discontented Discourses: Feminism/ Textual Intervention/Psychoanalysis*, ed. Marleen S. Barr and Richard Feldstein (Urbana: University of Illinois Press, 1989), 141–59.

37. Criticism of this novel is proliferating at an extremely rapid rate. It is an exemplary literary text for the current historical moment of criticism, because it gathers together so powerfully issues central to African-American, feminist, and cultural studies. *New Essays on "Their Eyes Were Watching God,"* ed. Michael Awkward (Cambridge: Cambridge University Press, 1990) contains a useful bibliography of recent criticism. Two critical works directly relevant to my concerns here are Elizabeth Fox-Genovese, "My Statue, My Self: Autobiographical Writings of Afro-American Women," in *The Private Self: Theory and Practice of Women's Autobiographical Writings,* ed. Shari Benstock (Chapel Hill: University of North Carolina Press, 1988), 63–89, and Barbara Johnson, "Metaphor, Me-

tonymy, and Voice in *Their Eyes Were Watching God*," in *A World of Difference* (Baltimore: Johns Hopkins University Press, 1987), 155–71.

38. Virginia Woolf, *The Waves* (New York: Harcourt Brace Jovanovich, 1931), 297. Subsequent quotations from this source will hereafter be cited parenthetically in the text by page number.

39. Note the contrast of the emptiness of Percival-as-center in *The Waves* to the crucial position of Percival in *The Waste Land*.

40. Virginia Woolf, *To the Lighthouse* (New York: Harcourt, Brace & World, 1927), 310. Subsequent quotations from this source will hereafter be cited parenthetically in the text by page number.

CHAPTER 7
AFTER MODERNISM

1. Andreas Huyssen, "Mapping the Postmodern," in *After the Great Divide*, 179–221.

2. In *Gynesis*, Alice Jardine provides a very different, but interestingly convergent, analysis of the gender configurations of American postmodernism. While Jardine finds contemporary male French writing (the characteristic writing of what she calls "modernity") the prime locus of "gynesis," where "'Woman,' 'the feminine,' and so on have come to signify those *processes* that disrupt symbolic structures in the West" (42), she sees American male postmodernist writing as I see it: a locus of masculine distancing from the fearsomely engulfing maternal feminine. Jardine ascribes this distancing not to the gender polarization of the early postmodernist period, as I do, but to the democratic tradition of American society and literary culture, which Jardine links to "matriarchy" (232–35).

3. Adrienne Rich, "Diving into the Wreck," in *Diving into the Wreck: Poems 1971–1972* (New York: Norton, 1973), 22–24. John Barth, "Night-Sea Journey," in *Lost in the Funhouse* (New York: Bantam, 1969), 3–12. Subsequent quotations from these sources will hereafter be cited parenthetically in the text by page number.

4. Adrienne Rich, "Transcendental Etude," in *The Dream of a Common Language: Poems 1974–1977* (New York: Norton, 1978), 76.

5. See Harriet Davidson, *The Located Self: Feminism and Postmodernism in Contemporary American Poetry* (Ithaca: Cornell University Press, forthcoming), on the shift in Rich's work in the late seventies, concomitant with the shift in postmodernism, from the simple affirmation of women and condemnation of men of her earlier feminist work to a view of "locatedness" that emphasizes more complex concatenations of difference.

6. "Natural Resources," in *Common Language*, 62–67.

7. Ezra Pound, from section V of *Hugh Selwyn Mauberley*, 1920, reprinted in *Selected Poems of Ezra Pound* (New York: New Directions, 1957):

There died a myriad,
And of the best, among them,
For an old bitch gone in the teeth,
for a botched civilization (64)

8. In *Stealing the Language: The Emergence of Women's Poetry in America* (Boston: Beacon, 1986), Alicia Ostriker sees "Diving into the Wreck" in a similar (though differently filtered) light of "woman-water identification":

Throughout our literature, descent into water signifies danger or death, consistently associated with the feminine. If Conrad recommends "in the destructive element immerse," he does not mean to minimize its alien quality. Women poets who make the same plunge also evoke the dangerous and the mysterious, but they tend at the same time to evoke a sense of trust. As the image of the flower shifts in women's poems to represent force instead of frailty, the image of water comes to mean security instead of dread. It is alien, and yet it is home, where one will not be hurt. Rich notes that relaxation rather than force is required to maneuver underwater, and she is confident of finding treasure as well as devastation. (109)

9. See Sylvia Plath's *The Bell Jar* (New York: Bantam, 1972) for a view of this cliché from the other side of the great early postmodern gender divide:

Now I knew Buddy would never talk to his mother as rudely as that for my sake. He was always saying how his mother said, "What a man wants is a mate and what a woman wants is infinite security," and, "What a man is is an arrow into the future and what a woman is is the place the arrow shoots off from," until it made me tired. (58)

The last thing I wanted was infinite security and to be the place an arrow shoots off from. I wanted change and excitement and to shoot off in all directions myself, like the colored arrows from a Fourth of July rocket. (68)

INDEX